NELL GWYNNE

1650-1687

" Like a mistress she must stand or fall,
   And please you to a height or not at all."

NELL GWYNNE.

From a portrait by Lely in the National Portrait Gallery.

NELL GWYNNE

1650-1687

HER LIFE'S STORY
FROM ST. GILES'S TO ST. JAMES'S

WITH SOME ACCOUNT OF WHITEHALL AND WINDSOR
IN THE REIGN OF CHARLES THE SECOND

BY

ARTHUR IRWIN DASENT

WITH ILLUSTRATIONS

BENJAMIN BLOM   New York/London

First Published 1924
Reissued 1969 by
Benjamin Blom, Inc., Bronx, New York 10452
and 56 Doughty Street, London, W.C. 1

Library of Congress Catalog Card Number 70-82824

Printed in the United States of America

PREFACE

IF it be asked whether it was worth while to portray the daily, and nightly, life of the Court of Whitehall two centuries and a half ago, I am content to leave the answer to my readers. I trust, however, that the task which I set myself to accomplish—the identification of the former abodes of men and women who played no inconsiderable part in the national life of their day—will not be deemed a work of supererogation. This congenial task has occupied my leisure hours for the last eighteen months.

My researches bring into a common fold celebrities so opposite in character and conduct as the mighty Ormonde, the *fine fleur* of British aristocracy, the volatile and engaging Mistress Nell (with whom these pages are mainly concerned), and the despicable Will Chiffinch,—all that was best and worst in the Court of the second Charles. I have also endeavoured to give a more detailed account of Nell's stage career than has hitherto been attempted.

Linking social manners and customs with history and topography, I claim to have made not so much a discovery as a *recovery*, precisely as it affects a limited area within the great City of Westminster, of which I am proud to call myself a native.

Some day a better-qualified historian may traverse the ground afresh and bring into prominence facts which I have overlooked. Meanwhile I am confident that none of Nell's previous biographers have studied the *terrain* of Drury Lane, Whitehall, Pall Mall, and Windsor more thoroughly than I have done, before putting pen to paper.

It remains to acknowledge my frequent indebtedness to Mr. Gordon Goodwin's admirable edition of Peter Cunningham's story of Nell's life, to Mr. Montague Summers, Professor G. Gregory Smith, and Mr. Thorn Drury, K.C. (all eminent authorities on the Restoration era), who have made many helpful suggestions during the progress of my researches. Without their assistance I should have found it difficult to write a serious book on what some may consider a frivolous subject.

Except for a temporary digression in Chapter V. which deals at some length with English sport and country life in the seventeenth and eighteenth centuries (wherein Nell's son and grandson played a conspicuous part) I have endeavoured to preserve the atmosphere of the Court of Charles the Second throughout.

I shall be grateful for any hitherto unpublished letters written by or for Nell Gwynne, and, especially, for a specimen of her autograph, if by chance one should be discovered.

ARTHUR IRWIN DASENT.

New Mile House,
Ascot, Berks,
February 2, 1924.

CONTENTS

CHAPTER I

CHAPTER II

CHAPTER III

CHAPTER IV

CHAPTER V

APPENDICES

ILLUSTRATIONS

CHAPTER I

DURING the sour and sullen rule of the Puritans, when the sports and amusements of the people, including theatrical performances of every description, were rigorously banned by the legislature, a new generation grew up, to which, on the entry of Charles the Second into Whitehall, the diversions of the stage were practically unknown.

An Ordinance of 1642 may be quoted as a typical example of the narrowness of vision which permeated the minds of the Parliamentary leaders in this respect at the outbreak of the Civil War.

It declared in measured terms that as public sports did not agree with public calamities nor stage plays with seasons of humiliation, such performances, too commonly expressing, as they were said to do, " lascivious mirth and levity,"

were forthwith to " cease and be foreborne."
Not only were the poor players effectually
silenced and deprived of their means of livelihood for nearly twenty years, but the liberties of
the subject were so curtailed in other directions
by a tyrannical Government, masquerading under
the name of liberty, that even the convivial
observance of Christmas was frowned upon.

These arbitrary restrictions were, however, re-
laxed, to a certain extent, before Cromwell's death.

Even before the Restoration was an accomplished fact the players, by slow and stealthy
steps, crept back to the stage from which they
had for so long been banished. In May 1656
Cromwell, at the solicitation of Sir Bulstrode
Whitelock, permitted Davenant to give a musical
entertainment, not, indeed, in a public theatre,
but at Rutland House in Aldersgate Street, in
which the singers appeared in costume. And, as
an additional attraction, something in the nature
of a scenic background was provided.

Three months later, when the same manager
produced his *Siege of Rhodes*, we reach a land-
mark in the history of the lyric drama in England.
This more ambitious opera, for such it may be
called, was quaintly described by its author as
" a representation by the art of prospective [1]
in scenes, and the story sung in recitative music."
Hitherto the English stage had known nothing

[1] ? Perspective.

better than the coarse hangings and rude tapestries which had served for a scenic background
since the days of Shakespeare and Ben Jonson.[1]

But now, for the first time, Davenant, with
the assistance of John Webb, who may justly
be described as the father of English scene-
painters, was able to present no less than five
changes of scene, eleven foot high and fifteen
in depth, "including the places of passage for
the music," whatever that may mean.

Nor was this the only novelty. While six
of the seven performers were men, the remaining
member of the cast was Mrs. Coleman, who took
the part of Ianthe. She was therefore the first
of her sex who was permitted to sing or chant,
though not to speak, upon the English stage, for
to the puritanical mind music was apparently not
considered to be so detrimental to public morals
as spoken dialogue.

No less than three composers, of whom the best
known was Henry Lawes, one of the fathers of
English music, provided the vocal numbers, Dr.
Coleman, the husband of the only woman in the
cast, being responsible for the instrumental music.

Two years later Davenant registered a further
advance by producing at the Cockpit in Drury
Lane an opera entitled *The Cruelty of the*

---

[1] The masques produced at Court in Elizabethan times were, undoubtedly, furnished with scenic accessories of a somewhat elaborate nature,
but these were, in all probability, not shifting scenes running in grooves,
but solid carpenters' work built up upon the stage and not easily removable.

Spaniards in Peru, and, to show that it was in the nature of a public performance, attention was called to the fact that there was " good provision made of places for a shilling."

It is probable that this particular entertainment was sanctioned by the Protector as being good political propaganda calculated to stir up popular feeling against the Spaniards and the enemies of the Protestant religion.

When Richard Cromwell succeeded his father the old unreasoning suspicion of the stage revived, and the toleration hitherto extended to Davenant suffered something in the nature of a relapse, for I gather from the *Public Intelligencer* of December 20 to 27, 1658, that "a Court is ordered for taking into consideration the Opera, shewed at the Cockpit in Drury Lane and the persons to whom it stands referred are to send for the poet and actors, to inform themselves of the nature of the work and to examine by what authority the same is exposed to public view."

But the hour of deliverance from the long persecution which the players had undergone was now at hand.

With the restoration of the monarchy a more tolerant disposition prevailed towards the recreations of the people ; otherwise the subject of this memoir, whose name to-day is a household word amongst English men and women, might, quite conceivably, never have been heard of.

When it was no longer a penal offence to laugh and be merry, in public or in private, the pleasure - loving Court and its immediate entourage (the maids of honour, and dishonour, whose names occur with tolerable frequency later on in these pages), the Cavalier aristocracy and its dependants became the mainstay of the two theatres which long sufficed for London's needs.

The citizen class was slower to acquire the theatrical habit, resenting, as it did quite naturally, the contempt and ridicule poured upon it by players and playwrights, poets and poetasters, alike.

Before Charles the Second had been three months upon the throne he empowered Killigrew and Davenant (than whom no better men could have been found for the purpose) to form two separate companies of players, and to purchase, build, or hire at their own expense, and in convenient situations, two theatres " for the representation of tragedies, comedies, plays, operas, and all other entertainments of that nature, in convenient places." This Royal grant — the earliest germ of the King's and the Duke's companies—though it passed the Privy Seal on August 21, 1660, was rendered to a great extent inoperative owing to the persistent opposition of Sir Henry Herbert, who had been appointed Master of the Revels so long before as the reign of James the First. Differences also arose between

Killigrew and Davenant, and, collectively, with Herbert, who had been accustomed to rule the unfortunate players with an iron hand, and more with a view to his personal profit than the interests of the profession as a whole.

Seeing that the sceptre was about to slip from his grasp, he petitioned the King against what he declared to be an infringement of his vested interests ; whereon Charles, in a well-meant attempt to find a satisfactory solution of the dispute between all the parties, suggested an amalgamation of the two companies.

The breach between the original patentees was now too wide to be healed by such a fusion as the King contemplated, and, though Killigrew eventually made his peace with Herbert, Davenant, after much manœuvring for position, seceded from the partnership and set up a company of his own, first at Salisbury Court in Fleet Street and then in Portugal Row, Lincoln's Inn Fields, thereby establishing the healthy principle of competition which was all to the advantage of the playgoer.[1]

The King's Servants, as they loved to be called, began to act at a makeshift theatre in Vere Street, Clare Market, on November 8, 1660, and Davenant's, or the Duke's company, only a week later at Salisbury Court.

---

[1] When Davenant opened the theatre in Portugal Row the revised version of his *Siege of Rhodes* was the first piece presented, and it ran for twelve consecutive days, which was probably a record up to that date.

Before they finally separated, Killigrew and
Davenant divided between them the old stock
plays of Shakespeare, Ben Jonson, Beaumont
and Fletcher, and a few dramatists of minor
importance, whereby Davenant obtained the
sole acting rights of *The Tempest*, *Measure for
Measure*, *Much Ado about Nothing*, *Romeo and
Juliet*, *Twelfth Night*, *Henry VIII.*, *King Lear*,
Macbeth, and *Hamlet*, and in the last-named
he had the inestimable advantage of the incom-
parable Betterton in the title-rôle. This left
Killigrew in possession only of *Othello*, *Julius
Cæsar*, *The Merry Wives of Windsor*, *Henry IV.*,
and *A Midsummer Night's Dream*. At first
sight this would seem to have been an unfair
division, but it must be remembered that at this
period Ben Jonson's plays were quite as much,
if not more, in favour than Shakespeare's. Killigrew now secured the monopoly of *The Fox*,
The Silent Woman, *The Alchemist*, *Catiline's
Conspiracy*, *Bartholomew Fair*, *The Devil's an
Ass*, *Every Man in his Humour*, *Every Man out
of his Humour*, and *Sejanus*, and he retained,
in addition, the best of Beaumont and Fletcher's
plays.

Davenant's employment of more elaborate
scenery than had yet been seen in London no
doubt acted as an incentive to Killigrew to
build, as soon as he conveniently could, an
entirely new theatre, designed for its express

purpose, sufficiently large to compete with, and, if possible, to eclipse anything that his rival could hope to show. On a cramped stage such as he possessed in Clare Market scenic effects of any magnitude were out of the question, and he, therefore (in conjunction with Sir Robert Howard, with whom he was associated at this time, financially as well as artistically), entered into negotiation for the lease of a piece of ground on the Earl of Bedford's Covent Garden estate, which had hitherto been used as a riding-yard.

Though the foundations of Killigrew's new theatre were laid early in 1661,[1] progress must have been slow, as two whole years elapsed before it was ready for opening. Meanwhile Davenant scored an initial advantage over his former partner by opening his new theatre in Portugal Row, Lincoln's Inn Fields, some time during the month of June 1661.

Building operations on the Drury Lane site must have been resumed in good earnest some time in 1662, as on April 25 of that year the King granted Killigrew a separate Patent, which not only clearly defined the status of His Majesty's servants but regularised the employment of women upon the English stage.

Under this charter of incorporation the vast

---

[1] " A very large playhouse, the foundations of it laid this month on the back side of Brydges Street " (Rugge's *Mercurius Britannicus*, March 2, 1661).

theatre on this historic site opens its doors to-day, and I make no apology for giving the terms of this remarkable theatrical document in full:

" Charles the Second by the grace of God King of England, Scotland, France and Ireland Defender of the Faith etc.

" To all to whom these presents shall come greeting know that we of our especial grace certain knowledge and mere motion and upon the humble petition of our trusty and well beloved Thomas Killigrew, Esquire, one of the grooms of our bed chamber have given and granted and by these presents for us our heirs and successors do give and grant unto the said Thomas Killigrew his heirs and assigns full power license and authority that they and every of them by him and themselves and by all and every such person or persons as he or they shall depute or appoint and his or their labourers servants and workmen shall and may lawfully quietly and peaceably frame erect new build and set up in any place within our cities of London and Westminster or the suburbs thereof where he or they shall find best accommodation for that purpose to be assigned and allotted out by the Surveyor of our Works one theatre or playhouse with necessary tireing and retiring rooms and other places convenient of such extent and dimensions as the said Thomas Killigrew his heirs or assigns shall think fitting wherein tragedies comedies plays operas music scenes and all other entertainments of the stage whatsoever may be shown and presented. And we do hereby for us our heirs and successors grant unto the said Thomas Killigrew his heirs and assigns full power licence and

authority from time to time to gather together entertain govern privilege and keep such and so many
players and persons to exercise and act tragedies
comedies plays operas and other performations of
the stage within the House to be built as aforesaid
or within any other House where he or they can be
best fitted for that purpose within our cities of London
and Westminster or the suburbs thereof which said
Company shall be the servants of us and our dear
Consort and shall consist of such number as the said
Thomas Killigrew his heirs or assigns shall from time
to time think meet.   And such persons to permit
and continue at and during the pleasure of the said
Thomas Killigrew his heirs and assigns from time to
time to act plays and entertainments of the stage of
all sorts peaceably and quietly without the impeach-
ment or impediment of any person or persons whatsoever for the honest recreation of such as shall desire
to see the same.   And that it shall and may be lawful
to and for the said Thomas Killigrew his heirs and
assigns to take and receive of such our subjects as
shall resort to see or hear any such plays scenes and
entertainments whatsoever such sum or sums of money
as either have accustomably been given or taken in
the like kind or as shall be thought reasonable by
him or them in regard of the great expenses of scenes
music and new decorations as have not been formerly
used.   And further for us our heirs and successors we
do hereby give and grant unto the said Thomas
Killigrew his heirs and assigns full power to make
such allowances out of that which he shall so receive by
the acting of plays and entertainments of the stage
as aforesaid to the actors and other persons employed

in acting representing or in any quality whatsoever
about the said theatre as he or they shall think fit
and that the said Company shall be under the sole
government and authority of the said Thomas Killigrew
his heirs and assigns and all scandalous and mutinous
persons from time to time by him and them to be
ejected and disabled from playing in the said theatre.
And for that we are informed that divers Companies
of players have taken upon them to act plays publicly
in our said cities of London and Westminster or the
suburbs thereof without any authority for that purpose
we do hereby declare our dislike of the same and will
and grant that only the said Company to be erected
and set up by the said Thomas Killigrew his heirs
and assigns by virtue of these presents and one other
Company to be erected and set up by Sir William
Davenant Knight his heirs and assigns and none other
shall from henceforth act or present comedies tragedies
plays or entertainments of the stage within our said
cities of London and Westminster and the suburbs
thereof which said Company to be erected by the said
Sir William Davenant his heirs or assigns shall be
subject to his or their government and authority and
shall be styled the Duke of York's Company.   And
the better to preserve amity and correspondence
betwixt the said Companies and that the one may
not incroach upon the other by any indirect means we
will and ordain that no actor or other person employed
about either of the said theatres erected by the said
Thomas Killigrew and Sir William Davenant or
either of them or deserting his Company shall be
received by the governor of the said other Company
to be employed in acting or in any matter relating

to the Stage without the consent and approbation of the governor of the Company whereof the said person so ejected or deserting was a member signified under his hand and seal. And we do by these presents declare all other Company and Companies before mentioned to be silenced and suppressed.

" And forasmuch as many plays formerly acted do contain several profane obscene and scurrilous passages and the womens parts therein have been acted by men in the habit of women at which some have taken offence for the preventing of these abuses for the future we do hereby strictly command and enjoin that from henceforth no new play shall be acted by either of the said Companies containing any passage offensive to piety and good manners nor any old or revived play containing any such offensive passage as aforesaid until the same shall be corrected and purged by the said masters or governors of the said respective companies from all such offensive and scandalous passages as aforesaid.

" And we do likewise permit and give leave that all the womens parts to be acted in either of the said two Companies for the time to come may be performed by women so long as these recreations which by reason of the abuses aforesaid were scandalous and offensive may by such reformation be esteemed not only harmless delights but useful and instructive representations of human life to such of our good subjects as shall resort to the same. And these our letters patent or the inrolment thereof shall be in all things firm good and effectual in the law according to the true intent and meaning of the same. Anything in these presents contained or any law statute act ordinance proclamation provision or restriction or any other matter cause or thing whatsoever to the contrary in anywise notwithstanding although express mention etc. In witness etc.

"Witness the King at Westminster the five and twentieth day of April (1662).

"PER IPSUM REGEM."[1]

Though the precise locality of the King's Theatre is not specified in the Patent, the site, ultimately decided upon, could not have been better chosen, for not only was it in close proximity to the great Piazza in Covent Garden, then one of the most fashionable centres in London, but it was also of easier access from the great thoroughfare of the Strand than was Davenant's rival playhouse in Portugal Row.

It is often described by contemporary writers as being situate in Covent Garden, nor until Rich built the first playhouse on the site of the existing Opera House in Bow Street, out of the profits he had made by the *Beggar's Opera*, was there a Covent Garden theatre properly so called.

Killigrew's company, with which these pages are more particularly concerned, continued to act for a time at Vere Street in Clare Market, a small and inconvenient theatre which had been originally, like Davenant's, a tennis court hastily adapted to theatrical uses.

---

[1] A similar patent was granted to Davenant on January 15, 1663.

The fact that Davenant, notwithstanding the cramped conditions of his stage, was able to introduce elaborate scenery in Portugal Row— and we have shown already that he was ahead of his time in this respect during the Common- wealth period—stimulated Killigrew to build an entirely new theatre, intended to surpass in the completeness of its appointments anything of the kind hitherto seen in London. The enterprising manager of the King's Company was probably his own architect on this occasion, though the second theatre on the site was de- signed by Wren. Different as the poles asunder from the huge building which extends to-day from Catherine Street, along Russell Street to the narrow lane from which it derives its name, the first "Old Drury" marked a great advance upon the Vere Street house.

Tom Killigrew, who was a man of good family, a prime favourite at Court, and the last of the King's jesters, seems to have been a man in advance of his time.

From his early youth he had a passionate and absorbing love for the stage. "Who will go on and be a devil he shall see the play for nothing," cried the manager of the Red Bull in Clerkenwell, a primitive playhouse of the inn-yard type, to a crowd of boys hanging round the entrance. And as a pantomime demon, besmeared with scarlet paint and equipped with a " property " tail, Killigrew acquired his first knowledge of the traffic of the stage.

Never losing sight of what he conceived to be his proper sphere in life—an actor-manager with ideas, energetic and resourceful—he was one of the first, if not the very first, to make an experiment, till then unattempted in London, which must, I think, have commended itself unreservedly to that indefatigable playgoer, Samuel Pepys, from whom we derive so much of our first-hand knowledge of the Restoration drama.

This was no less an innovation than the introduction of women upon the stage, instead of assigning female characters, according to long-established practice, to boys dressed in women's clothes. This novelty, like most new departures, did not at first meet with universal approval, but, thanks in great measure to the charm, ability, and beauty of an extremely young girl, who joined Killigrew's company within two years of the opening of the King's Theatre, the innovation once made had come to stay.

The absurdity of employing men to take women's parts is well illustrated by a story of old Chetwood's, who relates that Charles the Second, having come to the Duke's Theatre to see *Hamlet*, and being kept waiting for some time for the curtain to rise, sent Lord Rochester to inquire the cause of the delay. He returned with the information that " The Queen was not quite shaved." " Oddsfish," said the good-natured King, " I beg Her Majesty's pardon. We will wait till her barber has quite done with her."

Who was actually the first woman to grace the boards of Old Drury is still a matter of controversy. One of the Marshall sisters, " Nan " or " Beck " (said to have been the daughters of a Presbyterian minister), Mrs. Coleman, and " Peg " Hughes have all been named in this connection, but there was another girl, only thirteen years old when the King's Theatre opened its doors for the first time on May 7, 1663, who may well have been present at the first performance, although as yet she was merely engaged in the humble task of selling oranges in the pit.

Her name, so soon to become famous, from the sharp contrasts which her career affords and from the glamour surrounding her short life, was Nell Gwynne.

English men, and women too, have always entertained a peculiar liking for Mistress Nell, whilst rightly withholding their sympathy from such kittle cattle as Barbara Villiers and Louise de Querouaille, her two principal rivals in the King's affections. They, though of better birth, and exposed to fewer temptations, are remembered, if at all, as having been two of the most rapacious and unscrupulous harpies who ever disgraced an English court.

On the other hand, Nell's invariable kindness to the poor and needy—the class from which she sprang—after she had been raised from grinding poverty to comparative affluence, has been the mainspring of the remarkable interest which has centred round her name.

Successive generations have extended to her an indulgence seldom conceded to the fair and frail in any age or in any country, with the result that " pretty witty Nell " has been raised to a pedestal amongst the daughters of joy, from which she can never now be dethroned.

There is abundant evidence that she had a generous and a tender heart, frequently exerting her influence with the King (to whom she was not only sincerely attached but consistently faithful) for good and worthy objects, even if the credit of inspiring the foundation of Chelsea Hospital for soldiers broken in the Civil Wars belongs not so much to her as to Sir Stephen Fox.

Once she had given herself to the King, she never looked to the right nor to the left, though attempts were sometimes made, as I shall show hereafter, to seduce her from that allegiance.

In this respect her conduct compares very favourably with that of her chief rival, Barbara Villiers, whose expansive affections were notorious from their not being confined to any particular class. One of her many paramours was a rope-dancer from Bartholomew Fair, and this at a time when she was receiving an annual income of many thousands a year from the King.

She gave five thousand pounds of Charles's money to enlist into her service John Churchill, the future Duke of Marlborough, when he was still in his teens. One day the King surprised him at his lodgings with his mistress, under circumstances which left no doubt of the guilty intimacy between them. Young Churchill jumped out of the window to escape Charles's wrath, whereupon the King called after him : " I forgive you, because I know that you do this for your bread !"

Even the baby-faced French girl, Louise de Querouaille, granted a share of her favours to Danby,[1] with whom she was anxious, for political reasons, to keep on good terms.

She also made the King furiously jealous at an intrigue which she entered upon with Philippe de Vendôme, one of the handsomest men of his time, until Louis XIV., in the hope of maintaining Louise's ascendancy at Whitehall, hastily recalled him to France.

But when Sir John Germain, a Dutch adventurer of mean extraction, who had grown rich by gambling, endeavoured, shortly after Charles's death, to estrange Nelly from her allegiance to the King's memory, she told him,

[1] Thomas Osborne, 1st Duke of Leeds.

with characteristic terseness of expression, that "she was no such sportsman as to lay the dog where the deer should lie."

When, in 1852, Peter Cunningham published his entertaining, if not always strictly accurate, *Story of Nell Gwynne*,[1] he began his narrative, oddly enough, with what an archbishop of Canterbury in the making[2] said of her when preaching her funeral sermon. Cunningham tells us that Tenison "found much to say in her praise," taking, no doubt, the charitable view that such deviations from the path of virtue, as must inevitably be associated with her memory, had been forced upon her, in extreme youth, more from circumstance than from choice.

It may be remembered that the saintly Sir Thomas More, in an earlier age, pleaded similar extenuating circumstances in the case of Jane Shore's mode of life. She, however, left her husband, who was a well-to-do goldsmith in Lombard Street, to become the mistress of Edward the Fourth, whereas Nell was never legally married to any one.

More affirmed that, to his personal knowledge, "Jane never abused her influence to any man's hurt, but to many a man's comfort and relief," and the same might be said with equal truth of Nell.

---

[1] Since edited and extensively annotated by H. B. Wheatley (1892) and more recently by Mr. Gordon Goodwin, to whom I must acknowledge my frequent indebtedness.

[2] Dr. Thomas Tenison, the vicar of St. Martin's-in-the-Fields.

That there were other points of resemblance in the characters of these two Royal favourites is clear from More's statement that Jane was " merry in company, ready and quick of answer," a description which exactly fits the subject of this memoir. She was, in the words of a contemporary of her own sex,[1] one of those rare individuals who seemed " as if she had been made to put the whole world into good humour."

I shall return to Archbishop Tenison's funeral sermon at St. Martin's, and the controversy to which it gave rise, at a later page, but I prefer to reverse Cunningham's biographical method and to trace Nell's meteoric career, for such it deserves to be called, from the beginning and to leave her funeral to the last.

After the lapse of more than two hundred and fifty years it is difficult to determine to which of three Cathedral cities—one of them Metropolitan and the other two provincial—which have, at one time or another, claimed this " brittle beauty whom nature made so frail " as their daughter, should rightly be assigned the preference.

London, Hereford, and Oxford have had their respective adherents, but in each instance such evidence as is available (and I have endeavoured to sift it to the best of my ability) is conflicting as to the actual place of birth.

[1] Mrs. Aphra Behn.

To take the claims of London first, this much is absolutely certain, that if she was not born in a mean street off Drury Lane, that region, so redolent of the stage, was her nursery, her school-room, and her playground too.

The parents of this fascinating girl, who was destined to set so many hearts aflame before she attained the age of seventeen, including that of the most susceptible monarch who ever sat upon the throne of England, are believed to have been living in poor circumstances, in, or soon after, 1650, at a small house in a squalid alley, called the Coal Yard. It was, and is to this day, the last turning on the right or eastern side of Drury Lane, going northwards towards Holborn.

In modern times this slum, for it was never anything better, has, for no apparent reason, been renamed Goldsmith Street, and to this day there are houses in it, now mostly tottering to their fall, which may well date from the middle of the eighteenth century, if not earlier.

In an extremely scarce and scurrilous little book entitled *The Lives of the Court Beauties*, 1715, by Captain Alexander Smith, ranging from Fair Rosamond and Henry the Second to the end of the reign of Queen Anne, it is definitely stated that Nell was born in the Coal Yard in Drury Lane.

This *chronique scandaleuse*, of which there appears to be no copy either in the British

Museum or the Bodleian Library, contains a great deal of curious information not to be found elsewhere. It was reissued and enlarged in 1716 as *The Court of Venus*, and must, I think, have been known to William Oldys, who had some share in compiling the short history of the English stage published by Curll in 1741, as he adopts the view that Nell was a native of the Coal Yard.

When I began to make an independent investigation of the circumstances of her birth I was in hopes that the rate books of St. Giles' would settle the question once and for all. Unfortunately, in these valuable records, the touchstone of sane and accurate topography, there are many gaps, so far as this portion of the parish is concerned, the year 1650 being one of them.

Personally, though I must confess to having been baffled in the attempt to find any direct evidence to support my view either in parish registers or rate books, I incline to the opinion that Nell was a native of London, although the claims of Hereford and Oxford cannot be altogether ignored.

The first-named of these Cathedral cities rests its slender case principally upon the fact that her grandson, Lord James Beauclerk, the seventh son of the 1st Duke of St. Albans, who was Bishop of Hereford in the eighteenth century, did not formally repudiate the legend.

Until comparatively recent years a house in Pipewell Lane, which the good people of the City, in their anxiety to claim Nelly for their very own, have rechristened Gwynne Street, was pointed out as having been the place of her birth.

This house, of which there are two photographic views in Mr. Gordon Goodwin's edition of Peter Cunningham's memoir, was a mere hovel of brick and timber demolished in 1859.

That there were numerous Gwynnes resident in Hereford in the seventeenth century is incontestable, more especially in the parish of St. John the Baptist, but its registers are not of sufficiently early date to throw any light on the subject of Nell's birth or parentage. Charles the Second, it is true, gave the Cathedral its organ, but that is not in itself sufficient to support the contention that he desired to reward the City for having been his favourite's spiritual mother.

The City of Hereford is not many miles distant from the Welsh border, and the county adjoins that of Brecknock, where, as also in Carmarthen, the name of Gwynne was, and is, commoner still.

Hereford is, I believe, still the second largest hop-growing county in England, and in this connection I chanced to find recently amongst the Harleian Manuscripts in the British Museum, in a " Collection of choice poems " (all in the same handwriting and unprintable from their amazing coarseness, even for the age in which they were written), a somewhat different heading to the many printed versions of the " Lady of Pleasure."

In the manuscript version of this scandalous poem Nell's life is said to be described from " *Hop Garden*, Cellar, to the Throne," whereas in all the printed copies of this disgraceful lampoon the first of her early habitations mentioned is the Coal Yard.

This is, so far as I know, the only scrap of contemporary, or nearly contemporary, evidence which points to Hereford as the probable place of birth, and it is difficult to explain why the Hop Garden was omitted from the printed versions.

In 1883 the late Bishop Atlay allowed a memorial tablet to be fixed on the outer face of his garden wall, in order that no future uncertainty might exist as to the former site of the wretched little house in which it is alleged that Nelly was born.[1]

The memorial slab to Bishop Beauclerk in the Cathedral Cloisters merely records that he died in 1787, and enters into no genealogical retrospect whatever.

Oxford, too, would claim Nell as one of St. Frideswide's virgins. Even the parish in which it is said she was born has been mentioned,

[1] Note in Mr. Gordon Goodwin's edition of Peter Cunningham's book, 1908, p. 165.

but a search of the registers of St. Clement's
Church yields no trace of the name of Gwynne.
Her mother is said by Anthony à Wood to
have " lived some time in Oxford," and her
father is believed to have died in prison there,
though I have not been able to substantiate the
statement.   Anthony à Wood inserted in his
Life and Times (published by the Oxford Historical Society, vol. ii. p. 457) a fragmentary
pedigree in which he deduced Nell's descent
from Dr. Edward Gwynne, a canon of Christ
Church, whose son (? Thomas) married the
daughter of one Smith of St. Thomas's parish.
The vexed question of the Christian name and
social status of Nell's father might have been
settled had the baptismal registers of St. Thomas's
for 1650 been preserved, but, unfortunately,
the earliest now in existence does not begin
until five years later.

It is impossible, in considering the claims of
Oxford, to forget that the minor titles conferred
in 1676 upon Nell's eldest son were both
derived from that county.   He was created
Baron Burford and Earl of Headington before
being elevated to the Dukedom of St. Albans.

This might, conceivably, be held to indicate
a family connection on his mother's part with
the county, but I think it is safer to assume that
as Nell is known to have accompanied Charles
on more than one occasion to the races which

were held annually on Burford Downs, she may have expressed a preference for an hereditary title drawn from Oxfordshire, independently of her supposed birth in its Cathedral city.[1]

It so happens that a comprehensive history of the pleasant little town of Burford, containing much fresh matter relating to Speaker Lenthall and his family, has been published quite recently. But though this excellent specimen of English local history contains a voluminous index of inhabitants at various periods, I have searched its pages in vain for the name of Gwynne.

Whilst it is impossible to-day to say precisely whether Nell was born in London, Hereford, or Oxford, there is no doubt whatever as to the date of her entrance into the world.

When Peter Cunningham wrote the story of her life he relied for the date of her birth upon her horoscope, which he assumed to have been cast by William Lilly, though it is more likely to have been the work of one of his pupils, acting under his direction.

This interesting document, of which a facsimile is given on the adjoining page, is still to be seen in the Bodleian Library, to which it was transferred in recent years from the Ashmolean Museum.[2]

---

[1] The Burford races were the precursors of the Bibury Club meetings of a later age.

[2] It will be remembered that Ashmole acquired most of Lilly's manuscripts at his death in 1681.

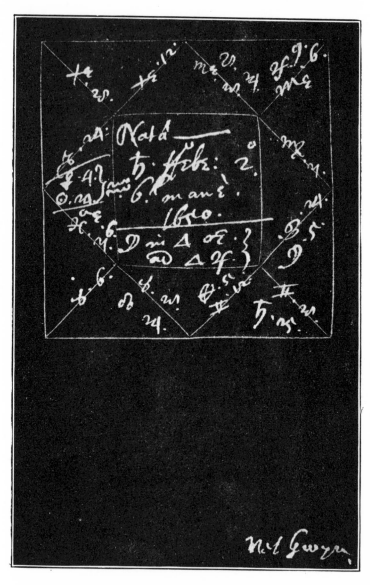

NELL GWYNNE'S HOROSCOPE.

From the original in the Bodleian Library.

This horoscope is of the utmost genealogical value, since it contains positive and convincing evidence, which all who run may read, that Nell's birth took place in 1650.

Since Cunningham wrote attempts have been made, as I now think without any justification, to prove that "1650" in this particular instance means "1651," and both Wheatley and Gordon Goodwin in their reissues and amplifications of Cunningham's memoir adopted the latter year as being the more probable date.

But whilst it is the fact that, according to the old style which obtained in England until the alteration of the Calendar in 1751, the official year was reckoned as beginning on the 25th of March (the Feast of the Annunciation) instead of on January 1, the almanac makers, of whom Lilly was admittedly the foremost and the most trustworthy, invariably adhered to astronomical dates in their annual compilations.

So far as I am aware there is not a single instance of an English " Ephemeris," " Merlin," Calendar, or Almanac of seventeenth-century date which does not begin the year with January 1 and end it with December 31.

After careful examination of the subject in all its aspects I am convinced that Cunningham was right in declaring for 1650, and that the claim, so confidently put forward in recent times to substitute the year 1651 for it, must henceforth be definitely abandoned. What is even more remarkable is that though such an accurate observer as Cunningham consulted the horoscope, he failed to decipher it in its entirety. For not only does it show the day of the month, the month itself, and the year, but it gives, in addition, something which is even more valuable in support of my contention. No one who has hitherto investigated the subject appears to have noticed that the day of the week is clearly indicated by the astronomical sign of the planet Saturn,[1] and on referring to Lilly's Almanack for 1650 I find that February 2 (Candlemas Day) fell upon a Saturday in that year. The Latin wording runs:

NATÂ ———
♄ FEBR 2ᴅ,
6 MANÈ
1650,

which, rendered into English, can only mean:

BORN AT ———,
SATURDAY, FEBRUARY 2ND,
AT SIX O'CLOCK IN THE MORNING,
1650.

This information, which must, I think, have been given to whoever cast the horoscope, either by Nell herself or by some one intimately acquainted with her and her family, not only

---

[1] Saturday.

clears up the misconception which has hitherto prevailed on the subject, but the tell-tale blank in the upper line reveals the interesting fact that Nell did not, apparently, know for certain where she was born, although she knew both the day and the hour. It is inconceivable that she would not have stated whether she was a native of London, Hereford, or Oxford had she been certain of the facts.

A learned friend, who has devoted years of study to the fascinating science of astrology, assures me that the movements of the heavenly bodies indicated for Saturday, February 2, 1650, correspond, in a remarkable degree, with the known facts of Nell's life, but that had it been true that she was born a year later than she actually was, the celestial signs and portents at the corresponding date in 1651, which fell upon a Sunday, are diametrically opposed to those indicated in 1650, and that so far as his observations go, they bear no relation to the well-ascertained course of her career, so accurately foreshadowed at the earlier date.[1]

It is a singular coincidence, which no one

[1] In the sign of Aries, which is believed to show personality, the Sun, Venus, Mercury, and Mars—the two latter in conjunction—were all in the ascendant, denoting charm, sociability, sexual attractiveness, self-confidence and quick wit, whilst the Moon being at the same date in the sign of Cancer, and therefore in her greatest dignity, is held to indicate popularity. I am also assured that the trine aspect of the Sun towards Saturn represented by the zodiacal sign of Gemini, " the house of children," correctly foreshadowed the birth of Nell's two sons.

appears to have remarked hitherto, that it was on Nell's thirty-fifth birthday, February 2, 1685, that Charles the Second was stricken down in the early hours of the morning by an apoplectic seizure, which resulted in his death four days later.

Nell's father was, I believe, one Thomas Gwynne, of respectable Welsh ancestry, and, as some say, a captain, broken in the Civil Wars, who married beneath him and came to London about the middle of the seventeenth century, though it is within the bounds of probability that he had lived in Hereford or Oxford at an earlier date.[1]

In confirmation of this theory it should be noted that in 1688, only a year after Nell's death, Frederick Van Bossen wrote a manuscript history of the kings of Scotland and the Royal House of Stuart, under the curious title of *The Royal Cedar*.[2]

Van Bossen, to the best of my belief, is the only *contemporary* writer who mentions the Christian name and rank of Nell's father, calling him "Thomas Gwine, a capitane of ane antient family in Wales." He is also responsible for the statement that it was in contemplation shortly

---

[1] A fourth Cathedral city is associated with Nell Gwynne's name, for, according to Horace Walpole, she gave two of the east windows of the choir aisles in Bristol Cathedral. (Horace Walpole to George Montagu, October 22, 1766.)

[2] This manuscript is preserved amongst the Laing Collections in the Royal University of Edinburgh.

before Charles's death to make Nell Countess of
Greenwich.

When she became prosperous, a coat of arms
was found for her by an obliging herald painter,
of which an illustration will be found on the cover
of this volume. The blazon, in a lozenge-shaped
shield, is " Per pale argent and or, a lion azure,"
and it will be noticed that it is based upon,
though not precisely similar to, the heraldic
bearings of the Gwynnes of Llansanor and other
allied Welsh families.

This interesting scrap of heraldic lore is contained in a manuscript volume in the British
Museum,[1] and on the opposite page to the illustration of Nell's arms is the shield of Gladstone,
a very early instance, if not the earliest, of the
occurrence of that distinguished name. To find
a Gladstone and Nell Gwynne in conjunction is
indeed a singular coincidence.

I have failed to discover the maiden name of
Thomas Gwynne's wife, but her Christian name
was Helena or Eleanor, and she belonged to
the parish of St. Martin-in-the-Fields, as was
recorded on a monument erected to her memory,
no doubt by her daughter, in the south aisle of
the old church. The inscription ran:

Here lyes interred the body of Helena Gwynn,
born in this parish, who departed this life ye 20th of
July MDCLXXIX in the LVI yeare of her age.

[1] Add. MSS. 26683, folio 59 B.

When St. Martin's church was rebuilt by Gibbs in 1721 this monument, with many others, disappeared.

Nell was not her parents' first-born child. She had an elder sister, called Rose, who was twice married, first to one John Cassells, whom I strongly suspect to have been identical with a highwayman of the same name.

It appears from the Calendars of State Papers that poor Rose was imprisoned in Newgate in December 1663, when Nell was only thirteen, but that she was lucky enough to obtain a reprieve before coming up for judgment at the Old Bailey.

She was visited in prison by Thomas Killigrew, with whom her younger sister was, in after years, to be so closely associated, and she also wrote to the Duke of York's cupbearer, whose name was Browne, begging him and Killigrew to procure her release " from this woeful place of torment," on the ground that her father having lost all he possessed in the service of Charles the First, it was hard that she should be left to perish in gaol.

A few days later she succeeded in obtaining her discharge.

John Cassells, whatever was his precise calling in life, must have had influential friends at Court, for, after committing other crimes of violence, when apprehended in 1671 for attempting to rob Sir Henry Littleton's house, he had the impudence to send a petition to the King pleading that "he had been seduced to aid in the robbery," and that, as his father also had lost "a plentiful estate in Ireland," through his loyalty to the Crown, he ought to be forgiven.

Instead of being hanged, as he probably richly deserved to be, he was pardoned and released, after which I find no further mention of his exploits on the road. He died in 1675, leaving his widow penniless, whereupon Charles gave Rose a pension of £200 a year, which she enjoyed until the accession of William and Mary.

From the date at which this pension was granted, it would appear as if she owed it to her more celebrated sister's influence with the King.

Rose married again, her second husband being a man named Guy Forster, whom Nell thought sufficiently well of to leave forty pounds in her will to buy a mourning ring with.

Whoever Mrs. Gwynne was, she was addicted to drink and had lax ideas as to morality, and, as I shall proceed to show, no young girl of beauty and spirit could possibly have had a worse bringing up than Nell had in those early years which go so far towards determining character.

Little or nothing is known of her father after he came to London, if, indeed, he ever did so.

Some imaginative writers, having read that his youngest daughter followed at an early age the calling of an orange-girl, have jumped to the conclusion that her parents plied the trade of fruiterers in Covent Garden, only a few minutes' walk, it is true, from the purlieus of Drury Lane.

But they conveniently forget that the sale of vegetables, fruit, and herbs, if it existed at all in Covent Garden in 1650, was then in its infancy, and that it was not until the end of the seventeenth century that it began to compete on anything like equal terms with the Stocks Market in the City of London, where the Mansion House stands to-day. It is true that in or about 1656 a few movable stalls were set up alongside the Earl of Bedford's garden wall, which abutted on the south side of the great piazza designed by Inigo Jones. Not until many years later was the open space in the centre encroached upon by stalls or booths, whilst the volume of trade, when Nell was born, would have been of negligible value.

Some colour, however, is lent to the statement that Nell's parents were connected with the sale of fruit and vegetables from a line in " Madam Nelly's Complaint," a coarse satire, formerly thought to be by Etherege, but not, in the light of recent research, now considered to have come from his pen.

> Pity poor Nell that's haunted by Moll Knight
> You that have seen me in my youthful age,
> Preferred from stall of turnips to the Stage.

Of Inigo Jones's piazza there is not a single house remaining which has not been rebuilt from its foundations, though, possibly, a few of the ancient cellars may remain. For when substantial houses dating from the seventeenth century are rebuilt or modernised, it not infrequently happens that the cellarage is left intact. At a later page I shall have something to say on this subject which directly refers to Nell Gwynne, after she left the neighbourhood of Drury Lane to take up her abode in the West End.

The National Sporting Club in King Street, though it did not form part of Inigo Jones's original design, was built towards the end of the seventeenth century for the Earl of Orford, the admiral who defeated Tourville at La Hogue.

From him the house, which contains a remarkable staircase, said to have been formed out of the timbers of one of the captured French ships, descended to Lord Archer, in whose possession it was when Vivares engraved a view of the façade. In 1774 it was opened as a family hotel, or *maison garni*, said to have been the first of its kind in London. In course of time it degenerated into Evans's Supper Rooms, which I am just not old enough to remember. For a brief space of time it was a mushroom proprietary club, prior to the acquisition of this interesting house by the present owners.

Before she became an orange-girl at the King's Theatre, Nell earned a precarious livelihood as a fish and oyster hawker on the unkindly streets surrounding her squalid home. She is alluded to in one of Rochester's cruel satires, only one of many which fell from his foul and vitriolic pen, as the King's "anointed Princess," and one

> Whose first employment was with open throat
> To cry fresh herrings even ten a groat,
> Then was by Madam Ross exposed to town,
> I mean to those who will give half-a-crown.
> Next in the Playhouse she took her degree
> As men commence at University.

There is reason to believe that she was employed as a menial servant, if not something worse, by this notorious hag, who inveigled young girls of attractive appearance, not only to sell apples and oranges in the theatres, but to act as decoys for houses of ill-fame in Lewkenor's Lane, or one of the other foul slums opening out of Drury Lane, in the immediate vicinity.

Lewkenor's Lane, which enjoyed, if possible, an even worse reputation than the Coal Yard, was called after Sir Lewis Lewkenor, Master of the Ceremonies in the reign of James the First. It will be remembered that some of Captain Macheath's fair friends in the *Beggar's Opera* hailed from it.[1]

---

[1] Only recently, nearly two centuries since its production at Lincoln's Inn Fields, Gay's lyric masterpiece has again delighted London audiences and broken all records for a work of this class.

It was long a favourite resort of thieves and thief takers. Jonathan Wild kept a house of ill-fame in it at one time, and here Jack Sheppard was captured, after his second escape from Newgate. It has recently been renamed Macklin Street.

One would like to think that her extreme youth may have protected Nell from greater indignities offered to girls of tender age in the abodes of misery and vice, controlled by the infamous Madam Ross and others of her tribe, of whom " Lady " Du Lake, alluded to by Dryden and other dramatists of the Restoration, was one. The house in which she was employed may have been identical with the " strong water " house alluded to by Pepys, on March 3, 1659–60, when he met with one Tom Harper, " who took me into a place in Drury Lane, where we drank a great deal of strong water, more than ever I did in my life at one time before."

This may well have been the case, for when, in after years, Nell had a quarrel with Beck Marshall, who reproached her with being Lord Buckhurst's mistress, Nell's spirited answer was: " I was but one man's mistress, though I was brought up in a bawdy house to fill strong waters to the guests, and you are mistress to three or four, although a Presbyter's praying daughter." A characteristic utterance which, though Pepys thought it " very pretty," was, perhaps, not strictly accurate, since it is not certain that the Marshall sisters were the daughters of a clergyman.

Enough has been said to show the dangers and difficulties which Nell was exposed to, partly from want of any parental guidance in her early girl-hood, and the next chapter must be devoted to showing how, by her own exertions, she extri-cated herself from the dregs of poverty and degradation, and how, having escaped from the thraldom of the vilest of her sex, she obtained an assured position upon the stage.

CHAPTER II

Stage Career, 1665–1671

I can readily imagine Nell noticing, as she ran wild in the narrow streets round about her squalid home in the Coal Yard, a large (and as it appeared to her eager eyes an imposing) building rising from its foundations in the spring time of 1661, when she would have been eleven years old.

And if she were sufficiently curious to enquire to what purpose this new building was to be put, she would have learnt that it was to be the King's own theatre, and the most perfect thing of its kind which the town had yet seen.

Such is the lure and glamour of the stage to young and impressionable minds that a real theatre such as this was to be, designed for its immediate purpose and shortly to be opened under the immediate patronage of the King, possessed from that moment an irresistible fascination for this waif and stray of the London streets.

At no time of her life was Nell devoid of
ambition, and she may well have conjured up
hopes that somehow, and at no distant date, she
might gain admission to it in some capacity,
however humble. But had any of her acquaintances predicted that she, the friendless Cinder-
ella of the Coal Yard, a fish-hawker on the
stony-hearted streets and a menial servant in a
house of ill-fame, would, within a few years,
become not only one of the theatre's greatest
attractions, but be taken under the King's protection, to live in comfort and luxury in a house
of her own in the most fashionable quarter of
the West End, she would have laughed outright
at the utter impossibility of such a miraculous
change being wrought in her condition.

Beauty, wit, and self-confidence were pre-
destined to accomplish for this precocious child
all this and much more. Nell may often have
watched the brave show of coaches and horses
issuing from the gates of my Lord Craven's big
house, little dreaming that within a few years
she would be the proud possessor of a coach of
her very own and the most envied member of
her profession.

"If only," she may have said to herself,
"I could obtain a footing in the new theatre,
who knows but that in time I might be taken
into Master Killigrew's company!" He had
befriended her sister Rose a few years before;

here, therefore, was a chance for Nell to extricate
herself from the miserable conditions in which
her girlhood had been passed.

Cold and hungry she had tramped the cruel
streets, in all weathers, for a bare livelihood, and
when, in the fulness of time, the dark nights of
sin and temptation were followed by a more
propitious dawn, this child of the people never
forgot the sufferings of the poor and needy,
or failed to relieve their necessities to the utmost
of her power.

Nell obtained a footing in the King's theatre
at, or soon after, its opening.[1] She now became
an orange-girl, and took her stand in the pit
with her back to the stage and a basket of fruit
covered with vine leaves on her arm. The cry
of the fruit-girls which Shadwell has preserved
for us, " Oranges, will you have any oranges? "
must, says Cunningham, have come " clear and
invitingly " from Nell's lips.

The beaux and wits who attended the playhouses were accustomed to crack jokes, and not
always very delicate ones, with the orange-girls,
and the latest recruit to their ranks soon proved
an adept at repartee. The usual price for an
orange was then sixpence, and it was thought
derogatory to the character of a gentleman to
haggle about the cost.[2]

[1] May 7, 1663.
[2] " Half crown my play, sixpence my orange cost," occurs in the
prologue to Aphra Behn's *Young King*.

The infamous Mother Ross, whom as I have shown was in the habit of sending young girls dressed as orange-women to act as decoys to houses of ill-fame, had not, apparently, a monopoly of this discreditable traffic, for it is on record that Mary Meggs, "a fruit-woman at Drury Lane," was apprehended on a warrant in 1669 for abusing one of the principal actresses [1] "to ye disturbance of His Majesty's actors and for committing other misdemeanours."

It may be that Tom Killigrew, ever on the look out for fresh talent, noted Nell's ready wit and powers of repartee, and decided to give her a chance of proving what she could do upon the boards.

Cunningham, following Oldys, was of opinion that Nell owed her promotion from the pit to the stage to the influence of a mysterious "Captain" Duncan, whom he confuses with a Robert Dungan who is mentioned in the Grammont Memoirs. He calls him a gentleman of merit who succeeded Louis de Duras, afterwards Earl of Feversham, in the post of Lieutenant in the Duke of York's Life Guards.

This Dungan, however, died in 1662, when Nell was only twelve years old, and a year before the King's Theatre opened its doors for the first time. Dungan, moreover, did not succeed Feversham, but was succeeded by him, and, who-

[1] Rebecca Marshall.

ever the other " Captain " Duncan may have been, he was certainly not identical with the man casually mentioned by Grammont.

In two abominable satires, " The Lady of Pleasure " and " Madam Nelly's Complaint," there are some coarse allusions to the supposed relations between Duncan and Nell, which I hesitate to repeat in their entirety. They were adopted, without investigation, by Oldys, who speaks of Duncan as a " merchant " instead of a " captain," adding that he took a fancy to Nell from her smart wit, her fine shape, and the smallness of her feet.

Whilst it is possible that some such person became acquainted with her during the short time she was employed in the theatre as an orange-girl, it is probable that she owed her advancement to Killigrew himself. That Duncan owed his appointment in the King's Guards in after years to Nell's liking for him is quite in keeping with what is known of her kind and generous disposition, but I see no reason to assume that because she helped him to obtain his commission she must necessarily have been his mistress at the tender age of fourteen.

Killigrew had a nursery for young actors and actresses, to which Pepys was an occasional visitor, and Nell's quickness in learning her part may have caused the astute manager to assume that she would be likely to do him credit as a regular member of his company.

Charles Hart, who was a great-nephew of Shakespeare, trained her to the business of the stage, and, if rumour does not lie, he taught her in addition much that it was undesirable such a young girl should know. Her proficiency in dancing she owed to Lacy.

Nell cannot have been an orange-girl for more than about eighteen months from the opening of the theatre, as I think that before the end of 1664 she began to study for the stage.

On April 3, 1665, when Pepys, to his infinite satisfaction, chanced to sit next to her and Beck Marshall at the Duke's Theatre,[1] he alludes to her as " pretty witty Nell at the King's House," clearly showing that by this date she was a regular member of Killigrew's Company. Pepys naïvely adds that the whole pleasure of the afternoon, so far as he was concerned, was that the King and Lady Castlemaine were present, and that he had the good fortune to sit next the beautiful young actress. The mere sight of her tiny foot peeping from beneath her petticoat and her shapely hand raised now and again to restrain a vagrant curl, held him in such a state of ecstasy that he altogether forgot to notice what was

---

[1] They had come to see the production of Lord Orrery's *Mustapha*, in which Betterton took the part of Solyman the Magnificent, with Harris in the title-rôle and Moll Davis as the Queen of Hungaria.

passing on the stage. Though she had neither
silver nor gold, in colloquial phraseology which
she would perfectly have understood, she had
plenty of brass, and there can be no manner
of doubt that her unfailing self-confidence and
ready wit, quite as much as her remarkable
beauty of face and form, played no inconsiderable part in her rapid rise from the dregs
of the underworld. Once she had shaken off
the company of mumpers, doxies, and brothel-
keepers amongst whom her early years were
passed, her meteoric theatrical career—for, as I
shall show, it extended only over five or six
years at the most—was an almost unbroken series
of triumphs.

She already knew, though only from the
outside, a primitive playhouse in a narrow yard
or alley off Clare Market, another in Drury Lane
itself which had been a cockpit, and a third,
hastily adapted from a tennis-court by Davenant
in Portugal Row.

Though we are more especially concerned
with Killigrew's Company in these pages, the
Duke's Theatre under Davenant's able direction
was always a formidable rival to the King's
servants.

Unlike Killigrew, who lived in the piazza in
Covent Garden, Davenant boarded the principal
actresses of his Company in a house adjoining his
theatre under the terms of an agreement by which

he bound himself to " maintain all the women
that are to perform."

Foreseeing the temptations to which they
would inevitably be exposed, he deserves credit
for the precautions he took to safeguard their
morals. Yet his well-meant efforts proved singularly ineffective, for, with the exception of the
virtuous Mrs. Saunderson, who became the wife
of his star actor, the famous Betterton, the others
were all living, within a short time, under the
protection of men of fashion.

Though their ranks were seldom thinned by
matrimony, the young and beautiful Mrs. Davenport was carried off and tricked into a sham
marriage with the last Earl of Oxford.[1] Moll
Davis became one of the King's many mistresses.
Mrs. Jennings, in the words of Downes, the
prompter at the Duke's House, was " by force
of love erept the stage "; Mrs. Long, celebrated
for the elegance of her appearance in men's
clothes, was annexed by the dissolute young
Duke of Richmond, the husband, in after years,
of _La belle Stewart_, whilst Mrs. Holden and Mrs.
Johnson were both taken into keeping by gallants
of the town.

Killigrew, perhaps deterred by Davenant's
want of success as a protector of morals, does not
seem to have taken upon himself any such heavy

---

[1] His daughter and eventual heiress married in after years Nell Gwynne's
elder son, the 1st Duke of St. Albans.

responsibility. Little, unfortunately, is known of the domestic concerns of the rival playhouses, though after Tom's death, and long after Nell's retirement, some dared to say that " Brydges Street is grown a strumpet fair." If Killigrew did not have so much trouble with the ladies of his Company as Davenant did, he had great difficulty at times in enforcing attendance upon his younger actors. An extraordinary device to which he resorted in order to ensure their regular presence at the theatre will be found in an entry which Pepys made in his diary on January 24, 1669, which it is not desirable to reproduce *verbatim* in these pages.

Building operations were resumed in earnest in Brydges Street when Killigrew became master in his own house, and on February 6, 1663, Pepys was able to write in his diary that he had walked up and down and looked upon the outside of the new theatre, " now a building in Covent Garden, which will be very fine."

It cost £1500 to build, and Killigrew paid the ground landlord, the Earl of Bedford, what sounds to-day the absurdly moderate rent of £50 a year.

Before either of the patent houses opened their doors, the diarist relates an unpleasant experience which befell him at one of the older playhouses. When sitting at the back in a dark corner of the pit, " a lady spat backward upon me by a mistake, not seeing me, but after seeing her to be a very pretty lady, I was not troubled at it at all." [1]

What, it may be asked, was the new playhouse like which Nell had watched the growth of with so much interest for two whole years? It so happens that as I write, in 1923, a theatre, to be called, I believe, The Fortune, is rising from its foundations in Russell Street, which must be the smallest playhouse in London; a mere pigmy in comparison with the bulk of its neighbour on the opposite side of the street.

Killigrew's house was not much larger than this chapel of ease to Old Drury. It measured little more than one hundred feet in length by sixty in depth, and it was by no means a lofty building, although it contained three tiers of seats.

Reopened so recently as 1922, after a complete reconstruction of the auditorium at a cost of £150,000, the great theatre as it stands to-day is not only one of the largest but, in all probability, one of the safest in Europe. It provides comfortable seating accommodation and an uninterrupted view of the stage, even from the topmost gallery, for nearly three thousand people, whereas I question if the audiences in Nelly's day ever amounted to that figure in any given year.

Built internally almost entirely of wood, the first Drury Lane must inevitably have proved a death-trap had a fire broken out when the house

---

[1] Pepys' Diary, January 31, 1661.

was crowded. And in less than nine years from its opening it was completely destroyed by fire, one of the actors of the Company, named Bell, unfortunately losing his life. Part of the Rose Tavern, a number of adjoining houses in Brydges Street, and Vinegar Yard were destroyed by the conflagration, which extended as far as the Lane itself.

The floor of the house was occupied entirely by the pit, for there were no stalls in the seventeenth nor, indeed, in the eighteenth century.

Killigrew was careful to provide an orchestra, which he placed in a recess beneath the stage, thus anticipating the practice of Bayreuth by more than two hundred years.

There being as yet no arrangements for lighting the auditorium, the performances began at three o'clock in the afternoon. A glazed cupola over the pit let in the daylight and, sometimes, in wet weather the rain, to the great discomfort of the audience, who, as Pepys tells us on more than one occasion, were " fain to rise," lest they should get wet through.

There were no footlights until long after the opening of the theatre, the stage being illuminated by wax candles placed on sconces. These, not unnaturally, were considered a great advance upon the tallow dips of an earlier generation.

Killigrew's new theatre was a three-tier house,

and so little were the private boxes raised above
the pit that it was possible for visitors to that
quarter of the house to converse with their
friends below, sometimes to the inconvenience
of the audience in the less expensive seats.

The prices of admission were four shillings
for the boxes on the first tier (some of which were
what would now be called " omnibus " boxes);
half-a-crown for the pit, a figure at which it
remained for a long period; eighteenpence for
the middle gallery on the second tier, and a
shilling for the upper (and noisiest) gallery, to
which footmen and attendants on their masters
and mistresses were admitted free after the
curtain had risen on the last act.

When a new play was produced it was
customary to double these charges.

The middle gallery was Pepys' favourite
quarter of the house, for after he became an
important public servant he considered it beneath
his dignity to frequent the pit, except when a
new play was to be produced, and the quality,
rather than miss an opportunity of passing
judgment upon it, could not find room elsewhere.

Another quarter of the house which Pepys
was occasionally privileged to enter was the
" tiring room." There were as yet no separate
dressing-rooms for the principals, and the diarist
has left it on record that Nell Gwynne and her
fair companions were in no wise disconcerted by

the intrusion, although he found them in various stages of picturesque unreadiness.

Even the citizens, who in their hearts the players despised, were sometimes invited behind the scenes, for in the *Gentleman Dancing Master*, a long-forgotten comedy by Wycherley, occur these lines:

> Into the pit already you are come,
> 'Tis but a step more to our tiring room,
> Where none of us but will be wondrous sweet
> Upon an able love of Lombard Street.

The social status of the habitual visitors to the pit was distinctly miscellaneous. Ladies of high degree rubbed shoulders with "vizard masks," the distinctive badge of women of the town who infested the playhouses in the seventeenth century after the wearing of masks by ladies had fallen into disuse. Originally they served to hide their wearers' blushes at the indelicacy of much of the dialogue upon the stage, whilst enabling them to keep a watchful eye upon their lords and masters without being themselves recognised.

It would be interesting to know the amount of the salaries which the principal actors and actresses received at this period, but, to a great extent, this is an unknown quantity, as the subject is scarcely ever mentioned in contemporary literature.

Killigrew once told Pepys that he had such a

high opinion of Mrs. Knepp's abilities that he
intended to give her an additional thirty pounds
a year, but as he omitted to mention what she
was in receipt of at the time, we remain in ignorance of the total amount of her salary. The fees
earned by authors are also largely a matter of
conjecture. They seem to have received a proportion of the takings at the doors on the third
day of a new play, but if, as not infrequently
happened, the play did not run more than one or
two days, the inference is that they were paid
nothing.

Etherege is said to have made money by *The
Man of Mode, or Sir Fopling Flutter*,[1] as he richly
deserved to do, for he was the virtual founder of
the comedy of intrigue, subsequently improved
upon by Congreve, and, in the eighteenth
century, by Goldsmith and Sheridan.

Even the mighty Dryden had his failures.
More than one of his plays did not survive the
ordeal of the first day's representation, whilst
numerous similar misfortunes could be quoted in
the case of lesser dramatists.

It is difficult to estimate at the present day
what it is that makes the difference between
lasting success and comparative failure. The
drama, we know, is the most ephemeral of all the
arts, yet a play which has been savagely attacked

---

[1] In the *Man of Mode,* produced at the Duke's Theatre in 1676,
Etherege reached his zenith as a writer of comedy.

by the critics, both amateur and professional, on the first night, will run for months, and sometimes for years, whilst a production praised by the press and launched under, apparently, the most hopeful conditions, and with a star cast, will fail to attract for more than a corresponding number of weeks. Perhaps the answer is that there are too many theatres, or that actor-managers are not always the best judges of what will attract the public.

I cannot find a single instance of a play in which Nell Gwynne appeared having been irretrievably damned on its production, though it may be that some inferior work, of which no record has survived, may have failed to draw, despite her remarkable skill in saving an awkward situation.

On May 7, 1663, after many delays and postponements, Killigrew opened his new theatre with Fletcher's *The Humorous Lieutenant*, which had held the stage since 1619, and continued to be popular with playgoers for generations after.

Pepys was not present at the first performance, but he witnessed the second representation on the following afternoon, when he found fault with some of the interior arrangements, alleging that the passages into and out of the pit were too narrow and the distance of the stage from the boxes too great. Nor did he like the fiddlers being placed below the stage, as he declared that he could not hear the basses at all and not much of the trebles.

One wonders what he would have thought of a theatre of the enormous dimensions of the existing Drury Lane, where he would have had to pay from ten to twelve shillings for a seat in the orchestra stalls.

In the seventeenth century an apron-shaped stage protruded much farther into the body of the house than is now the case. This arrangement enabled Nell Gwynne and her fellow-actresses of the King's Company to display their charms to greater advantage, and to deliver their prologues and epilogues in more intimate fashion than would be possible in a theatre constructed on modern lines, with a proscenium arch of the present type.

Whether Nell graduated at the nursery for stage aspirants or not, the triumvirate responsible for the productions at Drury Lane—Tom Killigrew, Sir Robert Howard, and Dryden—must have decided early in 1665 that the time was ripe for her *début*.

Dryden up till then had written only two comedies, the first of which was a failure and the other only a *succès d'estime*.[1]

---

[1] *The Wild Gallant*, first acted in February 1663 at the old playhouse in Vere Street, is said by Pepys to have been " As poor a thing as ever I saw in my life and so little answering the name that from beginning to end I could not tell which was the Wild Gallant." His next attempt, a tragi-comedy entitled *The Rival Ladies*, was rather more successful. Dryden soon after collaborated with Sir Robert Howard in *The Indian Queen*, and although there are some lines in it which could only have come from his pen, the play owed such moderate success as it achieved more to its elaborate scenic accessories than to the dialogue.

Early in the spring, and probably in the month of March, for the theatres were compulsorily closed in May owing to the outbreak of the plague, his first, and in many respects his best, tragedy, *The Indian Emperor*, was staged. It must, I think, have been one of the most thrilling moments in her career, when, soon after the curtain rose, Mistress Nell, in the springtime of her youth and beauty, first faced a public audience and opened her lips upon the stage.

The King, who was interested in everything which Dryden wrote, would certainly have been present, and no doubt there was a crowded house. Whenever a new play by a popular dramatist was produced, so great was the public interest in its success or failure—for in an era when there were no newspapers it was the first day's audience which decided the fate of a play—the quality would crowd into the cheaper parts of the theatre rather than lose the opportunity of passing judgment upon it.

So great was the crush at the first performance of one of Etherege's comedies [1] that, to Pepys' astonishment, his Grace of Buckingham in company with Lord Buckhurst and Sir Charles Sedley " sat openly in the pit," whilst a thousand people were unable to obtain admission to the theatre.

What were the first words ever spoken by

[1] *She Would if She Could*, a distinct advance upon *Love in a Tub*, was produced February 6, 1668, at the Duke's Theatre.

Nell on the boards of Old Drury? Appropriately enough they refer to the power of love
and its mastery of the human heart, and are
charming in their simplicity and insight into
character.

When Cydaria makes her entry her father,
Montezuma, is recommending her betrothal to
Orbellan, an Indian prince, and his daughter,
torn between filial duty and a disinclination to
bestow her heart to please her father rather than
herself, replies:

> So strong an hatred does my nature sway,
> That, spite of duty, I must disobey.
> Besides you warned me still of loving two;
> Can I love him, already loving you? [1]

We hear much of the indecency of the Restoration drama, but in *The Indian Emperor* there is
not a single line which could possibly give offence
to the most fastidious if it were to be revived to-
day. The dialogue flows melodiously in rhymed
couplets throughout five acts, not an objection-
able word being set down for Cydaria to speak
from the rise to the fall of the curtain.

Montezuma having bidden his daughter return
home, she exclaims, whilst gazing fixedly at
Cortez:

> My father's gone, and yet I cannot go:
> Sure I have something lost or left behind!

[1] Cydaria has not then seen Cortez (Charles Hart), with whom she falls
in love at first sight. Dryden, it will be noted, here uses " still " in the now
obsolete sense of " heretofore."

To which Cortez makes answer:

> Like travellers who wander in the snow,
> I on her beauty gaze till I am blind.

Cydaria then describes her growing passion for the noble young Spaniard:

> Thick breath, quick pulse and beating of my heart,
> All signs of some unwonted change appear;
> I find myself unwilling to depart,
> And yet I know not why I should be here.
> Stranger, you raise such torments in my breast,
> That when I go (if I must go again),
> I'll tell my father you have robbed my rest,
> And to him of your injuries complain.

After Cortez has spoken of her " conquering eyes," she, gradually becoming bolder, proceeds:

Cydaria. Where is that other world, from whence you came?
Cortez.   Beyond the ocean far from hence it lies.
Cydaria. Your other world, I fear, is then the same,
      That souls must go to when the body dies.
      But what's the cause that keeps you here with me,
      That I may know what keeps me here with you?
Cortez.   Mine is a love which must perpetual be,
      If you can be so just as I am true.

In the second act the love passages between the two are charmingly contrived and reveal the poet at his best.

Cydaria. I cannot love you less when I'm refused,
      But I can die to be unkindly used.
      Where shall a maid's distracted heart find rest,
      If she can miss it in her lover's breast?

Cortez.   Our greatest honour is in loving well.
Cydaria. Strange ways you practise there [in Spain] to win a
   heart,
   Here love is nature, but with you 'tis art.
Cortez.   Love is with us as natural as here,
   But fettered up with customs more severe,
   In tedious courtship we declare our pain,
   And ere we kindness find, first meet disdain.
Cydaria. If women love, they needless pains endure;
   Their pride and folly but delay their cure.

Cortez, having pleaded guilty to an earlier
attachment, proceeds:

   'Tis true I loved, but she is dead, she's dead:
   And I should think with her all beauty fled,
   Did not her fair resemblance live in you,
   And, by that image, my first flames renew.
Cydaria. Ah, happy beauty, whosoe'er thou art!
   Though dead, thou keep'st possession of his heart;
   Thou mak'st me jealous to the last degree,
   And art my rival in his memory;
   Within his memory!   Ah, more than so,
   Thou liv'st and triumph'st o'er Cydaria too.

In the fourth act there is a Spanish saraband
with a castanet accompaniment, but as Cydaria
does not appear in this scene Nell probably did
not take part in it.

It seems almost incredible that a girl of fifteen
could have committed such a long and exacting
part to memory—she had over two hundred lines
to speak,—and probably the prompter's voice
was heard somewhat oftener than was altogether
agreeable to the management. Yet, on the

whole, Nell emerged from her ordeal with credit, and concluded her performance by delivering a spirited epilogue, conceived in Dryden's most graceful vein.

Spoken by " a mercury " it is too long to quote *in extenso*, but the last four lines struck a personal note which the young actress was quick to take advantage of as she gained experience.

> Last for the ladies, 'tis Apollo's will,
> They should have power to save, but not to kill:
> For love and he long since have thought it fit,
> Wit live by beauty, beauty reign by wit.

Peter Cunningham not having been aware of this the first recorded appearance of Nell upon the stage, for it was the indefatigable Genest who made the discovery, I have dealt with *The Indian Emperor* at considerable length, fortified by the opinion of the greatest living authority on Dryden, who pronounces this play as exhibiting in a marked degree the peculiarity of his style. It drew upon him the attention of the artistic world and may be considered as a model of the heroic drama, wherein all the men are brave and all the women are beautiful, differing only from each other as the haughty or the tender predominates.[1] Moreover, it is wholly original,

---

[1] " The charm of the poetry and the ingenuity of the dialogue," says Professor Saintsbury, " render it impossible to peruse without pleasure, a drama, the faults of which may be imputed to its structure, whilst its beauties are peculiar to Dryden."

not even the captious Langbaine having been able to point to any borrowed source.

Dryden dedicated *The Indian Emperor* to the young Duchess of Monmouth, and so great a success did it prove that not only was it frequently revived but it held the stage for over half a century.

So greatly did it please the Court on its production that it was acted at Whitehall,[1] the Duke and Duchess of Monmouth and Mrs. Cornwallis taking part in it, as did a Captain O'Brien who danced admirably in the saraband scene. The Duchess, who was only sixteen at the time, was also a first - rate dancer, but having sprained her thigh in this same year, she never entirely recovered from the lameness caused by the accident.[2]

Little or nothing is known of Nell's life in London from the breaking out of the plague until the reopening of the theatres towards the close of 1666, but it is possible that she and her mother now removed for a time to Oxford.

Drury Lane was one of the first streets in which the dread disease made its appearance, and early in June 1665 Pepys noted houses

[1] On January 14, 1668.

[2] Dryden is known to have invented the names of many of his pseudo-classical characters, and it has been suggested to me that in casting Nell for the part of *Cydaria*, he intended to make a punning allusion to her supposed Herefordshire origin. If, as he may have supposed, she was born in the cider county, *Cydaria*, or Cyderia as Downes wrote it, may supply a clue to her actual birthplace.

there marked with a red cross with the touching inscription over their doorways:

> Lord have mercy upon us.

Killigrew took advantage of the compulsory closure of the playhouses to widen and improve his stage, but the theatres did not reopen until October 1666.[1]

On December 8, Nell was back again at Drury Lane, when she created the part of Lady Wealthy, a rich widow, in the Hon. James Howard's comedy *The English Monsieur*.[2] Howard, who was Dryden's brother-in-law, not only wrote plays, but he mauled and mutilated Shakespeare, notably in the case of *Romeo and Juliet*, which he provided with a happy ending. Evidently the management of the Duke's Theatre was doubtful of the expediency of the alteration, for the play was presented by Davenant on alternate days as Shakespeare wrote it and as Howard altered it.

There is not much story in *The English Monsieur*, and little force of character or lively dialogue. Yet Nell, unfitted as she was by nature and temperament to achieve any notable success in tragic parts, fairly revelled in comedy and contrived to make a success of Lady Wealthy,

---

[1] On October 29 Davenant produced, at the Duke's Theatre, Etherege's *Love in a Tub*.

[2] Drury Lane had reopened on the previous day with *The Maid's Tragedy*.

a part, no doubt, specially written for her. It is a matter of regret that she never had a chance of appearing in Shadwell's or Etherege's comedies, for they were able to bring real life upon the stage even more than Dryden. But they were both tied to Davenant at the rival playhouse,[1] and as long as he lived he enjoyed a monopoly of their talented pens, as well as the services of Betterton and his wife, of Nokes, and Sandford— the best representative of a villain, in the King's opinion, — of Elizabeth Davenport, and Moll Davis.

"A mighty pretty play. Very witty and pleasant; the women do very well but, above all, little Nelly," was Pepys' comment on his first visit to *The English Monsieur*. He saw it again on two subsequent occasions, but his thoughts were running all the time more upon the charms of the performers than the rather scanty merits of the play. On his last visit[2] he carried Mrs. Knepp, who was also in the cast, to a *tête-à-tête* supper at Kensington after the play was over.

The following brief extract from the printed text will give an idea of the quality of Howard's writing:

Lady Wealthy. It seems 'tis for my money you would have me.

Welbred. For that, and something else you have.

Lady Wealthy. I'll lay a wager thou hast lost all thy money at play, for then you're always in a marrying humour. But

---

[1] The Duke's Theatre in Portugal Row.   [2] April 21, 1668.

d'ye hear, gentleman, d'ye think to gain me with this careless way, or that I will marry one I don't think is in love with me?

Welbred. Why, I am.

Lady Wealthy. Then you would not be so merry. People in love are sad, and many times weep.

This is rather poor stuff, yet Nell's humour and admirable by-play redeemed the play from failure, so much so that James Howard was encouraged to write another comedy for her which proved even more successful.

There are one or two allusions in *The English Monsieur* to Nelly's former calling in the theatre, of which she was now one of the bright particular stars, and to the precarious nature of an orange-girl's means of livelihood.

Mr. Vain. I can't imagine how I first came to be of this humour, unless 'tis hearing how the orange wenches talk of ladies and their gallants. So I began to think I had no way of being in the fashion, but bragging of mistresses.

Farther on are these lines:

This life of mine can last no longer than my beauty; and though 'tis pleasant now, I want nothing whilst I am Mr. Welbred's mistress—yet, if his mind should change, I might e'en sell oranges for my living; and he not buy one of me to relieve me.

Early in the new year [1] Nell appeared as Celia in a revival of Fletcher's *The Humorous Lieutenant*. Genest does not mention this revival, but Pepys, who could never keep away from the King's Theatre when Nell or Mrs. Knepp were

[1] January 23, 1667.

in the bill, was present, and wrote in his diary: "Nelly, a most pretty woman, acted the great part of Celia to-day being fine and did it pretty well."

The original Celia, the only female character in the play, was one of the Marshall sisters. *The Humorous Lieutenant* would not appear particularly humorous to a modern audience, nor is it possible to feel much sympathy for the heroine owing to the indelicacy of much of the dialogue. Yet Celia has some good lines to speak, as for instance when, dressed in poor attire, and amidst a crowd, she perceives the King's son Demetrius[1]:

> Was it the prince they said? How my heart trembles!
> 'Tis he indeed! What a sweet noble fierceness
> Dwells in his eyes! Young Meleager like,
> When he returned from slaughter of the boar,
> Crowned with the loves and honours of the people,
> With all the gallant youth of Greece, he looks now—
> Who could deny him love?

After the play was over, Pepys went with his wife behind the scenes, through Mrs. Knepp's good offices; for she it was who brought them to Nelly: "I kissed her, and so did my wife, and a mighty pretty soul she is." As Sir Walter Scott pointedly remarked, "It was just as well that Mrs. Pepys was present on this occasion."

The Humorous Lieutenant was probably revived as a stopgap until Dryden's new tragi-comedy, in which Nell had the best comedy part she ever

[1] Charles Hart.

played, was ready.[1] The competition between the
rival houses was now very keen, and Killigrew
told Pepys on February 12 that the audiences at his
theatre were not half so large as before the fire.
Nell's next appearance was in Rhodes's *Flora's
Vagaries*, produced at Drury Lane February 14,
1667.

On March 2, 1667, Nell created the part of
Florimel in the poet's *Secret Love, or The Maiden
Queen*, a play which shows a marked improvement
upon his *Wild Gallant* or *The Rival Ladies*. The
King and the Duke of York and most of the
Court were present at the first performance.

The play was presented by Tom Killigrew
with a star cast. Nell was Florimel, a maid of
honour to the Queen of Sicily; Hart was Celadon;
Mohun, Philocles, and Burt, Lysimander. Beck
Marshall was the Queen[2]; Mrs. Knepp, Astoria
(a strangely American-sounding name to modern
ears); Mrs. Corey (Doll Common) was Melissa,
and Anne Quin, with whom Nell has so often
been confused, took the part of Candiope, Princess
of the blood.

Pepys, who was of course present, saw it no
less than half-a-dozen times, declaring that it was
impossible that any one could possibly have

---

[1] She was probably in the cast of the Duke of Buckingham's adapta-
tion of Beaumont and Fletcher's *The Chances* produced at Old Drury
February 5, 1667.

[2] The character of the Queen in *Secret Love* is said to have been modelled
on that of Christina of Sweden.

acted better than Nell. " The truth is there is
a comic part done by Nell, which is Florimel,
that I never can hope to see the like done again
by man or woman. So great performance of a
comical part was never, I believe, in the world
before as Nell did this, both as a mad girl, then
most and best of all when she comes in like a
young gallant, and hath the motion and carriage
of a spark the most that ever I saw any man
have."

" Florimel," says Cunningham, "must have
been Nelly's *chef-d'œuvre* in her art." Hardly
refined according to modern notions, there is
clearly discernible in it a strain of saucy freshness
which must have been, as acted by Nell, most
attractive. She won the hearts of her audience
by her individuality from the very first.

Seldom off the stage in five long acts, the main
burden of the performance rested on her shoulders.
She had to sustain all the loose rattle of the
dialogue, some of it none too delicate, though
after carefully studying the text I cannot see
that it is more suggestive than much of the
language to be heard on the modern stage at
half-a-dozen London theatres on any night of
the year. Charles Hart as Celadon was an ideal
courtier, more of a gentleman than Loveby, less
coarse and much more witty, whilst entirely free
from the brutality of Dorimant or Vainlove. As
Cunningham quotes but little of the text, a few

extracts will sufficiently explain what Pepys calls the " wit and strain " of the play.

At the beginning of the first act Astoria tells Celadon that Florimel, the Queen's ward, is " a new beauty, as wild as you, and a vast fortune," a sufficient description to cause him to fall in love with her at first sight. In the next scene Florimel is masked, a disguise which enables the dramatist to give a negative description of her personal attractions.

> *Florimel.* What kind of beauty do you like?
> *Celadon.* Just such a one as yours.
> *Florimel.* What's that?
> *Celadon.* Such an oval face, clear skin, hazel eyes, thick brown eyebrows, and hair as you have, for all the world.

To which Flavia, another maid of honour, adds:

> But I can assure you, she has nothing of all this.

Celadon then attempts to draw her portrait as he conceives her appearance to be from the limited point of view so far permitted to him.

> A turned-up nose, that gives an air to your face: oh, I find I am more and more in love with you!—a full nether lip, an out-mouth, that makes mine water at it, the bottom of your cheeks a little blub [1] and two dimples when you smile: For your stature 'tis well, and for your wit 'twas given you by one that knew it had been thrown away upon an ill face—Come, you're handsome, there's no denying it!

To which Florimel replies:

> Can you settle your spirits to see an ugly face and not be frighted! I could find in my heart to lift up my mask, and disabuse you.

[1] Puffed out.

In the third act there is some lively banter between the lovers, in which Celadon points out the disadvantages of her remaining unmarried.

Celadon. But dost thou know what it is to be an old maid?

Florimel. No, nor I hope I shan't these twenty years.

Celadon. But when that time comes, in the first place, thou wilt be condemned to tell stories, how many men thou mightst have had, and none believe thee: Then thou growest forward, and impudently weariest all thy friends to solicit man for thee.

Florimel. Away with your old commonplace wit: I am resolved to grow fat and look young till forty, and then slip out of the world with the first wrinkle, and the reputation of five and twenty.

One wonders if Nell felt any inkling of its prophetic truth, for though she long retained her youthful appearance she was not destined to attain the age of forty.

In the fifth act Nell danced a jig disguised as a boy, " a very jaunty fellow, *poudré* and *ajouté* as well as the best of 'em," which was received with thunders of applause. The King, of all people in the world, took exception to this act, contending that the travesty of marriage which Celadon and Florimel foreshadowed, in the presence of the Queen, was in the nature of a blot upon the play. People were unkind enough to say that the relations existing out of doors between Hart and Nelly were not exactly innocent, and Dryden's lines are certainly open to the objection that they imply some disparagement of the married state, if they do not actually hold it up to ridicule.

Florimel. But this marriage is such a bugbear to me. Much might be if we could invent but any way to make it easy.

Celadon. Some foolish people have made it uneasy, by drawing the knot faster than they need; but we that are wiser will loosen it a little.

Florimel. 'Tis true, indeed, there's some difference betwixt a girdle and a halter.

Celadon. As for the first year, according to the laudable custom of new-married people, we shall follow one another up into chambers, and down into gardens, and think we shall never have enough of one another. So far 'tis pleasant enough, I hope.

Florimel. But after that, when we begin to live like husband and wife, and never come near one another—what then, sir?

Celadon. Why, then, our only happiness must be, to have one mind, and one will, Florimel.

Florimel. One mind, if thou wilt, but pr'ythee let us have two wills; for I find one will be little enough for me alone. But how if those wills should meet and clash, Celadon?

Celadon. I warrant thee for that: husbands and wives keep their wills far enough asunder for ever meeting. One thing let us be sure to agree on, that is, never to be jealous.

Florimel. No; but e'en love one another as long as we can; and confess the truth when we can love no longer.

Celadon. When I have been at play, you shall never ask me what money I have lost.

Florimel. When I have been abroad, you shall never inquire who treated me.

Celadon. Item, I will have the liberty to sleep all night, without your interrupting my repose for any evil design whatsoever.

Florimel. Item, Then you shall bid me good-night before you sleep.

Celadon. Provided always, that whatever liberties we take with other people, we continue very honest to one another.

Florimel. As far as will consist with a pleasant life.

Celadon. Lastly, whereas the names of husband and wife hold forth nothing, but clashing and cloying, and dulness and faintness, in their signification; they shall be abolished for ever betwixt us.

Florimel. And instead of those, we will be married by the more agreeable names of mistress and gallant.

Celadon. None of my privileges to be infringed by thee, Florimel, under the penalty of a month of fasting nights, etc. etc.

It is impossible to say precisely how many times *Secret Love* was performed during the season, but Pepys saw it half-a-dozen times, his enthusiasm for Nell's rendering of her part growing with each visit; and it was revived on several later occasions. The last time he saw it was on New Year's Day 1669, when he and his wife were in a box, but, being in terror of his wife's learning of his intimacy with Mrs. Knepp, his enjoyment of the play was completely spoilt. " Knepp looked down upon us but I durst not show her any countenance, and as well as I could carry myself, I find my wife uneasy there, poor wretch, therefore I shall avoid that house as much as I can." A very human touch, but, of course, he did not act upon his resolution.

Shortly after its first representation, John Lacy, one of the principal actors in Killigrew's Company, who had been in trouble before for assaulting Ned Howard, was imprisoned for abusing the Court and " gagging " in his part in the *Change of Crowns.* Insolence on the part of a male player—the women could do pretty well what they chose—was more than the King could stand, and Lacy's impudence gave such offence in the highest quarters that the performances at Drury Lane were prohibited for some weeks, as a salutary lesson.[1]

The brief interruption of Nell's career owing to this *contretemps* conveniently paved the way for an episode which gave rise to much talk and conjecture in the theatre, and, not improbably, at Whitehall itself.

Early in the summer of 1667 she so far yielded to Lord Buckhurst's [2] importunities as to throw up her parts at Drury Lane and " keep merry house " with him at Epsom for a month or six weeks in July and August.[3]

> None ever had so strange an art
> His passion to convey
> Into a listening virgin's heart
> And steal her soul away.[4]

Buckhurst was now thirty and Nell seventeen. Though held to be one of the best-bred men of the age he was a notorious rake, haunting the play-

---

[1] Lacy's suspension took place in April 1667. He is said to have told Howard on one occasion that he was more of a fool than a poet, and Pepys notices the growing insolence of some of the actors towards the courtiers and would have welcomed their chastisement. Nor did the women always escape, for Mrs. Corey, an original member of Killigrew's Company, was imprisoned for mimicking the oddities of Lady Harvey upon the stage.

[2] Charles Sackville, Earl of Dorset and Middlesex, born 1638, died 1706.

[3] The house they stayed at was next door to the King's Head Inn, and some of the outbuildings are, I believe, still standing.

[4] From an interpolated song in Etherege's *Man of Mode, or Sir Fopling Flutter.*

houses much as Rochester, " the wicked Earl,"
was in the habit of doing.   Privileged to penetrate
behind the scenes owing to his intimacy with
Tom Killigrew, he early acquired habits of dalli-
ance with the actresses of the King's Company, and
he had known Nell since she was an orange-girl
in the pit.   Having a lively appreciation of her
powers of raillery, he may have had some share in
bringing about her promotion to the boards.

His attitude towards the sirens of the Restoration stage, in that era of loose morality, was not
dissimilar to that of his sovereign.

In the pursuit of his many fugitive amours
Charles seems to have been able to persuade
himself that every woman he fancied himself in
love with was the only one who could make him
happy.   But once his purpose was achieved, he
soon tired of the new plaything and began the
process afresh.

Yet he was astute enough to perceive that, with
one exception, his mistresses only cared for him
in so far as they derived some material advantage
from the connection.   This exception was Nell
Gwynne.   What he did not sufficiently realise
was that though most things, which men in their
ignorance imagine that they want until they
get them, can be procured by perseverance or
lavish expenditure, love is not one of them, for
it remains the one and only thing which cannot
be bought ready-made.

Included in the merry party at Epsom was
Sir Charles Sedley, who was little, if at all,
inferior to Buckhurst as a writer of graceful
verse.[1] Etherege, Buckingham, and Rochester,
as dissolute a trio as could well be found in all
London, were also Buckhurst's boon companions.

It so happened that this same summer a lady of
a very different temperament was staying in the
neighbourhood of Epsom. This was Mary Rich,
the pious Countess of Warwick, and the following
delightful extract from her diary exhibits the
current opinion as to Sedley's reputation.

August 5, 1667.—Went with Lady Robartes and
her Lord to Durdans[2] to see my Lord who was there.
At dinner that day dined Sedley, which was much
trouble to see him for fear he should be profane.
But it pleased God to restrain him: yet the knowledge I had how profane a person he was troubled
me to be in his company.

Nell, however, would have felt no such
scruples, and the delight she experienced at being
in the country in the summer time and in such
agreeable company, coupled with the freedom
from restraint and the abundant hospitality of
her protector, was sincere enough. But such
stolen pleasures are proverbially of short duration and are destined seldom or never to recur.

The fact that she was now at Epsom keeping

---

[1] Sedley's "Phyllis is my only joy" is better remembered to-day than
its author's name.

[2] Now Lord Rosebery's, at the foot of Epsom Downs.

house for Buckhurst raises the question whether
she had thus early succumbed to the blandish-
ments of any of her numerous admirers, some of
whose intentions may have been honourable,
whilst others were distinctly the reverse.

After this lapse of time no satisfactory solution
of the problem is possible, but by 1667 she may
have found herself in agreement with the woman
in Petronius Arbiter who wished herself ill-luck,
si unquam se meminerit virginem fuisse.

So to Epsom she went, and we can almost
fix the date, owing to Lacy's indiscretion and
also because Buckhurst is believed to have conceived a violent passion for her from seeing her
roll from side to side of the stage, and exposing
her shapely limbs in a ridiculous scene in James
Howard's *All Mistaken, or the Mad Couple.*[1]

This play was, I think, produced shortly
before the temporary closing of the King's
Theatre above recorded. It is true that Pepys
does not mention it until some months later, but
he does not then speak of it as a new play;
nor does Genest mention it so early, but whenever it was first acted it owed its success entirely
to Nelly and Charles Hart. The former took
the part of Mirida, a madcap girl, and the
latter that of Philador, a wild gallant, and a
kinsman of an Italian duke. Mirida, who is

[1] *All Mistaken, or The Mad Couple* was probably first acted in April
1667, and revived in August and December of the same year. In April
Nell also created the part of Samira in Sir Robert Howard's *The Surprisal.*

persecuted with the advances of a lean and a fat lover, declares that she will marry the thin one when he is fatter or perhaps the fat one when he is thinner.

A ridiculous though not a very delicate situation is created when the nearer the fat man rolls towards her the farther she rolls away from him, until rising with a merry laugh, she seizes a couple of swords from a passing cutler, disarms her fat admirer, and holds him up to the ridicule of the audience.

In a Panegyric dated 1681,[1] purporting to describe Nelly's career, are these lines:

> Much did she suffer first on bulk and stage
> From the Black Guard and Bullies of the age;
> Much more her growing virtue did sustain,
> While dear Charles Hart and Buckhurst sued in vain.
> In vain they sued, curs'd be the envious tongue
> That her undoubted chastity would wrong.

The references to virtue and chastity may have been meant ironically, but the allusion to Nell's early struggles on *bulk* and stage is interesting, since it appears to refer to the open stalls or shops, called bulk shops, in which vegetables are sold to this day in poor neighbourhoods such as Drury Lane.

There can be no manner of doubt that Buckhurst in his youth was very attractive to women. He was the finest gentleman in the voluptuous

---

[1] Harleian MSS. No. 7319.

court of Charles the Second, and he had as much wit as the King or Buckingham or Rochester, without the Royal lack of feeling or the " wicked Earl's " want of thought.[1]

He wrote admirable verse. His " To all you ladies now at land " is one of the best songs of its kind in the English language, and has been reprinted in most anthologies of the period. He was the friend of all the eminent poets of his day, a munificent patron of men of genius; he entertained lavishly and possessed the happy knack of making all his guests feel at home. No wonder was it then that Nell succumbed to him, and when she took the plunge and went to stay with him at Epsom, in the words of one of her admirer's own songs,

> All hearts fall a-leaping whenever she comes,
> And beat day and night like my Lord Craven's drums.[2]

Some misconception having prevailed as to a corrupt bargain alleged to have been entered into between Buckhurst and the King, whereby the former was to renounce all pretensions to Nelly, it is only necessary to state that well-ascertained dates prove that she was off with the old love before she was on with the new. Buckhurst was not sent, as Dryden insinuated, on a " sleeveless

---

[1] Congreve, who visited Lord Dorset when he was dying, declared that even then he "slabbered more wit than most men do when in the best of health."

[2] The lady here referred to was not, however, Nell Gwynne, but a Mrs. Barnes, familiarly known as " Bonny Black Bess."

errand " into France in 1667, though he was
appointed an envoy to Louis XIV. at a later date.
Nor was he offered an earldom to compensate
him for the loss of his mistress.

At the time this compact was supposed to have
been entered into Buckhurst was heir-apparent to
his father's earldom of Dorset, to which he succeeded in 1677, and two years earlier, having
inherited the estates of his maternal uncle,[1] he
had been created Baron Cranfield and Earl of
Middlesex in his own right.

In a letter which Nell wrote to Lory Hyde in
1678, which is printed at a later page of this
volume, she refers to him as " My Lord Dorset,"
and by that title he appears to have been more
generally known.

Whatever was the cause of the quarrel in 1667,
the two were quite good friends in after years,
and Dorset was selected as one of Nelly's trustees
when Burford House at Windsor was settled upon
her.[2] Yet I can imagine Nelly having told
Charles, after the disagreement, that if he wished
to bestow some signal mark of the Royal favour
upon Buckhurst, the office of " Remembrancer
of the first-fruits " might not be altogether
inappropriate! Who can tell at this lapse of
time?   Charles may, conceivably, have wanted to

---

[1] Lionel Cranfield, Earl of Middlesex.

[2] The warrant is preserved amongst the important series of manuscripts
at Knole House, Sevenoaks.

get Buckhurst out of the way, a little later, in consequence of a liking he had taken to Lady Falmouth, whose husband was killed in a sea-fight in 1665. However this may have been, the lady was installed in Whitehall, and though the King spent an enormous amount of money upon her in a few years, she ultimately married Buck-hurst, though not until 1674.

Nell's *liaison* with Buckhurst having proved of short duration, for they soon fell out—perhaps on account of a trifling matter of pounds, shillings, and pence, or because her protector was jealous of Sedley—in August she was back again at the theatre in one of many revivals of *The Indian Emperor*. Only ten days earlier Dryden produced his *Sir Martin Mar All* at the Duke's Theatre.[1] This was perhaps the most uniformly amusing of all Dryden's comedies, and if it had been staged at Drury Lane no doubt Nell would have taken the part either of Mrs. Christian or Mrs. Millisent. The revival of *The Indian Emperor* was followed a few days later at Old Drury by Nell's reappearance in her old part of Samira in Sir Robert Howard's *Surprisal*, and though it was "a very mean play" in Pepys' opinion, it was sufficiently popular to be again revived in the following winter season.

Her next appearance on record is as Panthea

---

[1] This would seem to have been a breach of the conditions of Killi-grew's Patent. See page 11 of this volume.

in a revival of Beaumont and Fletcher's *A King and No King* in September. This was followed [1] by a revival of Richard Rhodes's comedy, *Flora's Vagaries*. It had first been acted at Christ Church, Oxford, by Rhodes and his fellow-students,[2] and in London on November 3 of the same year. Pepys, of course, went to see it, but he does not say much about the play because on this occasion he was admitted to " the women's shift where Nell was dressing herself, and was all unready, and is very pretty, prettier than I thought."

The manner of her first acquaintance with the King is characteristic of Charles's habitual attitude towards women.

Towards the close of 1667, or early in 1668, it chanced that Nell was on friendly terms with a sprig of the Cavalier nobility—a cadet of the house of Villiers—with whom she had probably become acquainted through Lady Castlemaine, a most undesirable companion for a young girl possessed only of wit and beauty and struggling to earn her living on the stage.

Nell's personal appearance at this time—she was now seventeen—must have been extremely attractive.

She was of middle height, exquisitely formed, with the smallest foot and the neatest ankle in all the town. Her hair was bronze-red, sun-kissed

---

[1] October 5, 1667. [2] January 8, 1663.

with streaks of gold, her luxuriant tresses falling
in silken waves over shapely snow-white shoulders.

Her eyes were of the darkest imaginable shade
of sapphire blue, her mouth a perfect Cupid's bow,
revealing, when she smiled, two rows of small
but evenly-matched pearly teeth.

She had a complexion like the wild rose, a
skin of satin, and a well-shaped, if, as some say,
a tip-tilted nose.[1]

But perhaps the greatest beauty of her face,
and it is one that is seldom or never found in
those of plebeian birth, was that her eyebrows
and eyelashes were dark, in striking contrast to
her warm red hair.

In the springtime of her youth Nell must,
indeed, have been fair to look upon.

Young Villiers escorted Nell to the play one
afternoon,—probably to the Duke's Theatre, the
rival house to Old Drury,—and as chance would
have it, who should be seated in the next box
but the King himself!

The impressionable Charles was there *incognito*,
and at once entered into conversation with Nell,
much to Villiers's embarrassment. When the play
was over he insisted on inviting himself to supper
with the young actress and her cavalier. Quite

---

[1] Lely's portrait, which forms the frontispiece to this volume, does not,
however, represent her as having a retroussé nose. She was also painted by
Kneller shortly before her death, and in the Duke of St. Albans' possession
is a fine miniature of her by Cooper, as well as a fan, and some household
accounts.

Carolus 2.^{dus} D.G. Ang: Sco: Fra: et Hib: Rex. &c

Sr P. Lely pinx. F. Luttrell fe. E. Cooper ex.:

CHARLES THE SECOND.

From a rare Mezzotint by Luttrell, in the Author's Collection.

conceivably Nell was nothing loth to obey the
Royal commands, though she could not have
realised how momentous this chance association
with old Rowley was to prove.   Charles ingeniously brought with him the Duke of York, so
that his brother might talk to Villiers and leave
him an uninterrupted field.

They made a merry party of four at a neighbouring tavern, where Charles, who could make
himself well-nigh irresistible to women, once his
desires were aroused, paid such marked attention
to Nell throughout the evening that the quick-
witted girl could not fail to perceive the inner
meaning of his gallantry.

When the tavern-keeper, unaware of the
rank and quality of his guests, presented his bill
—and presumably it was not a short one—to the
King as the senior member of the party, Charles
fumbled in his pockets, only to find that he had
not enough money with him to discharge it.
The Duke of York being found to be equally im-
pecunious, Villiers had to pay the reckoning, not
only for himself and his inamorata, but for all four.

Nell, amused beyond measure at the comicality
of the situation, burst into fits of laughter and,
mimicking to perfection the King's tone and
usual mode of expression, exclaimed: " Oddsfish!   But this is the poorest company that ever
I was in before at a tavern."

Instead of being angry with her for laughing

at him, Charles was so captivated by her high
spirits that he promptly imagined himself to
be head over ears in love. No doubt he had
thought much the same dozens of times before,
but so rapidly did this new-born passion develop
that, before the party broke up, he declared his
Royal will and pleasure to be that Nell should
retire from the stage at the earliest possible
moment, and place herself under his protection.

And so it happened that Villiers, in the brief
space of one convivial evening, lost not only his
money but his mistress, whilst helping, incidentally,
to lay the foundations of what was to prove the
most enduring of all the King's fugitive amours.

Nell did not, however, at once exchange the
tinsel splendours of the stage for the solid comforts
of life at the West End of the town. On the
contrary, though her name soon began to be
freely associated with the King's, she remained
a member of the Drury Lane Company for some
considerable time longer.

Pepys noted in his diary on January 11, 1668,[1]
that "the King did send several times for Nelly,
and she was with him, but what he did she [Mrs.
Knepp, another member of Killigrew's Com-
pany] knows not. This was a good while ago."

On February 20, 1668, Nell, in speaking the
epilogue to Sir Robert Howard's tragedy, *The*

---

[1] On this date Killigrew revived Beaumont and Fletcher's *The Wild
Goose Chase*, in which Nell may have taken part, though the cast has not
been preserved.

Great Favourite, or The Duke of Lerma, said—
perhaps it was a gag of her own—" I know you
in your hearts hate serious plays, as I hate serious
parts," yet Killigrew, who must have been the
best judge of her capacity, continued to assign
tragic parts to her for the remainder of her
career.[1] In conjunction with Mrs. Knepp she also
spoke the prologue, " most excellently " according
to Pepys, whose allegiance to Nell was now somewhat weakened, owing to his growing infatuation
for her fellow-actress in the King's Company.

The English Monsieur was revived in March
and April 1668, and on May 7 Nell appeared, for
the only time in her life, in one of Davenant's
plays, *The Man's the Master.*[2] By right it
belonged exclusively to the Duke's Company, but
the death of Davenant in the previous month
enabled Killigrew to stage it at Drury Lane.
Nell wore boy's clothes and looked " mighty
pretty " in them.[3] In the same month, on May
30, she was seen in a revival of Beaumont and
Fletcher's *Philaster, or Love lies a-Bleeding,* a
tragi-comedy produced so long before as 1609.[4]
It owed its lasting popularity with theatrical
audiences to the touching character of Bellario,

[1] Sir Robert Howard's earlier play *The Committee* had been given at
Drury Lane on May 13, 1667, and at Court on February 8, 1668, and Nell
in all probability appeared in it, though of this there is no actual proof.

[2] To a certain extent *The Man's the Master* was borrowed from Scarron.

[3] There is no mention by Genest of this production at Old Drury.

[4] When *Philaster* was revived in 1695, Horden, who spoke the prologue,
said :—

and actually held the stage for one hundred and fifty years, being revived at Drury Lane so late as 1763 by the younger Coleman.

Pepys, who was present, does not on this occasion mention Nell, his vanity leading him to recall the fact that as a boy he had been cast for the part of Arethusa at Sir Robert Cooke's house. Still he had the grace to add: "What a ridiculous thing it would have been for me to have acted a beautiful woman," with which admission we are not inclined to disagree. It is probable that Nell appeared in Sedley's *The Mulberry Garden* on May 18, and in Lacy's *The Old Troop, or Monsieur Raggou* on July 31, though there is no positive proof of her having done so.

Before the season closed—there seems to have been usually a *relâche* in August and September—Nell created the part of Donna Jacintha in Dryden's new comedy, *An Evening's Love, or the Mock Astrologer*,[1] which was founded, to some extent, on the younger Corneille's *Le Feint Astrologue*.

In the preface to the printed text the poet ably defended himself against the charge of plagiarism, and quoted a saying of Charles the

---

"That good old play, Philaster, ne'er can fail,
But we young actors, how shall we prevail?
Philaster and Bellario, let me tell ye,
For these bold parts we have no Hart, no Nelly,
Those darlings of the stage."

[1] It was acted on June 12 and 20, 1668, revived in 1669 and in 1671, when Nell made her last appearance on the stage.

Second that he only wished that writers who
accused Dryden of piracy would confine themselves to stealing plays as good as his own.

The scene of *An Evening's Love* is laid in
Madrid at Carnival time, the Spanish atmosphere
being admirably expressed. Pepys, who, whatever else he was, cannot be accused of squeamish-
ness, thought it "very smutty," whilst Evelyn,
who was paying one of his infrequent visits to
the theatre, labelled it as profane.

Though Wildblood and Jacintha bear a
strong family resemblance to Celadon and
Florimel, the comic scenes are neither so spon-
taneous nor so irresistibly humorous as those in
the earlier and crisper comedy. Nell, no doubt,
romped through her part and contrived to
stamp it with the hall-mark of her personality,
but much of the dialogue allotted to the minor
characters is dull to the verge of boredom. There
is no scene in the play comparable with one in
Dryden's *Marriage à la Mode*, first acted in 1673.[1]
A duologue in it, on the ethics of flirtation,
between Palamede (Charles Hart) and Doralice
(Mrs. Marshall), a part which would certainly
have been played by Nell had she still been
on the boards, is, in its way, a masterpiece of
humorous characterisation.

In *An Evening's Love* there are four songs
conceived in Dryden's best lyric manner, but the

---

[1] Two years after Nell's retirement from the stage.

refrain with which each concludes is somewhat marred by suggestiveness. I will only insert the last, which takes the form of a duet between Damon (Charles Hart) and Celimena (Nelly):

Damon. Celimena of my heart
None shall e'er bereave you:
If, with your good leave, I may
Quarrel with you once a day,
I will never leave you.

Celimena. Passion is but an empty name,
Where respect is wanting:
Damon, you mistake your aim,
Hang your heart, and burn your flame,
If you must be ranting.

Damon. Love as dull and muddy is,
As decaying liquor:
Anger sets it on the lees,
And refines it by degrees,
Till it works the quicker.

Celimena. Love by quarrels to beget
Wisely you endeavour;
With a grave physician's wit,
Who, to cure an ague fit,
Put me in a fever.

Damon. Anger rouses love to fight,
And his only bait is,
'Tis the spur to dull delight,
And is but an eager bite,
When desire at height is.

Celimena. If such drops of heat can fall
In our wooing weather;
If such drops of heat can fall
We shall have the devil and all
When we come together.

In the epilogue, spoken by Nell, Dryden had one of his periodical flings at the critics, and I append the opening sentences, as they throw an instructive sidelight upon the demeanour of theatrical audiences at this period:

> My part being small, I have had time to-day
> To mark your various censures of our play.
> First, looking for a judgment or a wit,
> Like Jews I saw them scattered through the pit;
> And where a knot of smilers lent an ear
> To one that talked, I knew the foe was there.
> The club of jests went round; he, who had none
> Borrowed o' the next, and told it for his own.
> Among the rest, they kept a fearful stir,
> In whispering that he stole th' Astrologer;
> And said, betwixt a French and English plot,
> He eased his half-tired muse, on pace and trot.

On September 15 Pepys went to Drury Lane to see a new play "acted but yesterday," Flecknoe's *Damoiselles à la mode*, in which the author had designed the part of Lysette for Nell. This is in all probability only one of many plays in which Nell appeared of which little or no trace has been preserved.

No other mention of this performance has been found, but Pepys tells us that it was "so mean a thing" that when it was announced that it would be acted again on the next day, the pit "fell a-laughing," there being not a quarter of it full. So that on this occasion Nell may have come very near to seeing a play damned on its production.

The staid and sober Evelyn was shocked to
find how the drama had degenerated since the
earlier days of the Restoration, and when we
contrast the elegant rhythm of *The Indian
Emperor* it must be admitted that the charge
was a just one.

Dryden reached the high-water mark of indelicacy in *Limberham*, which proved so distasteful
to its audience on its production (in 1678) that it
was promptly withdrawn.   Later still, after Nell's
death, his prologues and epilogues spoken by
Mrs. Bracegirdle were as coarse as anything
which Wycherley or Aphra Behn ever wrote.

Except that she spoke the prologue to Ben
Jonson's tragedy, *Catiline's Conspiracy*, " in an
Amazonian habit," when that old play was
revived on December 19 and the following
day, Nell, after appearing as Pulcheria in a
revival of Shirley's *The Sisters*, was now absent
from the stage of Old Drury for some months.
In *Catiline's Conspiracy* she seems to have taken
no part, Mrs. Corey being the Sempronia.

But in the spring of 1669 she made a welcome
reappearance as Valeria in Dryden's *Tyrannic
Love, or the Royal Martyr*, in which Hart was
Porphyrius and Peg Hughes St. Catherine.[1]

Nell, having stabbed herself in the last act,

---

[1] Malone says that *Tyrannic Love* was first acted at the end of 1668 or
the beginning of 1669, but a reference in the prologue to " in the prime of
Easter term in tart and cheese cake time " seems to point to its having been
produced in the spring.

springs to life again, as she is being carried off
the stage, to speak a riotous epilogue in which
occur the oft-quoted words: " I die out of my
calling in a tragedy."

Oldys wrote that she so captivated the King
by her spirited delivery of this epilogue and the
humorous turn which she gave to the words, that
he promptly went behind the scenes and carried
her off to an entertainment that same night.

But, as I have shown, his affections had
been engaged long before this date, and, moreover, Curll's *History of the Stage* is notoriously
undependable, especially in the matter of dates.

Nell was not seen again at Old Drury for
several months, during which Dryden was engaged in writing his last important tragedy,
in two parts, *Almanzor and Almahide, or The
Conquest of Granada by the Spaniards*, a more
ambitious and extravagant work, though, in our
humble judgment, it is inferior in charm to
The Indian Emperor.

The new play, which was borrowed in part
from Scudéry, was intended by its author to be
staged in the spring, but, owing to the fact that
Nell was then about to give birth to her elder son,
the future Duke of St. Albans, it had, perforce,
to be postponed until the autumn.

When at last it was produced, Dryden, in
the outspoken fashion of the times, explained
the cause of the delay in the epilogue:

Think him not duller for the year's delay;
He was prep .·ed, the women were away:
And men without their parts can hardly play.
If they through sickness seldom did appear,
Pity the virgins of each theatre;
For at both houses 'twas a sickly year!
And pity us, your servants, to whose cost
In one such sickness nine whole months were lost.

In May 1670 Henrietta, Duchess of Orleans, came to England, with Louise de Querouaille in her train, to negotiate the secret Treaty of Dover, by which her brother bound himself hand and foot to Louis XIV. in return for an annual subsidy, paid over in French gold to Will Chiffinch. The Duchess brought over with her the latest French fashions in dress, amongst these being larger hats than were then the vogue at Whitehall. The men attending her wore extremely short coats and broad waist-belts which, for some unknown reason, seem to have provoked ridicule in this country.

James Nokes,[1] who had been a toyman in Cornhill before he took to the stage, was the principal low comedian at the Duke's Theatre, though the performance in question was given at Dover; an early instance of a London theatrical company making a provincial excursion. Killigrew's Company is said, however, to have been commanded to appear at Tunbridge Wells during

---

[1] Nokes was the creator of the part of Sir Nicholas Cully in Etherege's first comedy, *Love in a Tub.* He was renowned for his impersonations of " bawling fops," which he played with an unsurpassed reality of action and manner.

the plague. With what must appear to any age but his own the worst possible taste, Nokes seized upon the sartorial peculiarities of the French as a means of provoking laughter and by appearing on the stage in an even shorter coat, to which the young Duke of Monmouth contributed a sword and waist-belt of his own; until, in the words of Downes, the prompter at Davenant's theatre, he looked more like a dressed-up ape than the character he represented [1] in Caryll's comedy, *Sir Solomon, or The Cautious Coxcomb.*

In order to accentuate, if possible, this ridicule of the French, Nell spoke the prologue to *The Conquest of Granada* in an enormous hat the size of a cart-wheel, and an even wider waist-belt. [2]

She apologised to the audience for the absurdity of her make-up by saying:

> This jest was first of t'other House's making
> And five times tried, has never failed of taking;
> For 'twere a shame a poet should be killed
> Under the shelter of so broad a shield.
> This is that hat whose very sight did win ye
> To laugh and clap as though the devil were in ye.
> As then for Nokes, so now I hope you'll be
> So dull to laugh once more for love of me.

As many of the Duchess's suite attended the performance they may well have been disgusted at the execrable taste of the imitation. But the

[1] Sir Arthur Addle.
[2] The beautiful young Countess of Kildare, who is believed to have been the last of Charles the Second's mistresses, was painted by Wissing in one of these cart-wheel hats—her portrait is reproduced facing page 271.

Court, headed by the King, received Nell's caricature of a caricature with roars of laughter and thunders of applause.

If Nell spoke the epilogue to the second part of the play, the folly of this ridicule of the French fashions was, to some extent, redeemed by Dryden's masterly review of the English drama from Ben Jonson to his own times:

> They who have best succeeded on the stage,
> Have still conformed their genius to their age.
> Thus Jonson did mechanic humour show,
> When men were dull, and conversation low.
> Then comedy was faultless, but 'twas coarse.
>
> .   .   .   .   .
>
> Wit's now arrived to a more high degree;
> Our native language more refined and free.
> Our ladies and our men now speak more wit
> In conversation, than those poets writ.
>
> .   .   .   .   .
>
> Yet though you judge (as sure the critics will),
> That some before him writ with greater skill,
> In this one praise he has that fame surpast,
> To please an age more gallant than the last.

We shall see how, in his next play, he falsified his claim to refinement in comedy, whilst justifying his assertion of " freedom."

Both parts of *The Conquest of Granada* were acted at Court on two successive days, the 10th and 11th February 1671, probably with the same cast as at Drury Lane.

In this same year *An Evening's Love* was revived. Peter Cunningham thought that the character of Almahide in *The Conquest of Granada* was the last which Nell appeared in on the stage of Drury Lane, and probably it was her last original creation, whereas the presentation of *An Evening's Love* in 1671 was only a revival.

Unfortunately for posterity, Pepys ceased to write his immortal diary in 1669, so that we have not his guidance in these latter days of Nell's stage career, but Oldys credits her with yet one more appearance at Old Drury —in Dryden's comedy, *The Assignation, or Love in a Nunnery*. In the cast given by Scott and Saintsbury her name does not occur, the only actresses mentioned being Mrs. James, Mrs. Marshall, Mrs. Knepp, Mrs. Boutell, and Mrs. Coxe. Genest makes no mention of Nell having acted at Drury Lane in 1672, nor was *The Assignation* printed until 1673, by which date she had certainly retired. A brief quotation from the printed text will show how much Dryden's dialogue had deteriorated since her triumphs in *The Indian Emperor* and in *Secret Love*.

In the first scene of the first act a song, which Oldys says Nell sang " with great archness," is introduced by a young lady, Violetta, being asked the following question by her sister:

Laura. Are you fit at fifteen, to be trusted with a maiden-head?
It is as much as your betters can manage at full twenty.

Whilst a little later on Violetta is made to say:

How! I a novice at ripe fifteen? I would have you to
know that I have killed my man before I was fourteen, and now
am ready for another execution.

The epilogue to *The Assignation* is also highly
indelicate, and we prefer to think of Nell's
undoubted successes in tragedy and comedy
achieved, as they were, without any such unworthy
lapses from decorum.

Though, after the most diligent study of
contemporary evidence, it has not been possible
to recover the names of more than a score of rôles
in which Nell is definitely known to have
appeared, all of them at Drury Lane, she must,
I feel sure, have acted many other parts, of
which all trace has been lost, between 1665 and
her retirement from the stage.

It may be that in years to come further
research will reveal other parts created by her,
or revivals of old plays in which she either acted
or spoke the prologue or epilogue.

Oldys mentions her having spoken a new
prologue to Beaumont and Fletcher's *Knight of
the Burning Pestle* at some unascertained date,
but, owing to the absence of any printed bills
of the play during the whole period of her
theatrical career, the scanty record of her share
in the varying fortunes of the Restoration stage
under Killigrew's management will not easily be
amplified.

The late Mr. Joseph Knight, who wrote the notice of Nell Gwynne in the *Dictionary of National Biography*, erroneously supposed that she created several other parts after the year 1671, but, misled by Genest, he fell into the mistake of confusing her with Anne Quin, an actress who was undoubtedly on the stage so late as 1682.

Anne, who is said to have possessed considerable personal attractions, bore no facial resemblance to Nell. She was apparently an actress of some importance, as in 1667, possibly during Nell's temporary absence from Old Drury, Killigrew assigned to her a separate dressing-room at the King's Theatre " with a chimney in it," this room to be " only for her use and whom she shall admit."

Anne, whose name is variously spelt Quin and Guinn, was perhaps the creator of the part of Alicia in Lord Orrery's tragedy *The Black Prince*,[1] which Pepys saw on three separate occasions without mentioning Nell in connection with it. He also tells us that he fell asleep the last time he saw it, which he would hardly have done had Nell been on the stage.

Alicia was intended by Lord Orrery for Alice Perrers, the mistress of King Edward III., and though historically inaccurate and insufferably tedious, the play contains a few good lines, some

---

[1] *The Black Prince* was produced at Drury Lane, October 19, 1667.

of which, had they been written a year or two later, would have been singularly appropriate to the real Mistress Nell:

Alicia. You know, dear friend, when to this Court I came
My eyes did all our bravest youths inflame;
And in that happy state I lived awhile,
When fortune did betray me with a smile;
Or rather Love against my peace did fight;
And to revenge his power, which I did slight;
Made Edward our victorious monarch be
One of those many who did sigh for me.
All other flames but his I did deride;
They rather made my trouble than my pride;
But this, when told me, made me quickly know,
Love is a god, to which all hearts must bow.

The italics are my own, and the lines seem so applicable to episodes in our heroine's life that the writer may well have had her in mind when he wrote them. Had not the King been present the play would probably have been damned on its production, but though Lord Orrery shortened it considerably and improved it, by omitting some of the more tedious passages, it achieved no permanent success.

Peter Cunningham unhesitatingly awarded Alicia to Nell, but Mr. Gordon Goodwin points out that Downes in his *Roscius Anglicanus* habitually spells Anne's surname with an *i* in order to distinguish her from her more famous contemporary. On the other hand, I have frequently found Nell's name similarly spelt, hence the inevitable confusion between the two actresses.[1]

The characters wrongly attributed to her by the *Dictionary of National Biography*, but which belong by right to Anne Quin, are seven in number: Angelica Bianca, "a famous courtezan," in Aphra Behn's *Rover*, 1677; Astrea, in *The Constant Nymph, or The Rambling Shepherd*, an anonymous pastoral; Thalestris, in Samuel Pordage's rhymed tragedy, *The Siege of Babylon*; Lady Knowell, "an affected learned woman," in Aphra Behn's *Sir Patient Fancy* (licensed, January 28, 1678); and Lady Squeamish, in Otway's comedy, *Friendship in Fashion* (licensed, May 31, 1678). All these were staged at the Dorset Gardens Theatre.

To these characters must be added: Sunamira, in Thomas Southerne's *The Loyal Brother, or The Persian Prince*, and Queen Elizabeth, in John Bankes's tragedy, *The Unhappy Favourite, or The Earl of Essex*. These two plays were acted at Drury Lane in 1682, and in each case Dryden supplied both prologue and epilogue.

Aphra Behn, whose maiden name was Amies or Amis, according to her latest and most competent biographer, Mr. Montague Summers, was not only a capable dramatist but the first Englishwoman to support herself by her pen. Had her plays not been disfigured by frequent lapses from

---

[1] It is therefore possible that Nell did appear in Lord Orrery's play, and I have included it in the tabulated list of her stage appearances in Appendix I.

decency her reputation would have stood higher than it does to-day. After writing a novel she succeeded in getting her first play, *The Forced Marriage*, produced at the Duke's Theatre in December 1670. Her next was *The Amorous Prince*, and her *Abdelazar*, founded on Marlowe, opens with a fine song, "Love in fantastic triumph sat." *Sir Patient Fancy* she took from Molière, but a rattling pantomimic farce, *Scaramouch*, appears to be wholly original. Aphra Behn had a genuine admiration for Nell, dedicating her *Feigned Courtezans, or A Night's Intrigue* (produced at the Duke's Theatre in 1679) to her in terms of fulsome adulation.

This many-sided woman, before she took to literature, acted as a spy during the war with Holland. She was married to a Dutchman, and having learnt in Antwerp that it was Cornelius de Witte's intention to send a fleet up the Thames and, if possible, to burn Chatham, she communicated the intelligence to London, where, however, it was ridiculed and unheeded.

What a loss Nell Gwynne must have been to the management of the King's Theatre is evident from the fact that *Secret Love* was not revived for ten years after her last appearance in it, for there would have been no use in presenting it with another Florimel; whilst *The Indian Emperor*, in which she probably reappeared so late as 1670, was not staged again at Drury Lane until eleven years later.

CHAPTER III

WHEN, some twenty years ago, that enterprising municipal body, the London County Council, formed its new thoroughfare from Holborn to the Strand, it wisely retained, at the lower end, the ancient place-name of Aldwych. Before the Council's alterations Drury Lane led, at its southern extremity, into Wych Street, which, within my recollection, contained a number of picturesque timbered and gabled houses similar to those which existed, until recently, in Cloth Fair, Smithfield. Drury Lane commemorates in some vague degree the Roman Via de Aldwych, which, for centuries, was one of the principal means of communication between the highway of the Strand, St. Giles's, and Bloomsbury. The lower portion of the Lane, where it debouched into the Strand, being only a narrow footway, wheeled traffic, perforce, followed the line of Wych Street; the foot passage to the Strand being marked in old maps of the neighbourhood as Maypole Alley or Little Drury Lane.

Wych Street, Holywell Street (so called from
a famous spring of clear water near St. Clement's
Church), Clare Market (which derived its name
from the Earls of Clare, its ground landlords), and
many lesser-known courts and alleys, disappeared
at one fell swoop when Kingsway and Aldwych
were constructed to meet the ever - growing
requirements of modern street traffic. The
inevitable removal of ancient buildings, which
the formation of an entirely new thoroughfare on
a large scale entails, sweeps into oblivion many
an interesting page from the life story of London,
for, when whole streets are blotted out, a generation which knew them not pays little heed to
their historical associations.

Bush House, the latest Anglo-American Moloch,
which, from its enormous bulk, completely dwarfs
St. Mary's Church, stands right athwart the site
of Maypole Alley, through which Nell Gwynne,
when she lodged on the west side of Drury Lane
at the Cock and Pye tavern,[1] must have passed
on that May morning when she stood at the doorway of her humble lodging, looking "mighty
pretty," to watch the milkmaids, with garlands
twined round their pails, dancing from sheer
lightness of heart to the merry strains of a fiddle.

---

[1] The Cock and Pye tavern, a building said to have been as old as the
reign of Henry the Seventh, remained until 1891, when it was pulled down
and rebuilt, only to be finally swept away on the formation of Aldwych.
Another old house in the Strand, called Nell Gwynne's dairy, disappeared
about the same time.

Standing at her own door and looking down Little Drury Lane, Nell could have seen the tall maypole, surmounted by a gilded crown, which had recently been re-erected in the Strand. Lacy, who first taught her to dance, was a neighbour of hers, and no doubt other members of Killigrew's Company also lived near the playhouse. Lacy's house was two doors from Lord Anglesey's, and near Cradle Alley.

No one who has the curiosity to visit the Lane as it exists to-day, with the intention of reconstructing in the mind's eye the vanished past, would imagine for a moment that the Via de Aldwych could ever have been a fashionable quarter of the town. Yet within a stone's throw of the " mazy courts and dark abodes " of which Gay wrote so piquantly, a great deal of British history was made. I use the word " British " advisedly, for England, Scotland, Ireland, and Wales are all represented in the catalogue of its former inhabitants.

Neither Peter Cunningham nor his learned continuator, Mr. Wheatley, give an adequate picture of Drury Lane's former residential importance, at any rate as regards the lower portion of it towards the Strand, for the upper part belonging to St. Giles's parish was never, at any time, anything better than a squalid slum. So completely has the neighbourhood changed, owing to the continuous process of urban expansion from east to west, that it is difficult to realise that the southern portion of this ancient thoroughfare, now a congeries of mean shops and blocks of artisans' dwellings, was once the chosen home of men and women who have left a more or less indelible mark upon the history of their time.

Crowned heads, great nobles, statesmen, lawyers, of course, and celebrities in nearly every walk of life were to be found in Drury Lane until the close of the seventeenth century, when the street underwent a rapid decline in social esteem. The vagaries of fashion often revolutionise the character of a street within a comparatively short period, and as nothing is so fatal to the reputation of a residential quarter as the admixture of business premises with private dwelling-houses, it would be impossible to set a limit to the extent of the metamorphosis which three centuries of change and progress can effect.

Ideas as to the comparative attractions of any particular London street as a place of residence are apt to undergo rapid transformations. Few would now be found willing to endorse Charles Lamb's opinion that Bow Street was the best place in London for a man to live in. He declared that he would not exchange it for any other street, as when he looked out of his windows he could see Drury Lane Theatre on one hand and Covent

Garden on the other, and he desired no better prospect.

This was in the first half of the nineteenth century, but at the present day I doubt if there is a single private house, either in Bow Street or in any of the once fashionable streets in the vicinity of the Piazza. The old police - station in Bow Street was reopened as an hotel not many years ago, and as the house was not rebuilt at the time, the cells have, presumably, been converted into bedrooms, a circumstance probably unique in the history of the metropolis.

When Nell first knew the neighbourhood there stood towards the Strand end of the Lane, on the east side, a great house in a spacious garden, surrounded by high walls to screen it from the vulgar gaze, which was then in the occupation of the Earl of Craven.[1] It had been built about 1530 by Sir William Drury, a member of an ancient Suffolk family which contributed a Speaker to the British House of Commons, and a Lord Justice to Ireland in Elizabethan days. Sir William obtained a grant of the land on which the house stood from Henry VIII., and the Clares were, I think, even earlier residents in the same locality.

It requires, as a rule, more than a generation

---

[1] The old Olympic Theatre in Wych Street, which was demolished within my recollection, stood upon a portion of Lord Craven's garden. Lord Craven is said to have given £50,000 to Charles the Second in exile.

of continuous residence for a family to bestow
its patronymic upon a London street or to oust
a more ancient nomenclature from popular
remembrance. Somehow the Drurys contrived
to stamp their cognomen upon this unlovely
quarter of the town, nor is their name likely
to be forgotten owing to the proximity of the
great theatre which has flourished on its present
site for more than two centuries and a half.

Yet the King's Theatre, to give it its first
name, was not actually in the Lane until the late
Sir Augustus Harris, when he became lessee
and manager, acquired some slum property at
the back of the stage for the purposes of a scene-
dock. Part of this property is at present let
out in shops, but the great theatre, owing to
Harris's foresight, thus became possessed of an
island site, the advantages of which are so rightly
insisted upon by the County Council in licensing
new buildings for theatrical purposes.

When Harris first came to Old Drury he told
me that the scenery was painted and stored, with
a quantity of highly inflammable material, under
the stalls and pit, and it was this very real danger
which prompted him to acquire the additional
space at the back of the stage.

It has been stated in print that there are few
streets in London of any considerable length in
which there cannot be found a tree or a patch
of green to relieve the dreary expanse of brick,

stone, and plaster, though it might well be imagined that Drury Lane, as it stands to-day, would be found to be an exception to the rule. Yet to my surprise, on a recent visit, I found two catalpa trees, not only growing but flourishing in the London smoke, in a small plot of ground (on the west side of the narrow street), which has wisely been converted from a burial-place to a playground for the children of the poor of this squalid neighbourhood, to whom the West End parks are practically inaccessible.

The plane is usually considered to be the most suitable tree for London, and the gardens of Lincoln's Inn Fields and Berkeley Square prove the truth of the saying. The catalpa, however, runs it close in smoke-resisting power. It flourishes exceedingly in New Palace Yard, Westminster, and deserves to be more extensively cultivated in our London parks and gardens than it has been hitherto.

Drury, afterwards Craven, House was a five-storied building with eleven small windows on each floor intersected by Doric and Ionic pilasters.[1] It was pulled down in 1809, when Craven Buildings were erected on the site. These, in their turn, disappeared on the formation of Kingsway and Aldwych.

Lord Craven placed his mansion at the disposal

---

[1] There is a good view of Craven House, which was an unusually lofty one for the date of its erection, in Wilkinson's *Londina Illustrata*.

of the Queen of Bohemia when she visited London
soon after the Restoration. She was, I think,
the only crowned head whom Drury Lane can
claim for its own, though her stay under Lord
Craven's roof was a short one.[1]

Archibald Campbell, 7th Earl of Argyll, who
became a Catholic in 1618 and fought for
Philip III. of Spain in Flanders, was born about
1575 and was an early resident in the Lane.
In 1619 he was declared a rebel and a traitor,
though the sentence was subsequently reversed.
His second wife died in the Lane in 1635, and
probably he did too,[2] although a contemporary
record speaks of his house as being in Covent
Garden, an elastic term at that date which often
included Drury Lane as well. His two successors
in the title were not so fortunate as to die in
their beds. The 1st Marquis, son and heir of
the 7th Earl, who is described by Clarendon as
a man of extraordinary cunning and ambition,
was instrumental in bringing Charles to Scotland
in 1650, and, with his own hands, Argyll placed
the crown upon the King's head at Scone. He
seems to have entertained hopes of marrying the
young King to his daughter, but, as nothing came
of the project, he gave in his adhesion to Cromwell. At the Restoration he had the effrontery to

[1] The King not being anxious for the Queen of Bohemia to come to England, she received no official welcome, whereupon Lord Craven offered her
asylum in Drury Lane. She soon removed to Leicester House, but died within
a week of her going there, on February 13, 1662.   [2] In 1638.

come to London to wait upon the King. I do
not know whether he still retained the family
house in the Lane, but in any case he would not
have required it long, for he was promptly lodged
in the Tower. Sent back to Edinburgh, he was
tried for high treason, attainted and executed at
the Market Cross, his head being exposed on
the top of the Tolbooth, just as Montrose's had
been in 1650.

His son, a staunch Protestant, was restored
to the Earldom, but he, too, was subsequently
imprisoned and twice sentenced to death. Escap-
ing to Holland, he joined in a conspiracy hatched
in that country to place Monmouth on the throne.
He headed a rising in Scotland with that object,
but being taken prisoner at the ford of Inch-
innan he was summarily beheaded, by the
express order of James the Second, on the old
charge preferred against him in 1681. His
head, like his father's and Montrose's, was exposed
on the Tolbooth, and it is doubtful if history
can supply a parallel case wherein three successive
holders of a title, father, son, and grandson, all
of whom bore the same Christian name, were
condemned as traitors, two of them actually
perishing on the same scaffold.

A near neighbour of the Earl of Argyll in the
Lane was William Alexander of Mains Menstrie,
1st Earl of Stirling and Viscount Canada, to whom
James I. granted, in perpetuity, enormous tracts

of land, including the whole of Nova Scotia and the greater part of the territory now represented by the United States and Canada. His career is one of the most extraordinary to be found in history. Notwithstanding splendid opportunities, his schemes of colonisation, which, had they succeeded, would have made him rich beyond the dreams of avarice, ended in complete failure, and he died in the Lane, insolvent, on September 12, 1640.

When the Earl endeavoured to obtain emigrants for his "Nova Scotia" he offered such poor terms that he failed to attract the right class of colonist. His next enterprise, the institution of an Order of Baronets, who were to receive grants of land six square miles in extent in return for a cash payment of £150, yielded no better results. James the First, who seems to have believed in him, helped him liberally, not only with money, but with valuable monopolies, including royalties on the copper coinage of Scotland, the grant of patents for printing the psalms, and by further gifts of land in Ireland. All of these proved equally unproductive. In his way Stirling was something of a playwright and a poet too; his earliest lyrical work, *Aurora*, being dedicated to his neighbour, the Earl of Argyll's wife.[1]

---

[1] On the death of the 5th Earl of Stirling in 1739 the Earldom became dormant. It has been unsuccessfully claimed on at least two occasions, the

Turning from Scotland to Ireland, another distinguished man who made his London home in Drury Lane was Sir Arthur Chichester, soldier and ambassador, Lord Deputy of Ireland from 1605 to 1615, and Lord High Treasurer of that country from 1616 till his death in 1625. He came to London in order to enter the profession of the law at Lincoln's Inn, so conveniently near to Drury Lane. Mountjoy wrote of him to Cecil:[1] "You must make one governor of all Ulster, and the fittest man that can be chosen in England or in Ireland is Sir Arthur Chichester."[2]

Chichester was a successful governor for over eleven years, though he was not, apparently, sufficiently zealous to altogether please the Court in enforcing the penal laws against the Catholics.

Another distinguished Irishman lived next door to him in the Lane. This was Arthur Annesley, Earl of Anglesey, who, like his friend, was a member of Lincoln's Inn. He was, I think, in some way dependent upon Chichester for his advancement in life.

---

latter of these preferred, in 1825, on the strength of a document which was found to be a forgery. In right of my own descent from Harry Alexander of Mains Menstrie, nephew of the 5th Earl (who died without issue), I am one of the coheirs to this peerage.

[1] October 2, 1601.

[2] It is interesting to recall that Sir Arthur Chichester was a collateral ancestor of the Rt. Hon. Hugh O'Neill, the first Speaker of the first Parliament of Northern Ireland, on whom devolved, in great measure, the onerous task of starting in Ulster an entirely new Parliamentary machine, in accordance with the provisions of the Government of Ireland Act of 1920.

Sir Lewis Lewkenor, Master of the Ceremonies, *temp.* James I., was another resident, and from him the notorious Lewkenor's Lane took its name.[1] Sir Francis Windebank had a house in the Lane in 1641, and there must have been people living in it when Nell Gwynne first knew it who remembered Oliver Cromwell as one of their neighbours. After living for a time in Long Acre[2] he flitted across the stage of Drury Lane before taking up his abode in Lord Pembroke's old quarters in the Cockpit at Whitehall.

Another notorious character whom Nell may have encountered in her walks was Moll Cutpurse—her real name was Mary Frith—who carried on a lucrative business in Fleet Street as a receiver of stolen goods. She was also a fortune-teller and a forger, frequently donning male attire and keeping a bodyguard of young thieves in her service. She is said to have been the means of bringing to justice the five women barbers of Drury Lane who treated a young girl in a very cruel manner.

Tom Killigrew wrote a song about them, which he sang to the King, beginning:

[1] On a recent visit to this unsavoury spot (it is now called Macklin Street) I noticed that the doorway of one of the houses bears the legend: " Cleansing station for women." No doubt it fulfils as useful a purpose in the twentieth century as it would have done in those far-off days when Madam Ross kept a house of ill-fame in Lewkenor's Lane.

[2] From 1637 till 1643.

> Did you ever hear the like?
> Did you ever hear the fame?
> Of the five women barbers
> Who lived in Drury Lane?

The other verses have not come down to us. One of these women is believed to have been the mother of Nan Clarges who married General Monk, thus supplying yet another link between Old Drury and Whitehall. It seems a curious occupation for the weaker sex to adopt as a means of livelihood, but history is continually repeating itself, and as there have been women barbers in the Strand within quite recent years, there may be still, for aught I know.[1]

At Nell's birth in 1650 the 2nd Earl of Salisbury and Lord Howard were living in the Lane, and, a few years later, I find in the parochial books the names of several ladies who were householders there: the Countess of Carlisle, Lady Paget, Lady Foster, and Lady Diana Curzon amongst the number.

Of these the first named was the most notorious. She was Lady Lucy Percy, a daughter of the Earl of Northumberland. In her youth she was a famous beauty and in her middle-age the Erinnys of her time. She it was who told Pym that Charles the First intended to go to the House of Commons and seize the five members. In 1649, when she was imprisoned in the Tower

---

[1] Moll Cutpurse is said to have died at her house in Fleet Street, July 26, 1659.

for corresponding with Charles the Second in Holland, it is said that she was threatened with the rack in the hope of extorting information as to the doings of the Royalist party.

Another lady, whose father [1] was living in the Lane at the Restoration, was the Duchess of Norfolk, who became one of Nell's friends in after years.

Strype, the continuator of Stow, writing in 1720, calls the Coal Yard "a place of very ordinary account," nor is he enthusiastic about the Lane generally, speaking of it as "inhabited by shopkeepers and others," whilst the courts out of Weld Street on the west side bore, in his day, an even worse reputation, being "not over well inhabited, except some of them noted for the reception of the kinder sort of females," which is an euphemistic mode of saying that they were nests of prostitution.

Humphrey Weld, who bought the Lulworth estate in Dorsetshire from the Earl of Suffolk, bought Weld House on the east side of the Lane from Sir Edward Stradling, who built it about 1630. It was a large mansion containing no less than thirty-three rooms on a floor, with a frontage of 150 feet towards the Lane and a large garden at the back. Persons of distinction, such as ambassadors, were frequently lodged there in the days of its social importance.

[1] The Earl of Peterborough.

The great Duke of Ormonde, a grandee of
the first class amongst his peers, with a wealth
of minor titles hanging to his name, ranks as
one of the greater ghosts of Drury Lane. His
grandfather, Walter, 11th Earl of Ormonde,
who was imprisoned in the Fleet for several
years, had his estates sequestered and his income
greatly reduced. On recovering his liberty he
took Weld House. His grandson, the 1st Duke,
had an adventurous youth. Born at Clerkenwell
in Sir John Poyntz's house, he was sent over to
Ireland when only three years of age. Returning
six years later, he is next heard of at a Catholic
school at Finchley, kept by one of the Conyers
family. A little later he was placed under the
charge of Archbishop Abbot at Lambeth Palace
until he was sixteen. He then came to live with
his grandfather at Weld House on the slender
allowance of £40 a year. He seems, however,
to have entered into all the gaieties of the town,
and, becoming a constant playgoer, he made
acquaintance with the leading actors of the time.

At eighteen he volunteered to serve under
the 1st Duke of Buckingham in a final attempt
to relieve La Rochelle. He hurried down to
Portsmouth, where the expeditionary force was
then fitting out, in the hope of being allowed to
take part in the enterprise, but the Duke, not
having obtained his grandfather's consent, refused
to take him with him. The very next day

Buckingham was assassinated by Felton at a house which is still standing in Portsmouth High Street, and young Lord Thurles, as he then was, returned discomfited to London.

At Christmas 1629, when still a minor, he married, in London, his cousin, Lady Elizabeth Preston, only daughter and heiress of the Earl of Desmond and Baroness Dingwall in her own right. He became Lord-Lieutenant of Ireland in 1643, and thenceforward his life was devoted to the service of his country in a Court, honey-combed with intrigue, wherein all the forces of corruption were arrayed against him. The Duchess of Cleveland worked hard to bring about his downfall because, forsooth, he pre-vented her from obtaining a grant in fee of the Phœnix Park, whilst the 2nd Duke of Buckingham, an equally unscrupulous opponent, connived at, if he did not actually contrive, the infamous Colonel Blood's attempt upon his life. None of his enemies could, however, disprove the truth of Ormonde's proud declaration: " How-ever ill I may stand at Court, I am resolved to lie well in the chronicle." [1]

After Ormonde's connection with Weld House ceased, persons of distinction frequently lodged there. Evelyn mentions his having dined there with Ronquillo, the Spanish ambassador, on

---

[1] The Duke of Ormonde's eldest son, Lord Ossory, who predeceased his father in 1680, was also a man of unblemished character.

April 26, 1681, the repast being half-English and half-Spanish.

The house, or one of its wings, was wrecked in an anti-Catholic riot in the reign of James the Second, when the ambassador's valuable library was burnt, though, to Ronquillo's great delight, the sacred Host in the Chapel was miraculously preserved. In this connection it is interesting to note that so many Catholics were living in the Lane in the seventeenth century that at one time it was commonly called "little Rome."

In 1694 Weld House was advertised to be let in the *London Gazette*, but the neighbourhood having by this time sunk appreciably in public estimation, it was soon after demolished and the site built over. Pope, writing in 1708, says: "In the town it is ten to one but a young fellow may find his strayed heart again with some Wild Street or Drury Lane damsel." No vestiges of the mansion inhabited by the mighty Ormonde remain, but to this day some old houses still standing in Great Wild Street, but fast tottering to their fall, may well date from the seventeenth century. Mean shops and blocks of artisans' dwellings, named, for the most part, after theatrical celebrities (although as yet Nell Gwynne is not so commemorated), now cover the former sites of many aristocratic homes. Their gardens also have long been built over, so that it seems safe to predict that Drury

Lane can never again, under the changed conditions of London life, be a residential street.
Between Holborn and its lower end it was
originally nearly half a mile long, but its
dimensions have been much curtailed by the
formation of Aldwych. In the Lane and its
tributaries there are still some oil and colour-
men's shops. A hundred years ago the Lane
was noted for them, but they have been for the
most part replaced by cheap fruit stores, and
humble little shops without windows, where coal
is sold by the scuttle and potatoes by the pound
—the bulk shops of an earlier age. There are
also numerous public-houses (of which the rebuilt
White Hart is amongst the oldest) and gin-
palaces galore. One of the former taverns in the
Lane, the old Mogul, has been converted first into
a music hall, and, more recently, into the Winter
Garden Theatre, which, under its present management, bids fair to revive in great measure the
traditions of the old Gaiety in the Strand.[1]

Covent Garden Market, from the nature of
its trade, has changed less in two centuries than
Drury Lane. Although there remain the great
theatre and the perfume of innumerable oranges
to remind us of Nelly and the scenes of her childhood, the importance of the Lane as a residential

---

[1] Nell Gwynne's name having been somewhat vaguely associated with
the old Mogul, Mr. Grossmith has formed at his theatre an interesting
collection of portraits and views relating to her life and times; an example
which other London managers would do well to follow.

quarter has vanished.   Never again can it be the
chosen home of fashion, any more than can Inigo
Jones's noble piazza in Lincoln's Inn Fields be
recovered from the lawyers and men of business.
It seems almost incredible that such a plague spot
on the map of London, where bullies, knights
of the road, cut-purses, and brothel-keepers
preyed upon one another and their betters,
should not have deterred members of the higher
aristocracy from living literally within a stone's
throw of the " mazy courts and dark abodes "
which opened right and left out of a lane so
narrow that it must have been an impossibility
for my Lord Craven to turn his coach and six in
it.   To pass through it in safety, as he rolled city-
wards or to Court, his running footmen thrust
humble men's carts and barrows into the side
alleys, to allow him to proceed.

In the next two chapters I shall show Nelly
and her Royal lover at the west end of the town,
at Whitehall when the Court was in residence in
the Metropolis, and at Windsor Castle where
Charles passed so much of his time in the summer
months.

CHAPTER IV

WHITEHALL AS NELL GWYNNE KNEW IT,
1675–1685

To reconstruct in the mind's eye, with any approach to accuracy, the Whitehall of Charles the Second's Court and the Palace as Nell Gwynne knew it from within, a plan [1] drawn about the year 1668 by an otherwise unknown cartographer named John Fisher should be carefully studied. This elaborate survey shows not only the exact position of the State apartments, private lodgings, Government departments, and menial offices, numbering some hundreds, but it supplies, in addition, what is even more valuable for our purpose, the name of every official of the Royal household who was living in the Palace at that time. This plan was engraved and published by George Vertue in 1747, but the date then ascribed to it, 1680, must from internal evidence be at least a dozen years too late. [2]

[1] Hereafter referred to as The Plan.

[2] This is proved, to give but three instances out of many, by the inclusion of the names of Sir Thomas Clifford, Sir John Denham, and the Duke of

RIVER-FRONT OF WHITEHALL PALACE IN THE REIGN OF CHARLES THE SECOND.

Taken in conjunction with the view of the river façade appended to Morgan's map of London and Westminster in 1682, it becomes possible to visualise Whitehall as it was more than two hundred and fifty years ago.[1]

Nell Gwynne comes quite naturally into the picture, as she was made an extra lady of the Queen's—I had almost written the King's—household in 1675. It has been questioned if she ever received such an appointment, but in a deed relating to some house property in Windsor, which she rented from the Dean and Chapter, I find her specifically described as "Eleanor Gwynne of the parish of St. Martin's in the Fields in the County of Middlesex, one of the ladies of her Majesty the Queen's Privy Chamber." And although she seems seldom or never to have occupied rooms in the Palace (her own well-appointed house in Pall Mall being so conveniently near Whitehall), there is abundant evidence of

Albemarle (better known as General Monk). Clifford was raised to the peerage in 1668; Sir John Denham died in 1669, and the Duke of Albemarle in 1670.

[1] Morgan and Ogilby's map, although dated 1682, was probably surveyed some years earlier. It is without doubt the most valuable plan of London published up to that date. It shows clearly, what no earlier map with which I am acquainted does, the actual boundaries of individual houses and the extent of garden ground attaching to them in the principal streets and squares—an important detail which not even Rocque in his great survey of London in 1746 attempted to portray.

Another valuable contemporary view of Whitehall from the river is Griffier's picture (in the Royal Collection) of the Lord Mayor proceeding to Westminster in his State barge attended by the City Companies in 1683. This painting is reproduced at p. 119 of this volume.

her having formed one of the merry group which surrounded the King there in the latter years of his life. When Nell first came to know the Palace from within, little or nothing of York Place (Wolsey's great mansion as altered by Henry VIII.) remained, with the exception of Holbein's Gate and a dining-hall, less than a third the size of Inigo Jones's great Banqueting House.

Holbein's Gate was the more ornamental of two substantial towers which the most autocratic of the Tudors built in defiance of an immemorial right-of-way from Charing Cross to Westminster, in order to secure a greater amount of privacy for himself and Anne Boleyn.

This celebrated gate was a lofty tower of tessellated brick with stone dressings, not unlike the even more ornate gate tower at Layer Marney. It had several good rooms on the upper floors and commanded an extensive view over St. James's Park. It had been occupied during the Civil Wars by General Lambert, the most powerful man in the Commonwealth after Cromwell, and the prime favourite of the soldiery, and stood nearly opposite to the old Tilt Yard where Dover House [1] stands to-day.

The other gate was at the entrance to King Street, where Downing Street opens into modern Whitehall. So early as 1314 several members of the Court petitioned Edward II.

[1] Now the Scottish Office.

to repair the highway from Temple Bar to
Westminster Palace, as it had become so dangerous that those who were compelled to use it in
bad weather were, in the quaint Norman-French
phraseology of the fourteenth century, " des-
turbez de lor busoignes suivre par profoundance
del dit chemin." Nothing, however, was done
until, in the next reign, Edward III., who called
Parliaments with the greatest regularity every
year,[1] ordered it to be paved from end to end
and the expense defrayed by a tax upon all
merchandise going to the Staple at Westminster.
This was defined to extend from Temple Bar
to Tothill.[2]

Three hundred years later, Henry VIII., with
an utter disregard for the general convenience,
closed the intervening space in front of the
Palace by the erection of these twin obstructions
of the public highway—for such in effect they
were—nor were they removed until the eighteenth
century, long after Whitehall had ceased to be
the residence of the sovereign.[3]

A better approach to Westminster from Charing Cross was then secured by the formation of

[1] Edward III. summoned 57 Parliaments in all.

[2] *Rot. Parl.* vol. i. p. 302.

[3] The King Street Gate was demolished in 1723 and Holbein's Gate in
1759. Whilst I do not suppose that the land approach to Parliament and
the Abbey was ever entirely prohibited to members of Parliament, the
interference with the right-of-way must have compelled humbler citizens
to travel either by the silent highway of the Thames, or to make a long
detour by road in order to reach Westminster.

an entirely new street which we now know as
Parliament Street. When this, too, was widened
on the erection of a huge block of Government
offices facing Parliament Square and extending along Great George Street to Storey's Gate,
the last vestiges of old King Street were swept
into oblivion. Delahay Street and Gardener's
Lane (which marked the course of a stream which
had formed one of the boundaries of Thorney
Island since Saxon times) disappeared at the same
time.

The Matted Gallery, the Vane Room, and
the great Stone Gallery, a long narrow structure
lying to the east of the Privy Garden, may have
been built either late in the sixteenth or at
the beginning of the seventeenth century; but
when Charles the Second entered into possession
of Whitehall, the Palace was, with few exceptions,
little better than a maze of inconvenient, and
probably insanitary, two-storied buildings, congested courtyards and narrow passages, leading
nowhere in particular, but containing in the
aggregate hundreds of small rooms huddled
together in picturesque confusion.

No wonder was it that foreigners, with any
perception of architectural taste, when they
visited London after the Restoration, expressed,
almost without exception, their astonishment
that the King and Queen of England, to say
nothing of their respective households, could

rest content with such cramped and inadequate accommodation. To a Frenchman accredited to the English Court by the *grand monarque* this apology for a Royal residence must have seemed a sorry substitute for Versailles; even William of Orange, when he came to London to wed the Princess Mary, may have contrasted it unfavourably in his mind with the dignified repose of " the pleasantest village in Europe," as Lord Chesterfield, in after years, happily termed the Court capital of Holland.

Nor was St. James's, until Charles called in Wren to remodel the Tudor apartments (which had presumably fallen into disrepair during the Civil Wars) and to add the existing south front towards the park, more calculated to impress the stranger within our gates. With the exception of the Banqueting House—the only portion ever completed of a sumptuous palace which Inigo Jones designed for James the First—there was scarcely an architectural feature of outstanding merit within the confines of Whitehall between Scotland Yard and the Privy Garden. Yet within this congested area an army of politicians, placemen, pensioners, pimps, and prostitutes entrenched itself, some amongst the number contriving to secure for their ignoble selves (and notably the King's French paramour, Louise de Querouaille) free quarters far exceeding in comfort and luxury the apartments of the Queen

Consort. It is said that the Duchess of Portsmouth's house, built in 1681 at the Privy Garden end of the Stone Gallery, was pulled down and rebuilt at vast expense no less than three times before she expressed herself satisfied with it. We will enter it later in order to show how this cormorant from the shores of Brittany squandered the public money.

The King's private apartments, as one would expect to find, faced the Thames, as did the Queen's, both being built round three sides of a small court or garden.

The outlook must have been a cheerful one when we remember that the Thames at this period was the principal means of communication between the cities of London and Westminster. Dotted with scores of rowing-boats, and when Hentzner visited London in 1598 by hundreds of swans which, as royal birds, were strictly protected, the river lapped the walls of the Palace and sometimes overflowed its banks to the great inconvenience of its inmates. The Thames was seen at its very best when the Lord Mayor in his State barge, attended by the greater City Companies, distinguished by the heraldic insignia of those ancient guilds, proceeded to Westminster by water. When the civic fleet arrived off the Palace the King set out from the Privy Stairs in his own resplendent barge, gilded from end to end, and with the Royal Standard fluttering in the breeze, and joined in the procession.

When the King alighted at the Privy Stairs his private apartments lay immediately to the left of the landing-place, and the Queen's to the right.

If the Plan is to be trusted, the King's rooms did not number more than a dozen on each floor, nor, until altered and heightened by Wren, were they at all regal in appearance.

From the earliest days of the Restoration I find three clearly defined classes of residents in the Palace. If it takes all sorts and conditions of men to make a world, the same holds good in the case of Courts.

First there were the men of outstanding ability, such as Ormonde and Albemarle—the one representing the flower of the ancient nobility, the other the foremost soldier and diplomatist of his time. Never worsted in battle on land or sea, invariably successful in the weightiest affairs of State, and always on the winning side, such was Monk's sense of duty that when, in 1665, the majority of the King's ministers fled from London for fear of the plague, he remained at his post and took sole charge of the government of the City.

Manchester, a stout Puritan, until he ranged himself in opposition to Cromwell on the question of bringing the King to trial, comes within the same category, as, in lesser degree, does Lauderdale, the virtual ruler of Scotland for many years. His influence with Charles was at all times considerable, until his health failed and he was driven from office.

Clifford, one of the Catholic lords, was sincerely attached to the King, though the advice which he tendered was not always judicious, as, for example, his recommending Charles to be the slave of one man [1] rather than of five hundred, meaning the House of Commons.

Though both Lauderdale and Clifford were members of the Cabal, the latter alone knew the terms of the infamous secret Treaty of Dover by which Charles became the vassal of France, in return for an annual subsidy which rendered him practically independent of Parliament, or rather it would have done so, had he not squandered so much of the money upon unworthy objects.

Sir Stephen Fox and Sir Christopher Wren, in widely different spheres, were valuable public servants, deserving well of their country.

Lord Peterborough, Laurence Hyde (as a young man he was Keeper of the King's Wardrobe), and Lord Lauderdale were three of the most highly favoured courtiers, as they had separate houses of their own on the west side of the long Stone Gallery with doorways opening out of it; all of these looked over the Privy Garden, and Lory Hyde's was the centre of the three.

[1] Louis XIV.

The Stone Gallery, wherein Charles hung such
of the Royal pictures as he was able to recover,
was a favourite promenade of the King and his
Court in bad weather. Members of both
Houses of Parliament were often found there in
friendly conclave, and in it the King transacted a
good deal of such business as his ministers could
induce him to attend to, walking up and down
the gallery at his usual rapid pace and declaring
his Royal will and pleasure in this highly uncon-
ventional fashion. Pepys was often seen there
after he made his mark as a capable public
servant and gained the confidence of Charles and
the Duke of York, whose interest in naval affairs
was one of the best traits in their characters.

Lauderdale was the bigger man of the trio
who lived in the Stone Gallery. Making it his
business never to be far away from the King's ear,
he gradually acquired the sole management of
Scottish business, until, at one time, his political
influence was well-nigh predominant. In this
connection it should be remembered that Nell,
who had no great liking for him or his methods,
once advised Charles to make his Parliament a
present of a " Scotch Collop," a " French *ragoût*,"
and a "calf's head," meaning Lauderdale, her pet
aversion the Duchess of Portsmouth, and Lord
Sunderland, whose features were supposed to
resemble a calf's. Another of her nicknames for
Louise de Querouaille was " the weeping willow,"

from her habit of resorting to tears when engaged in an attempt to wring some fresh concession from the King.[1]

The Killigrew family, which had originally been domiciled in Lothbury, in the heart of the City, obtained a firm foothold in Whitehall in the reign of Charles the First, and was still extensively represented there at the Restoration.

Sir William, Tom's eldest brother, was located in rooms in the most desirable quarter of the Palace—the river front.

Madame Charlotte, Tom's Dutch wife, had her separate apartments, and although her husband, the manager of Drury Lane, had a perpetual right of entry as Court Jester, he seems to have lived, for the most part, in the Piazza at Covent Garden in order to be near his theatre.

Nor was Tom the last of the family to be found here, for Sir Philip was well housed in the outer portion of the Palace comprehensively known as the Cockpit; whilst Mrs. Kirk, whose mother was a Killigrew, had not one but two suites of apartments, one of them a very large building with, apparently, fifteen rooms on a floor.

The Cockpit, which, next to the river front, was the most sought after place of residence in Whitehall, lay opposite to the Privy Garden on the park side of the roadway, which ought to have

[1] Yet another nickname which Nell conferred upon her French rival was Squintabella, in allusion to a slight cast in one of her eyes.

been a public thoroughfare but was not, owing
to the arbitrary action of Henry VIII. in closing
it.   Hereabouts the 1st Duke of Albemarle was
in possession of a great number of rooms near
the Cockpit itself.   Some of his apartments overlooked St. James's Park, and, in addition, he had
the use and enjoyment of a small private garden.

The Duke of Ormonde had not one but a
whole group of houses, fifteen in all, assigned to
him in the same quarter.   These buildings lay
immediately to the south of what remained of
Henry VIII.'s Tilt Yard and closely adjoined
Holbein's Gate.   The Duke's emoluments as Lord
Steward were only £100 a year, but his perquisites
entitled him to sixteen dishes daily at each meal,
besides wine and beer from the Royal cellars.
As he was one of the most hospitable of men, and
never so happy as when surrounded by his sons
and daughters and grandchildren, such an ample
allowance of free victuals must have been welcome, even to a man of his wealth.

The Duke of Monmouth had a house of eleven
rooms on a floor, also in the Cockpit area, but
rather shut in by surrounding houses.   An old
tennis-court which had been built by Henry VIII.
was converted into lodgings for him, and a new
court was built upon what had been Lord Sandwich's private garden.[1]

[1] Although Lord Sandwich's name does not appear in the list of names
printed on the Plan, it is certain from Pepys' frequent allusions to his
lodgings here that it should have been so included.

The name " Cockpit," as applied to the Treasury and other ministerial offices on the St. James's Park side of the roadway, lingered until the early days of last century, but is now only a memory.

It is possible that Ormonde, by virtue of his office, was empowered to grant rooms which he did not require for his personal use to people whose presence in the Palace cannot otherwise be accounted for.

In the absence of Lord Sandwich's name on the Plan, it is probable that his actual place of abode may be concealed amidst the long array of rooms in the occupation or gift of the Lord Steward.

Barbara Villiers was living at her grandmother's house on the east side of King Street (immediately outside the gate tower which stood at the entrance of the street) when her eldest son was born.

She was born, I think, in old Lady Villiers' house, where her parents, Lord and Lady Grandison, usually resided when not in Ireland. On searching the baptismal registers of St. Margaret's, Westminster, for another purpose, I accidentally came upon the entry of her christening there on November 27, 1640. She was therefore ten years older than Nell Gwynne. The Duchess of Mazarine was six years younger than Barbara, and Louise de Querouaille was Nell's senior by one year.

Barbara Villiers' knowledge of the Palace was extensive and peculiar. Born, as we have shown, in the immediate vicinity, she obtained a foothold there in April 1663, when she is said by Pepys to be " removed as to her bed from her own house to a chamber in Whitehall next the King's own."

A little later in the year apartments were assigned to her in the Cockpit, next door to Lord Sandwich. One October day the tide rose so high that her kitchen was flooded, just as she was expecting the King to sup with her. When the cook told her imperious mistress that it would not be possible to roast a chine of beef which she had ordered, she replied, " Zounds, she [the cook] must set the house on fire, for it must be roasted." Eventually Lord Sandwich's house-keeper, " Mrs. Sarah," obligingly cooked it for her, and the supper party was duly held.

In January 1664 there was an outbreak of fire at her lodgings, when she offered a reward of forty pounds to any one who would save a valuable cabinet from the flames. In May the ever-inquisitive Pepys descried from the Privy Garden Barbara's finest smocks and linen petti-coats, edged with real lace, hanging out to dry in the sun, and went into raptures at the sight, as might have been expected from a man of his peculiar temperament. This looks as if she was still living at her grandmother's house, which was divided only by a low partition from the Palace precincts. In May of the same year Holbein's Gate was allotted to her, and on the King's birthday Charles danced there with a band of fiddlers, almost all night long, in defiance of all convention. In July Barbara returned for a time to King Street, but only to return to the Palace in October, when she gave a ball at her new lodgings.

In June 1666 she was ordered to leave the Court, whereon she went to a private lodging in Pall Mall; but the quarrel being soon afterwards patched up, she returned to the Palace, until in May 1668, partly on account of the King's growing infatuation for Miss Stewart, she was relegated to Berkshire House in St. James's, the King cheerfully paying £5000 for it in order to keep her at a safe distance.

Though Barbara's name does not appear as a resident in the Palace on the Plan, " Lady Castlemaine's kitchen " is duly marked. This is another proof that the Plan must have been drawn in 1668, because she then withdrew to Berkshire House. The fact of her kitchen being marked can only have been an oversight on the part of the draughtsman or a reminiscence of a state of affairs no longer in existence.

According to the custom of the times, kitchens and larders were often detached from their owners' residences, and at St. James's, in the

eighteenth century, the whole of the food for
the Royal table was prepared and cooked in a
building some little distance from the State
apartments, which Kent remodelled for George
the Second. Each dish had to be carried from
the kitchen across an intervening open space
into the Palace, and to be carried quickly, lest
it should reach the Royal table stone cold. At
the present day, when Ministerial dinners are
given at St. James's, they are held in George the
Fourth's banqueting room, which has an overhead
passage of communication to Kent's kitchen.

At Whitehall the various kitchens, cellars,
pantries, and serving rooms are, for the most part,
shown on the Plan as detached buildings.

After the great officers of the Household who
were accommodated in the Palace came some of
lesser note who, having been with the King in
exile, sharing his privations in the Low Countries,
in the dark days between 1649 and 1660, were,
not unnaturally, rewarded with household appointments, many of them virtually sinecures, with free
quarters in Whitehall in gratitude for their loyalty.

At the other end of the scale were the syco-
phants and hangers-on whom Charles was too
good-natured to shake off and too indolent to
dispense with. Of these parasites of the Court,
alike the most influential and the most contempt-
ible, was Will Chiffinch. The following lines
sufficiently describe one of his principal duties:

As England's Monarch in his closet lay
And Chiffinch stepped to fetch the female prey.[1]

Pandering year in and year out to his master's weaknesses, and entrusted by him with the expenditure of large sums of money which were never subjected to public scrutiny, he attained such a powerful position that many who in their hearts despised his methods found it advisable to stand well with him. His wife, nominally the Queen's sempstress, was, in point of fact, the *entremetteuse* whose congenial task it was, in collusion with her spouse, to usher into the Royal apartments, at all hours, mysterious visitors, often closely veiled, whose business none might enquire, whose identity no man must discover.[2]

The Plan shows clearly how admirably the position of Chiffinch's rooms lent themselves to the purposes of clandestine intrigue. Visitors who were conducted through this *salle des pas perdus* connecting the keeper of the backstairs' apartments with those of the King and the maids of honour could, if they came on foot, leave by water and *vice versa*, thus attracting less attention than if they left the Palace by the route they entered it.

In a few years over £10,000, derived from the Secret Service Fund, stuck to the fingers of the pimp and the procuress as " bounty," in

---

[1] *Poems on Affairs of State*, 1697.

[2] Mrs. Chiffinch's mother, it may be added, was Mrs. Nunn, the Queen's laundress.

addition to which Mrs. Chiffinch had an annual
salary of £1200.[1]

Charles at one time would have been willing
to break with Louise de Querouaille were it not
that he was mainly dependent on her good
offices for the punctual payment of his pension
from Louis XIV. As the Parliament which he
called in 1679 was unwilling to grant him any
considerable sum for his private needs, he was
in constant terror lest the stream of French gold
should be diverted to another channel. He was
therefore compelled to preserve friendly relations
with Louise, who not only maintained, but
positively increased, her baneful influence over
him in his later years.

A fresh element of disturbance was introduced into the Palace when Hortense, Duchess

---

[1] The curious volume of the Secret Service Expenses of Charles and his
successor, published in 1851 by the Camden Society from a manuscript then
in the possession of Mr. Selby Lowndes, throws a flood of light upon the inner
life of the Court. The share which Nell received from this source out of
a gross total of more than half a million was inconsiderable compared with
the huge amounts paid to other Royal favourites, and notably in the case of
the Duchess of Portsmouth, whose total emoluments in one year reached
the almost incredible figure of £136,668. This was in 1681, when she was
building a new house at the Privy Garden end of the great Stone Gallery,
with a south aspect over the Bowling Green.

In studying the accounts for this year I was puzzled by the sudden
increase in the sums paid to Louise from this source alone, until I remembered
that she was then furnishing her new apartments in a style of luxury and
splendour far surpassing those of the Queen. The whole of this extrava-
gantly planned house, reflecting at every turn the insolence of ill-gotten
wealth, was burnt to the ground, with some other buildings extending to
the waterside, in 1691, the year of the first of two great fires which broke
out in the Palace, the still greater conflagration of January 1698 destroying
practically the whole of the Royal apartments.

of Mazarine, entered the Court, like Armida in
the camp of Godefroy, in January 1676. She
was then under thirty, her beauty unimpaired
by the vicissitudes of a singularly adventurous
and unhappy married life. She had come to
England in the hope of reviving in Charles's
susceptible heart a passion which he was supposed
to have felt for her in his youth. Her arrival
was received with mixed feelings by the King's
entourage. For though all the men spoke of
her with admiration, all the women regarded her
with jealousy and distrust.

> Now through the world fair Mazarine had run
> Bright as her fellow traveller the sun.
> Hither at length the Roman eagle flies
> At the last triumph of her conquering eyes.

So wrote Waller, and an even closer analysis
of her fascination by a Frenchman who accompanied her to England may be quoted:

> La couleur de ses yeux n'a point de nom, c'est ni
> bleu, ni gris, ni tout à fait noir. Ils n'ont rien de
> languissant ni de passionné, comme si elle n'était née que
> pour être aimée et non pour aimer. Sa bouche n'est
> si grande ni de la dernière petitesse, mais tous les
> mouvements en sont pleins de charmes.

Posterity should be grateful for this contemporary pen portrait, as it enables us to form
some conception of the glamour exercised by this
voluptuous beauty, not only in her prime, but
in her later years, when most of her contem-

HORTENSE, DUCHESS OF MAZARINE.

From the Painting by Pierre Mignard, in the possession of the Earl of Sandwich.

poraries were either dead or forgotten. She soon declared war both upon Barbara and Louise, and although the latter contrived, despite occasional set-backs, to retain her hold over the King, their relations gradually assumed a platonic rather than an amatory complexion. Louise was no beauty, but only a moderately good-looking girl, when she first came to England, her " baby " face being noted by Evelyn, who happened to be one of the house party at Euston when she was installed *maitresse en titre*. But in point of looks she was not to be compared with Nell Gwynne at any time of her life.[1]

Voltaire admired Louise, and pronounced her to be at least as good-looking as Madame de Montespan, but no likeness of her which I have seen discloses any trace of real beauty. Had she possessed any great distinction of face or figure, so skilful an artist as Pierre Mignard (judging from the sheer loveliness of his portrait of the Duchess of Mazarine at Hinchingbrook) would surely have succeeded in reproducing it. But his likeness of her in the National Portrait Gallery (where to this day Nell fearlessly challenges comparison with Louise and Barbara in the Stuart room) reveals " Madam Carwell " as only a moderately good-looking young woman, with small slitty eyes, no eyebrows to speak of,

---

[1] Shakespeare's line, " Between two girls, which hath the merriest eye," would, unhesitatingly, have been answered by Charles in Nell's favour.

dark hair, and a rather peevish expression of countenance. At her side is a negro boy, offering from a shell a number of loose pearls and a branch or two of red coral.

The Marquise de Seignelay's portrait by the same artist in the National Gallery has a somewhat similar attendant—a winged cupid instead of a blackamoor also humbly offering pearls and coral.

Hortense brought a negro boy to England with her, to make her coffee, she said; but the fashion did not take root in England to any great extent.

Of Louise's portraits, of which I have only seen reproductions from original paintings, the one attributed to Lely, in the Duke of Richmond's collection at Goodwood, is by far the most pleasing.

Unlike her French rival, Nell, who was never a political schemer, preferred to be a sleeping partner in the State, and, in consequence, she was the only one of Charles's mistresses for whom he felt anything approaching lasting affection.

The Italian enchantress, whose dazzling white skin and flashing black eyes proved irresistible to young and old—one of her nephews made protestations of undying love for her when she was already a grandmother, and fought a duel with another of her admirers—soon set up a *salon* of her own, whereat flirtation and witty conversation alternated with high play at cards and dice.

It so happened that Lady Sussex, one of the King's natural daughters, who was herself endowed with great personal attractions, conceived a passionate admiration for Hortense, and became her inseparable companion. This provided the Duchess with abundant opportunities for meeting the King in private, much to the chagrin of Lady Sussex's mother (Barbara Villiers), who, by reason of her daughter's infatuation, was powerless to exclude the newcomer from the innermost Court circle.

Charles was closely watched at this time by Louis XIV.'s spies, acting under Louise's orders. Successive ambassadors faithfully reported his daily and even his nightly movements. One of them, Honoré Courtin, wrote to Pomponne[1] when Hortense had been only six months in England:

La fille du roi, de la Duchesse de Cleveland, avait été mariée tout enfant au Comte de Sussex ; elle se prend d'une tendresse ardente pour la Duchesse de Mazarin, Le Roi s'arrange pour rencontrer chez sa propre fille Madame Mazarin. Quand il est là, nul n'entre, pas même les musiciens français.

L'appartement de Madame de Sussex est le même qu'occupait Madame de Cleveland sa mère dans le temps de sa faveur. Il est situé au dessus du cabinet du Roi, et ce prince y peut monter sans être vue.

Madame Mazarin y est à toute heure, elle y passa même hier la nuit.

[1] July 1676.

This amateur detective then proceeds to give a pretty picture of Lady Sussex:

> Elle est encore un enfant qui ne songe qu'à danser et à sauter depuis le matin jusque au soir.

On another day she is reported to have played battledore and shuttlecock the entire afternoon.

Eventually the feud between Louise and Hortense was patched up, and an armed neutrality succeeded openly avowed hostility.

The same inquisitive ambassador wrote a little later to the same correspondent, confirming to the letter the part which Will Chiffinch habitually played in effecting these clandestine meetings:

> Madame Mazarin a été depuis trois heures jusqu' à sept avec le Roi. Il y a deux appartements qui tiennent du sien où l'on entre par plusieurs portes différentes, dont il n'y a que lui *et un valet de chambre de confiance* qui aient la clef.

One is almost inclined to pity Charles, in spite of his infidelities, for being so persistently spied upon by Louise's agents. It is possible that he was aware that his footsteps were dogged even in the most secret recesses of Whitehall, but by this time he had become so callous that he was probably past caring what was said of him.

Whatever else they accomplished, these French spies, continually eavesdropping in search of incriminating evidence, certainly earned their

pay; though one wonders whether it was worth
Louis's while to spend so much money in order
to learn, at second hand, what was common talk in
the City, in Parliament, and in Whitehall itself.

The lodgings assigned to the maids of honour
were in closer proximity to the King's than to
the Queen's apartments, and from the circum-
stantial account which Grammont gives of Charles's
surprising *la belle Stewart* and the Duke of
Richmond when they would much rather not
have been disturbed, it is evident that the King
could pass from his own rooms on the level by a
passage which led directly to those occupied by
the ladies-in-waiting.

These young ladies had over them a mother
of the maids, Lady Sanderson, who was supposed
to look after their morals as well as their creature
comforts, but as, like most duennas, she habitually
took the line of least resistance, her influence
was all but negligible.

Adjoining the Queen's private rooms, which
like the King's were built round three sides of
a small court facing the river, lived her chamberlain, Sir William Killigrew, and close to him
again was Father Patrick, her Irish confessor.

Beyond him resided her secretary, Sir Richard
Bellings, in a lofty embattled stone building, apparently of Tudor date. This adjoined the ordinary
landing-place for the Palace. Its site is now
occupied approximately by the huge block

of flats called Whitehall Court, whilst the
National Liberal Club beyond it covers the
ground allotted in the seventeenth century to
the menial offices of the Palace.[1]

Behind Sir Richard Bellings's rooms were a
chapel (probably the same which Wolsey had
used) and a dining-hall, or " great Chamber,"
about a third of the size of the existing Banqueting House. This smaller hall had a high-pitched
roof with a louvre in the centre to let the air
in and the smoke out.

Lady Suffolk, Queen Catherine's groom of
the stole, was not far off from her mistress,
and several other ladies of her household, Lady
Arlington and Lady Falmouth amongst the
number, were domiciled in this part of the Palace.

Lady Suffolk's maiden name was Barbara
Villiers, but she must not be confounded with
the more notorious woman who practically
dominated the King's affections for some eight
years until he discovered that she was habitually
unfaithful to him and beyond any hope of reformation. Not that Charles ever actually cast her
off. In the language of the card-table, he never
discarded. He merely added to his hand.

In June 1675 Nell bought herself a sedan-
chair, and from the maker's bill, which, by a

---

[1] The new War Office, Whitehall Court, and the National Liberal
Club have, between them, obliterated the whole of that portion of the
Palace, formerly known as Scotland Yard.

lucky chance, has been preserved, it is evident
that it was an exceptionally fine one. So studded
over was it with nails, and gilt with the best water
gold, that its leather body could scarcely be seen.
It was to have cost £34, but as Nell paid for it
within a month, she obtained a discount of £4
for settling the account so promptly. So the
King's mistresses were not always such bad
paymasters, as Nell, in a letter she wrote a few
years later, admitted was the general opinion.

About the same time she seems to have set
up her own coach. I have not ascertained what
this fresh departure cost her or any particulars
of its build, except that it bore on its panels
her cipher E.G., and, probably, the coat of arms
which had recently been found for her by an
obliging herald painter.

No doubt Nell now felt that it was incumbent
on her to have her own coach and horses to transport her between Pall Mall and Whitehall; for,
on becoming a member of the Household, she
would have considered it derogatory to her
position to go to Court in a hackney carriage like
a mere knight of the shire or a common burgess.

Her coach was drawn by four horses, though
Barbara Villiers considered nothing less than six
sufficient to support her dignity. Yet what an
advance it represented for Nell since the days
when she trudged on foot from her shabby
lodgings in Drury Lane to the theatre and back

again. And yet only ten years had passed since her first appearance on the stage.

Another circumstance which seems to point to her having been admitted to the Court circle in the summer or early autumn of 1675 is that the post may have been offered to her as a sop. She had been indignant when "Madam Carwell," as the common people would persist in calling Louise de Querouaille, had her French name anglicised under the resounding title of Duchess of Portsmouth only a year after her arrival in England. But when her rival's son was made Duke of Richmond at the tender age of three, Nell's wrath knew no bounds. "Even Barbara's brats," she cried, "were not made Dukes until they were twelve or thirteen, but this French spy's son is ennobled when little more than an infant in arms!"[1]

Well might she exclaim, "I have no name to call my sons by," until, in the following year, she was appeased by her first-born being made Baron Headington and Earl of Burford, both in the county of Oxford, though he did not become Duke of St. Albans until 1684.

It is a singular coincidence that the titles of Plymouth and Portsmouth found their way into the British Peerage almost simultaneously; the one conferred by the King on his French mistress

---

[1] Another son of the King's by the same mother, George Fitzroy, who, according to Evelyn, was the most promising of the family, was not created Duke of Northumberland until much later.

and the other on his natural son " Don Carlos," neither of whom had the remotest connection with either of the great naval ports. Portsmouth was a Royal dockyard in the reign of Henry VIII., and one of the smaller stone docks still to be seen there is probably of Tudor date. It was from Plymouth, as every schoolboy knows, that Drake set sail to destroy the Spanish Armada then approaching our shores, but it did not become a Royal dockyard, in the modern sense of the word, until the seventeenth century.

It is possible, without unduly stretching the imagination, to picture Mistress Nell, still in the prime of her remarkable beauty—she was only twenty-five at the time referred to—being carried through the Mall in her new chair, on a fine summer's day, beneath the grateful shade of the sweet-smelling limes which fringed one of three long alleys which ran parallel to one another in St. James's Park. At the farther end towards the open fields stood Arlington House, until it was unfortunately burnt down in September 1674. As it was promptly rebuilt, it may have risen from its ashes by the following summer. At the farther, or Charing Cross, end of the Mall was the Spring Garden.

Sedan-chairs were allowed to use the side avenues, but the middle alley was strictly reserved for the *jeu de maille*, the game from which the locality derives its un-English name.

So few Malls remain in England that it is
the more to be regretted that by the formation,
a few years ago, of a brand-new Processional
road from Buckingham Palace to the Admiralty
Arch, a genuine and pleasing relic of seventeenth-
century London has been obliterated.[1] Gone
alike are the lime trees and those level walks
strewn with powdered cockle-shells in each recurring spring and continually rolled in order to
attain the smoothest possible surface. Our rulers
in their wisdom have put in its place a *sieges
allee*, on approved Teutonic lines, which, from
its very width, is one of the most dangerous
thoroughfares for foot passengers in all the West
End. In robbing London of the Mall, as it
existed for more than two centuries, a large slice
was taken out of St. James's Park in order to secure
a " vista " for the Victoria Memorial, that clumsy
group of statuary which the ex-Kaiser is said to
have admired so much when he unveiled it in 1911.

Between St. James's and the Spring Garden,
Nell, in her progress to Whitehall, would be
sure to meet with one or more young men of
fashion of her acquaintance, all of them living
much the same pleasurable existence, with no

[1] Many Malls remain, however, in France and in Holland, little if at
all altered since the date of their formation. The Lange Vorhout at the
Hague is a good example of the Dutch type, and may well have suggested to
Charles the Second the plan of his own Pell-mell alley. At Tours, and I
believe also at Lyons and Bordeaux, it is easy to identify the locality where
this now obsolete game was played in the land of its origin.

thought for the morrow, in exuberant spirits, and intent only on enjoying life to the utmost as they conceived it should be spent.

Such was the fascination which Nell exercised over all beholders, that gallants would pause in their game to cast admiring glances in her direction, which she, all smiles and dimples, leaning out of the window of her latest new toy, would acknowledge with a wave of her shapely hand or a word of greeting. A single encouraging look from those alluring blue eyes would be enough to make any one of her admirers happy for the remainder of the day. Clasped in her arms would, quite likely, be a little spaniel, nor does it require much guessing to name the kennel that it came from.

Peter Cunningham tells a good story of an honest cavalier who, pressing forward to see the King enter Salisbury, came so near the Royal coach that Charles warned him to be careful lest one of his little black spaniels should bite him. Taking no heed of the caution, he clung so close to the door of the Royal coach that a spaniel seized him by the finger, whereupon the sufferer cried out: " God bless Your Majesty, but God damn your dogs!"

The "little dogs' kennel" near the duck decoy in St. James's Park was almost on the identical spot inhabited by the pelicans at the present day.

After playing at Pell-mell all the morning the

gallants would dine at Long's, a noted ordinary in the Haymarket and a favourite place of resort, from its proximity to the Gaming House, where so many of them lost and so few won large sums.

In the afternoon they would usually be found at the King's or the Duke's Theatre, especially when comedy replaced tragedy in the bill. Often when far from sober they came in late, sometimes without paying for their seats, and disturbed orderly frequenters of the pit by discordant cries and interruptions. By way of illustration an episode at the Duke's Theatre in Dorset Gardens on February 16, 1680, is worth recalling.

A drunken man, coming into the pit, espied Nell in one of the side boxes and shouted an opprobrious epithet at her, which many of the audience hotly resented. Young Mr. Herbert [1] constituted himself her principal defender. Swords were drawn, and such a hubbub arose in the house that the performance could not proceed for some considerable time. Many of the Restoration dramatists refer to similar unseemly interruptions and to the vile manners of a section of theatrical audiences at this period.

Wycherley at his worst made a stronger appeal to these rowdies than Dryden at his best. They enjoyed Aphra Behn and Etherege more than

[1] He succeeded his brother as 8th Earl of Pembroke in 1683, married three wives, and had a long and distinguished political career. He was also an executor of Nell's will.

anything that Shakespeare or Ben Jonson ever wrote, and they applauded vigorously when Nell Gwynne, in male attire, danced a jig [1] in the last act of *All Mistaken, or The Mad Couple,* or rolled from side to side of the stage to escape the importunities of a fat lover, incapacitated by his bulk from keeping pace with her.

The delivery of a risky epilogue by Mrs. Knepp, of whose talents Tom Killigrew had such a high opinion, roused them to a pitch of enthusiasm which the graceful lines set down for Nell to speak in *The Indian Emperor* would fail to arouse in their sordid minds. Then would come a prolonged carouse at the Rose in Covent Garden, or one of the many other taverns in that neighbourhood. "A man could not go from the Rose tavern to the Piazza once but he must risk his life twice," wrote Shadwell in *The Scowerers.* When they were lucky enough to escape being mixed up in a street brawl, they staggered home to bed at midnight, to pass their time in precisely the same manner the next day. There being as yet no clubs in the modern sense of the word, the Hectors, the Mohocks, and the Tityre Tus were compelled to dine at taverns where they were charged exorbitant prices for food and drink. Instead of mixing only with their own class, they associated with a lower

---

[1] This jig was called "I care not a pin for any man," which I am afraid was not very applicable in this particular case.

stratum of society, in which men with money to spend swore, drank, and gambled in company with women of the town imported from Lewkenor's Lane and the other dens of infamy which abounded in and about Holborn and Drury Lane, and even, I think, in the precincts of the Parliament at Westminster.

Young Lord Gerard, who died suddenly in a drinking bout at the Rose, had been imprisoned in the Counter when only fifteen for running an apprentice through the body in a scuffle in which he was mixed up at Bedlam; whilst Robert Villiers, Lord Purbeck, who hired a big house in St. James's Square for a ball which he gave to the Masqueraders, at which the only ladies present wore masks, was another wild young rake of the same type. He was imprisoned a few years later in the Tower of London for challenging one of the Prince of Orange's suite, and was killed in a duel at Liége in 1684. But the Lord Pembroke who married Louise de Querouaille's sister was a worse offender than any of these. He killed a perfect stranger to him at a Haymarket tavern by jumping upon him and kicking him as he lay upon the floor; and though he was tried by his peers and found guilty of manslaughter, he managed to escape the penalty of his crime by pleading the privilege of his order under a Statute of Edward VI. Worn out by dissipation and disease, he died unremembered and unmourned, whereon his widow returned to Brittany, carrying with her a shipload of valuable property which her sister had helped her to acquire.

These hotheads habitually ate more than was good for them. They gambled and drank far too much for their pockets and their health. Uttering strange and fearful oaths in a futile endeavour to give some point to their conversation, ridiculous disputes, arising out of their dissipated habits, often led to their fighting duels on the flimsiest pretexts. Many a young blood met his death at daybreak in the Royal parks or in the open fields which then lay round about the Mulberry Garden, Knightsbridge, and Pimlico, in defending what he conceived to be his honour, in order to decide such trivial problems as the comparative beauty of rival actresses at the two patent houses, their probable ages, and even the colour of their hair and eyes. Leading the reckless life they did, it is small wonder that they died like flies, burnt to a cinder with hot liquor, or were carried off by the smallpox and other kindred diseases which the medical skill of the age was not sufficiently advanced to cure permanently. Rochester died at the early age of thirty-three, having drank most of his friends dead, and the Lord Pembroke who married Louise de Querouaille's sister was precisely the same age.

To realise the accustomed mode of life of

a young man of fashion in the later years of the seventeenth century, the works of contemporary dramatists, intent on holding up the mirror to nature, are more valuable for our purpose than the solemn diatribes of the clergy and the moralists, which fell, for the most part, on deaf ears. Shadwell, and to a greater extent Etherege, brought actual life upon the stage, and prepared the way for the more polished comedy of manners, initiated by Congreve in his masterpiece *The Way of the World*.

Whilst it would be untrue to say that all the fops were rakes, gamblers, spendthrifts, and drunkards, it is unquestionable that the ever-decreasing standard of morality which prevailed at Court, especially during the last decade of Charles's reign, when things were said and done upon the public stage unfit for decent men and women to see and hear, was reflected in the lives of many men of good birth, who, if not actually members of the Court circle, were quick to adopt the latest extravagance in dress or frivolity of conduct in which Whitehall chose to indulge. The bad example set in the highest quarters spread downwards through London society like a contagious disease.

Reading Dryden's earlier plays, such as *The Indian Emperor*, in which there is not one risky line, or his graceful epilogues of the same period, and comparing them with the declension of style so apparent in *Limberham* and his later comedies, it will be seen that he swam with the stream and prostituted his talents in order to suit the vicious tastes of his audiences.

Returning to Nell and St. James's Park, if "Lory" Hyde—he was not Lord Rochester then—was taking the air on the morning I have selected for her progress from Pall Mall to the Palace, her chair would halt awhile, for Nell and he were firm friends; but if by chance she should meet the "wicked Earl"[1] I do not think she would have wished to stop for a moment. The coarse gibes of Etherege—if he really did write *The Lady of Pleasure*, which is not certain—would not trouble her long, but the unutterable filthiness of some of Rochester's lampoons in which her name occurs was more than any woman of spirit, whether a daughter of joy, a siren of the stage, or a Royal favourite, could forget or excuse.

It may be that some of the more disgraceful libels attributed to Rochester were the work of others, although the *State Poems on Various Occasions*, first printed in 1697, undoubtedly contain many verses which flowed from his facile and vitriolic pen. Compared with the originals

---

[1] John Wilmot, Earl of Rochester, one of the most depraved men of his age. Born 1647, died 1680. Many of the satires and lampoons attributed to Rochester were, however, the work of others. George Julian, whom Buckingham called "The Newsmonger of the Muses," made a living by circulating manuscript libels on defenceless women, and Andrew Marvell was another writer who prostituted his pen in the same way.

in the Harleian MSS. these will be found comparatively decent reading, as they were drastically
altered and toned down before they could be
given to the world in book form.

Rochester's licence was frequently endorsed,
if we may coin the phrase in this connection, by
periodical enforced absences from Court. Yet
Charles, too lenient by nature to banish him permanently, allowed him to creep back again after
a few months' rustication, only to offend decent
opinion afresh by further outrages upon good taste.

That, like most bullies, he was also a coward
is proved to the hilt by his backing out of a duel
which he had entered upon with Lord Mulgrave,
on the plea of ill-health.

Nor was the writing of obscene verse his
only outrage on propriety. He probably did not
know, or if he did he did not care, how serious
an offence it was to strike a man within the
verge of the King's Court. So sacred was the
Sovereign's place of residence held to be that any
one so offending was liable to the direst penalties,
such as losing his right hand, or being imprisoned for life in addition to the infliction of a
heavy fine. Yet when this frantic rake assaulted
Tom Killigrew in the precincts of the Palace, he
was promptly let off by the easygoing Charles
and only told not to do it again.[1]

---

[1] In one of his drunken frolics Rochester threw down the sundial in the
Privy Garden, which was esteemed one of the rarest in Europe.

Colonel Colepepper, a half-crazy swaggering bully, was not so lucky in the next reign when he assaulted Lord Cavendish [1] within the verge of the Court. He was imprisoned in the Marshalsea and condemned to lose his right hand, though this savage sentence was not carried out.

The quarrel between the two broke out afresh when Cavendish, who had become Earl of Devonshire in the interval, struck Colepepper a blow with his cane in the Vane Room at Whitehall. For this he was fined £30,000, and he only obtained his release from prison by giving a bond for double the amount and proving that he had advanced Charles I. an equivalent amount of money during the Civil Wars. The Earl withdrew for a time from public life and occupied himself with building Chatsworth, nor did he return to London until William the Third, more generous than James, cancelled this outrageous exaction and took him into favour.

In contrast to so much that was scurrilous and profane in Rochester's writings, the well-known epitaph on the King, which he wrote at Charles's request, was the truest bit of verse he ever penned:

> Here lies our sovereign Lord the King,
>   Whose word no man relies on;
> Who never said a foolish thing,
>   And never did a wise one.

But how witty was the reply it promptly elicited:

[1] Afterwards the 1st Duke of Devonshire.

" The matter was easily to be accounted for—
his discourse was his own, but his actions were
his Ministry's " !

Another of Nell's acquaintance who positively
haunted the Mall was Sir Carr Scrope. He
lived close by in bachelor quarters in Duke
Street, and though singularly ill-favoured by
nature and handicapped by a pronounced squint,
he seems to have thought himself irresistible to
the opposite sex. When savagely attacked in
print by Rochester, who described him as being
" spit at and shunned by every girl in town," the
mere sight of him being enough to make a woman
" start back for shame and straight turn chaste for
fear," Scrope scored neatly by replying:

Thou canst hurt no man's fame with thy ill word,
Thy pen is full as harmless as thy sword.

Leaving Rochester to the contempt of honest
men, we pass on a little farther and meet with a gay
young spark, immaculately dressed and singularly
handsome, but much spoilt by the ladies of the
Court. This was the luckless Duke of Monmouth,
who, rightly or wrongly, had persuaded himself
about this time that he was the legitimate heir to
the throne. Nell always liked him, although she
did call him " Perkin " to his face on one occasion.
When in disgrace a few years later, she not only
gave him excellent advice (which, of course, he
did not listen to) but pleaded hard with the King
to take him back into favour. In this she was, for

once in a way, unsuccessful, and it was left to
the beautiful Lady Kildare, whom Charles had
recently taken into favour, to bring about a
reconciliation between father and son.

Taking the route across what is now the
Horse Guards Parade, Nell would leave her
chair at the foot of a long staircase which
adjoined the Tilt Yard of former days.[1] Tripping
lightly up the steep stairs, she would pass into
the famous gallery built by Henry VIII., to
which allusion has already been made.

By 1675 this Tudor relic had been merged
in Ormonde's apartments, but, although much
altered and subdivided, it was still possible
to walk on the level through a number of
communicating rooms. Therefore Nell, having
passed across Holbein's Gate, would have to
descend another staircase in order to reach the
main court of the Palace. She would then make
her way to those labyrinthine quarters set apart
for the maids-of-honour and the Queen's ladies-
in-waiting, to which, as has already been shown,
there were so many means of ingress and egress.

[1] This external staircase is shown in some of the older prints of Whitehall as seen from St. James's Park. Masell's view, reproduced in Gordon
Goodwin's edition of Peter Cunningham's *Story of Nell Gwynne*, conveys
an excellent idea of it. By it Charles was accustomed to enter the park
on foot, to feed his ducks and exercise his dogs, chatting meanwhile with
friends and acquaintances in that easy familiar style which did so much to
make him popular with all classes of his subjects. The staircase stood
almost exactly where the Scottish Office (Dover House) fronts the Horse
Guards Parade, and a little to the northward of the Treasury and the Privy
Council office.

By 1675 many of the residents in the Palace, whose names are shown on the Plan, had either died or been replaced in office by others. Ormonde still lived there occasionally, though he removed from time to time, first to Clarendon House, Piccadilly, and afterwards to a great house on the north side of St. James's Square, which had been built by the ground landlord, the Earl of St. Albans, for his own occupation. Monk had died five years before. The King's chief ministerial adviser was now Danby, though I am not sure whether he lived in the Palace, although he had his offices there. Arlington was still in residence, and in power, and so was Will Chiffinch. Nor was the Duke of Buckingham far away, for Wallingford House, now the Admiralty building, was only just across the road.

I do not suppose that Nell troubled her pretty head much about Tudor or any other style of architecture, or that she knew anything of Anne Boleyn's sad story. But she may have felt some slight interest in Holbein's Gate, if only because her rival Barbara had been installed there, before the King began to weary of the connection.

Another reason which may have prompted Nell to enter the Palace by this route was that she was always sure of a friendly reception by Ormonde. To this day there are preserved in the muniment room at Kilkenny Castle more of her letters (none, unfortunately, autographs,

but the work of an amanuensis whose spelling
was simply atrocious) than are known to exist in
any other collection yet examined and reported
on by the Historical Manuscripts Commission.

The reason which prompted Nell to correspond with the Duke so frequently in later
years was that she had been granted a pension
on the Irish establishment derived from the
Crown rights at Dundalk and Carlingford. This
pension was constantly falling into arrear. It
would have been surprising had it been otherwise, seeing that it was drawn from a country
where the punctual payment of rent has always
been a custom more honoured in the breach
than the observance.

From one of her many dictated letters to
Ormonde, preserved at Kilkenny Castle, I gather
that Nell could write if she chose, but that she
thought it kinder not to trouble her friends with
what she humorously described as her "wild
characters." Some day a letter in her own handwriting may be discovered in some old library or
muniment room, after lying unheeded for two
centuries and a half, but at present her autograph is as rare as that of Shakespeare. She had,
in addition to her pension, a charge of some
description upon Lord Dungannon's property,
the precise nature of which is not divulged in
any of the Ormonde papers in which her name
occurs. The first Viscount Dungannon, who

died in 1670, had personally encountered Cromwell and claimed to have wounded him with his
sword at the battle of Marston Moor. It would
seem but a poor reward for his loyalty and bravery
in the field that the King should grant one of his
mistresses a pension derived from a charge upon
his successor's estate. But at this period Irish
lands were often burdened in like manner in
order to enrich men, and women too, who never
set foot in that unhappy country in their lives.

The entries of foreign ambassadors accredited
to Whitehall were marked by elaborate ceremony.
The Prince de Ligne, the representative of Spain,
had seventeen coaches in his retinue in 1660;
and the Muscovite a suite of one hundred and
sixty-five, bearing presents—mantles of sables
and ermine, Persian carpets, and hawks—the
like of which was never seen before. When the
Russian ambassador presented his credentials [1] he
was much annoyed because his coach was not
allowed to drive into the Palace courtyard, fearing that his master would be offended if he
omitted to observe the least punctilio. Sir
Clement Cotterell, the Master of the Ceremonies,
contrived to pacify him by telling him that
no ambassador's coach was ever permitted to
drive into the Court. He, too, brought Persian
carpets, tapestries, sables and ermines, but the
ambassador himself was nothing like so splendid

[1] In October 1681.

and exotic as the one who preceded him twenty
years before.

The State entry of Colbert was witnessed by
Evelyn, who, standing by His Majesty at dinner,
was presented by Charles with a slice of West
Indian pineapple off his own plate. Evelyn did
not think much of it, though he admitted that
whilst it had a grateful acidity its taste more
resembled that of a quince or a melon, from
which it may be gathered that it was unripe.

When Hamet, the ambassador from Morocco,
arrived in London in 1682, he came up to the
throne without making any sort of reverence or
bowing his head or body—not that this was
intended as a mark of disrespect, since it was in
strict accordance with the manners and customs
of his country. His legs and arms were bare,
and he wore leather socks like the Turks.[1] As
gifts he brought with him two lions and thirty
ostriches, at which the King said to some of his
entourage that he could not think of anything
more appropriate to offer his master in return
than a flock of geese!

A few days later the ambassador and his
suite were entertained at " a banquet of sweet-
meats and music " in the Duchess of Portsmouth's
newly finished house at the farther end of the

---

[1] Another account says that his feet were bare, and that, feeling the
cold of the marble floor, he balanced himself first on one leg and then on the
other, at which the King could not help laughing.

great Stone Gallery.[1]   They behaved with extraordinary moderation and modesty, placed at a
long table, between every two Moors a lady.
Amongst the company were the King's natural
daughters, the Countesses of Lichfield and Sussex,
the Duchess herself, and of course Nell Gwynne,
" as splendid as jewels and excess of bravery could
make them."   There cannot, however, have been
much conversation at the banquet, unless the
services of an interpreter were requisitioned for
the occasion.

The King undertook to provide the wedding
clothes of both his daughters, and their mother,
the Duchess of Cleveland, ordered them.   Somehow the bills were not paid as promptly as they
should have been, and eventually they were
defrayed out of the Secret Service Funds after
Charles's death by James the Second.

These accounts are instructive, as showing not
only the cost of dressmaking and millinery two
hundred and fifty years ago, but the names of
the tradesmen who supplied the finest wares worn
at the Court.   £646 was paid to William Gostling
and partners for gold and silver lace, whilst other
bills due to Nicholas Fownes, Richard Bokenham,
Benjamin Drake, and John Dodsworth brought
the sum total of the trousseaux of the Royal
brides up to £1046, the accounts not being finally

[1] Her new house is duly marked in Morgan's map of London and
Westminster, 1682.

settled until ten years after the date of the first wedding.

When Charles gave a dinner to the Knights of the Garter on St. George's Day, 1667, the cheer was extraordinary in its profusion. Each knight had forty dishes to his mess, piled up five or six high. The King sat alone on an elevated throne and the knights at one long table on his right hand, which reached the whole length of the Banqueting House. Over against them was a buffet or sideboard covered with rich gilt plate, and in a gallery above were placed the wind and percussion instruments— trumpets and kettledrums.

About the middle of the banquet the knights drank the King's health standing, or such of them as could stand, and the King drank theirs, whilst the trumpets sounded and the guns at the Tower were fired to let the whole town know how His Majesty celebrated the feast of St. George in proposing the toast of " Merry England."

Pepys, who was present, remarked that what was not eaten of " the banqueting stuff " was flung about the room, adding that " in truth the crowd was so great that I stayed no longer than this sport began, for fear of disorder."

It is conceivable that Wolsey lived in greater state at York Place than did any of the Stuart kings. His rooms were hung with cloth of gold or silver, and the Cardinal's meals, it has been stated, were served on plate of solid gold. This, however, I take leave to doubt. At no time in English history was any large amount of plate assayed of unalloyed gold. Even the so-called gold plate at Windsor Castle, frequently referred to in our own times by imaginative writers, is only silver gilt. Yet, deceived by its colour, the credulous persist in believing that it is wrought entirely of the more precious metal. A small quantity of real gold plate, salvers, bowls, and spoons and forks, made to William the Third's order, was carried off to Hanover by George the First, and these are said to be still in existence at Gmunden.

Wolsey may have numbered amongst his treasures one or more pieces of plate resembling the famous Royal drinking-cup, embellished with translucent enamel, which is now in the British Museum, or a somewhat similar one belonging to the Corporation of King's Lynn. Both of these date from Plantagenet times; but such secular pieces are excessively rare both in England and on the Continent, and the bulk of Wolsey's plate in daily use must have been of silver, water-gilt perhaps, but not wrought of solid gold.

Amongst the altar vessels in his private chapel there may have been relics of an earlier age than his own, but, as a rule, such priceless works of art were only to be found in the greater cathedrals and monasteries, where they were

jealously guarded and held in especial venera-
tion by the faithful. Autocrat as he was, it is
doubtful whether the Cardinal would have dared
to remove any of the altar plate from York to
London without obtaining permission from Rome.
Merely to read the inventory of the gorgeous
works of mediæval art belonging to Salisbury
before the Reformation helps posterity to realise
the irreparable loss which Henry VIII., in his
greed to destroy the Catholic Church, inflicted
upon England.

What would not any one with the slightest
feeling of reverence for mediæval art, as practised
in England in the fourteenth and fifteenth
centuries, give to-day for a glimpse of the waggon-
loads of sacred relics—the jewelled crosses and
gold chalices encrusted with precious stones—
torn from the shrines of Edward the Confessor
and Thomas à Becket!

All have been lost or melted down, though
a single ruby stolen from one or other of the
shrines at Westminster or Canterbury is said to
have been worn by Henry VIII. on his burly
thumb. But this, like the story of the jewel said
to have been worn by Henry the Fifth on his
helmet at Agincourt, may well be apocryphal.

There is, I believe, not a single piece of pre-
Reformation plate now at either Westminster or
St. Paul's, and of the Regalia only one spoon,
and that without a hall-mark.

The destruction of such specimens of ancient ecclesiastical art as escaped the Reformation was rendered all but complete by the fanatical zeal of the Puritans in the Civil Wars, till, at the present day, a few colleges at Oxford and Cambridge, which did not melt their plate for the good of the Royal cause, and some of the City companies, are almost the only possessors of any considerable amount of mediæval silver. Whitehall was stripped bare of its treasures after the execution of Charles the First, but, to his credit, his son endeavoured, though only with partial success, to buy back such pictures, books, and furniture as he could trace.

Whatever else was lacking in the domestic economy of the Palace, there was always plenty to eat and drink. The Plan is dotted over with kitchens, bakehouses, scalding houses, pastry ovens; meat, fish, and game larders; butteries; wine, beer, and cider cellars, necessitating a large staff of cooks, scullions, bakers, dairymen, cellarers, and waiting men and women. No doubt there was an enormous amount of waste, and probably peculation too. There always is, and always will be, in palaces, as in private dwellings, where the head of the house is indifferent to such minor considerations as the punctual payment of household accounts. One redeeming feature of the profusion which obtained at Whitehall was that every day the

poor were regaled with what was left over from
the Royal table.

In the joy with which the English people
welcomed the restoration of the Monarchy and
the rebirth of a merry England, the provincial
corporations vied with one another in enabling
the King to live once more in regal style. Plymouth presented Charles with a magnificent
silver wine-fountain and Exeter with a highly
ornate salt-cellar to grace the high table, and
these, happily, have survived to the present day.[1]

Silver wine-cups, though still in frequent use,
were not such a necessity as they had been a
generation or two earlier, owing to the gradual
introduction of glass drinking vessels. Spoons
had been in use for centuries, but forks were
still something of a rarity in noble and gentle
households. This made it necessary to rinse
the fingers after each course, and waiting men
charged with this duty proffered a bowl of
fresh water and a napkin to each guest in turn.
When forks came into general use, such relics
of barbarism as eating with the fingers disappeared
for good and all.

The gorgeous clothes worn by the Cavalier
aristocracy were in the nature of a reaction from
the enforced shabbiness of the King's Court in

---

[1] The salt-cellar, which bears the maker's initials I. H. in a shaped shield
but no other marks, cost £700. The wine-fountain was bought from Sir
Robert Vyner, goldsmith, and Lord Mayor of London.

exile. French silk or velvet coats, trimmed with gold, silver, or fur, antique lace ruffles, powdered periwigs, hats with waving ostrich plumes, and jewelled shoe-buckles were now the only wear for men of fashion. Great courtiers, who had gone threadbare at the Hague, now appeared at Whitehall in clothes which, in some instances, entailed an expenditure running into hundreds of pounds for a single suit.

Nor were the dresses worn by the ladies less costly or profuse. The brave show of silks and satins, taffetas and brocades, worn at Court by the fairest in the realm, rivalled the hues of the rainbow. The brightest colours, scarlet and sapphire, emerald and orange, rose-pink and green, were worn in competition with silver, gold, or virgin white.

In the majority of instances the natural charms of their wearers were enhanced by the flash of diamonds, the fire of rubies, and the sheen of pearls. Their clothes were, for the most part, of English make, but even then ladies preferred to get their gloves from Paris, where a maker named Martial was reckoned the best *gantier* in Europe. Some of the dressmakers had to wait a long time for the settlement of their bills, as we have already noted.

Nell, whose income from all sources was never a tenth part of that of the twin cormorants Barbara Villiers and Louise de Querouaille, gave upwards of £4000 for a necklace of fifty large and evenly matched pearls, which had once been the property of Prince Rupert's mistress, "Peg" Hughes.

The interest which great ladies took in the clothes worn by the King's mistresses, and their curiosity to learn the latest fashion of dressing the hair, is illustrated in a letter written by Ursula Wolryche to her daughter, Lady Wrottesley, about 1670: "They say that there (at Whitehall) is the greatest gallantry, silver and gold lace all over the petticoats and the bodies of their gowns, but sleeves and skirts black, abundance of curls [1] very small on their heads, and very fine (are) their head dresses."

It was long a point of contention which of the actresses of the King's Company was the handsomest. Blows were exchanged and duels fought by hot-headed young men holding opposite views. In one of these encounters one of the players' brothers was unfortunately killed, as if to demonstrate the folly of such a controversy being satisfactorily decided by an appeal to arms.

Nell's celebrated necklace appears in Gascar's print, which, from its rarity, invariably fetches a high price when offered for sale. Essentially French in character and conception, it depicts her in a lace chemise, and not much else, reclining on a bed of roses from which her two children,

---

[1] This must refer to Nell's luxuriant tresses.

as winged Cupids, are withdrawing the curtains.
Charles is seen in the mid-distance apparently
in the act of addressing his inamorata, from whom,
however, he is separated by a sheet of water.

The artificiality of Gascar's composition compares unfavourably with Lely's treatment of
Mistress Nell in the National Portrait Gallery,
where, limned to the life in studied negligence,
she is shown without any extraneous ornament,
" hair loosely flowing, robes as free." [1]

These pearls of great price—a necklace with
a pedigree if ever there was one — are now, I
am credibly informed, heirlooms in the Duke
of Rutland's family, but what became of her
" crochet of diamonds," alluded to in one of
her few extant letters as " the finest thing that
ever was seen," I have not been able to discover.

Their Graces of Cleveland and Portsmouth
counted their jewels by the bushel. According
to Ruvigny, Charles gave the latter lady, by way
of compensation for an alleged injury which it is
not possible to describe in cold print, a rope of
pearls valued at four thousand Jacobuses, and a
diamond necklace costing six thousand. Reckoning the Jacobus at twenty-five shillings, the two
together represented about £12,500 of English
money.[2] Both were in bad health at the time,

---

[1] In none of Lely's portraits which I have examined is Nell depicted
with a necklace, a pendant or a brooch, or even with a ring upon her finger.

[2] Ruvigny to Pomponne, May 14, 1674, quoted by H. Forneron, *Louise
de Querouaille*, Paris, 1886.

and Louise paid several visits to Tunbridge, Bath, and the waters of Bourbon before she recovered.[1]

On a former occasion I endeavoured to follow Charles the Second in an imaginary perambulation of one of the London Squares, noting whom he called upon and whom he passed by. It will, I think, not be thought inappropriate if I describe, quite briefly, a single day's doings in the Palace, and show how the Court amused itself from day to day and night to night. I have taken as an illustration the summer of 1675, because, though money was scarce and Parliament indisposed to grant further supplies until it knew how they were to be applied, the Court, so far as can be ascertained, lived in precisely the same atmosphere of luxury and extravagance as in the earlier years of the Restoration. This was the year in which Nell Gwynne first became officially connected with Whitehall, thus realising her early dreams of advancement when living in rags and misery in the Coal Yard.

The Royal dinner-hour was one o'clock, and when the King entered a number of his loyal

---

[1] When Miss Blagge, afterwards Lady Godolphin, whose salary as a maid-of-honour was only twenty pounds a year, appeared at Court in the *Masque of Calisto*, she wore diamonds of the estimated value of £20,000. But as the Queen had no cause to be jealous of her, for she was a saint amongst sinners thrust into an uncongenial atmosphere, it is likely that Catherine, with her usual kindness of heart, lent her some of her own jewels for the occasion. Even little Miss Frazer, the daughter of the King's doctor and one of the best dancers at Court, dressed so well that envious tongues declared that such an expenditure could not have been honestly come by.

subjects usually crowded into the gallery of the Banqueting House to watch their Majesties eat. It must have been a red-letter day in Pepys' calendar when on July 25, 1666, he was able to write in his diary: " By and by the King to dinner, but, Lord! how little I should be pleased to have so many people crowding about me." He afterwards had his own dinner " at the Back-stairs," where, as he relates with great satisfaction, he " dined nobly," eating the same meat as had been put before the King, and drinking the same liquor.

There is much divergence of opinion as to what constitutes enjoyment, but I have been told that, to this day, numbers of highly respectable and presumably sane citizens derive considerable satisfaction in sitting for hours in the gallery of the Guildhall to watch the Lord Mayor and his guests eating and drinking. The semi-barbarous custom of Royalty dining in public was a survival from early times, when it was thought that the sovereign ran less risk of being poisoned if he dined *coram populo* than if he ate in private.

Charles once bade Grammont remark that at dinner he was served upon the knee, an observance peculiar to the English Court, whereon the audacious Frenchman, who seems to have been privileged to say anything he liked to the King, replied, " Is that so, sire? I thought it was by way of apology for giving you such a bad dinner!"

This practice of Royalty dining in public, which one would think must have been extremely irksome to the persons chiefly concerned, was now beginning to fall into desuetude. Yet, on the whole, it does not seem to have been one of those ceremonial observances which were better managed in France. Madame de Sévigné has drawn rather a dismal picture of a State banquet at St. Germain which she was privileged to attend as a spectator:

Le roi et la reine mangent tristement, Madame de Richelieu, dame d'honneur de la reine est assise et les autres debout: celles qui n'ont point dîné sont prêtes à s'élancer sur les plats. Celles qui ont dîné, ont mal au cœur et sont suffoquées de la vapeur des viandes. Ainsi cette troupe est souffrante.[1]

Royalty dined early in England so as to allow of a visit to one of the theatres, at which the performances began at three o'clock precisely. Dryden's five-act tragedies, so much in vogue at Drury Lane, must have occupied from two to three hours in representation, but time was usually found for a rapid drive round the ring in Hyde Park in the evening, or, if the weather was favourable, for a water picnic on the Thames, a form of amusement in which Charles much delighted.

The evening entertainments at the Palace were of a less formal nature than the dinners,

[1] Madame de Sévigné to Madame de Grignan, January 22, 1674.

and were all the more enjoyable because Royalty was exempt at supper-time from the intolerable nuisance of being stared at by strangers.

It is safe to assume that the ceremonial banquets and balls were invariably held in Inigo Jones's Banqueting House, but there was another and smaller building, shown on Morgan's map, and called on the Plan " The Great Hall." It had a high-pitched roof with a *louvre* in the centre, to let in the air and let out the smoke. Standing as it did nearer to the river than the great Banqueting Chamber, it was conveniently situated for the King's and Queen's private apartments, as it had its own separate range of kitchens and offices and its private cellar. Moreover, the master cook, a very important personage in the daily life of the Palace, lived not far from it. This hall may have been a survival of Wolsey's building, as may also have been the private chapel of Charles the Second's Court. If this was so, it returned to the use of the ancient faith when James the Second came to the throne, only to relapse once more into Protestantism under William of Orange.

Wolsey's chapel, which figures, if I mistake not, in Visscher's conjectural view of Whitehall from the river, appears to have been a large building with a lofty spire, but it is easy to be misled by panoramic views of London, such as were drawn by van Wyndegrade, Agas, Visscher, and other artists of the sixteenth century. They took great liberties in the matter of perspective and proportion, and not until the age of Hollar is reached is it possible to ascertain with certainty what any particular building in London really looked like.

The daily life of the Palace was an incessant round of amusement and convivial extravagance. Sometimes, perhaps, in the ceaseless pursuit of pleasure, the gaiety may have been more apparent than real, owing to the intrigues of rival factions within the Court. These, as a rule, originated in the constant bickerings and jealousies of the King's mistresses. But though these intrigues seldom failed to bring disappointments in their train, on the surface all went smoothly enough.

Poor Queen Catherine when she came to England brought with her (in addition to Tangier, Bombay, and a dowry of £300,000) a number of Portuguese ladies-in-waiting, whose personal attractions were inconsiderable. From the moment they landed at Portsmouth they seem to have given trouble to the officials responsible for their housing and maintenance. Amongst other complaints which they preferred, they one and all firmly declined to occupy any bed in which a man had ever slept before. On the difficult and delicate situation which this gave rise to being referred to the King, he professed himself (as indeed might have been expected) at a loss

to understand such a mental attitude, and advised
their being sent back to Portugal at once.   And,
accordingly, back they went, their places being
promptly filled by English ladies, Barbara Villiers
amongst the number, who were less disposed to find
fault with the accommodation provided for them.[1]

Every evening the especial favourites of the
hour either played cards, often for higher stakes
than they could afford, with their male friends
and admirers, danced to their heart's desire to
the invigorating strains of an excellent string
band, or listened to more or less erotic songs,
rendered by native and foreign artists to the
twanging accompaniment of a guitar.

Taking the card-players first, we find that
basset was the most popular game, though the
Queen is said to have preferred the more compli-
cated ombre, perhaps because she had seen it
played in the land of her birth.   At ombre only
three could play, whereas basset provided amusement for five.   When there were French guests
at Court the tables were set for faro and trente-
et-quarante.   I am not sure whether the simpler
but more fascinating roulette (originally known
in this country as roly-poly) had yet found

---

[1] For a description of something else which greatly shocked the modesty
of these unfortunate ladies, reference must be made to an entry in Lord
Chesterfield's MS. letter-book and diary in the British Museum, as it would
be quite impossible to print the details in these pages.   To have done so
would have resulted in this book being placed upon the Index Expurgatorius
immediately on publication.

its way over from Paris, though if it had, how
it would have delighted the gay throng at
Whitehall! A casino in the Green Park, under
Royal patronage, would have rendered Charles
independent of Louis XIV. or Parliament!
In the next century, Sarah, Duchess of Marlborough, played at roulette fast and furiously,
and such became its vogue in England that
Acts of Parliament were passed to restrain its
growth. At basset, weekdays and Sundays, the
tables were heaped high with gold, for as yet
there were no bank-notes. Nell was never very
lucky at the card-table, and probably she was too
careless to pay strict attention to the rules of the
game. She once lost £1400 at a sitting to the
Duchess of Mazarine. Yet this was a bagatelle
compared to the high play of the Duchess of
Cleveland, who had been known to drop five or
six times as much in a single night. Charles
did not care much for gambling either at cards
or dice—"spotted ivory and painted cardboard,"
as Nell called them. He never staked more than
five pounds at a time, either at cards or hazard,
but he always insisted on having music, of which
he was an excellent judge.

No doubt some of his own compositions, of
which a song on "the pleasures of love" was
about the best, occasionally formed part of the
programme ; but if he did not dance much himself in his later years—in his youth he had been

one of the best dancers in Europe—he liked to look on at others, and in the great ball-room we shall be more likely to find him, and Nell Gwynne also, than in the antechamber set apart for the gamblers.

The lighting of so large a room as Inigo Jones's Banqueting House must have been no easy matter. Some spluttering flambeaux held by the Yeomen of the Guard provided a portion of the illumination and a good deal of smoke. In addition, a profusion of wax candles cast their mellow rays upon a pageant of dress which surpassed in wealth of colour and elaboration the glories of any other European Court.

Mistress Nell, though she always affected the *négligé* style of dress, was fond of bright colours, and she contrived by sheer force of beauty and natural grace to hold her own with, if not to outshine, the Duchesses of Cleveland and Mazarine, although they spent ten times the amount on their clothes which she could afford. But then she possessed the incalculable advantage of being considerably younger than either of them!

It would seem as if, on her entrance into the Court circle, Charles's long-suffering Consort bore no ill-will to the ex-orange-girl of Drury Lane. Nell, of course, had turned her back on the theatre for good and all, as it would have been incompatible with her position in the Queen's household to act in public. Yet it is not im-

probable that she took part in some of the theatrical
representations of a more or less private nature
which were given in the Palace from time to time.

The Queen must often have seen Nell on the
stage, and admired her comic powers, as well as
her dancing, and that she cannot have been ill-
disposed to her is, I think, proved by her
having given her son [1] (after his mother's death)
the handsome allowance of two thousand pounds
a year out of her own privy purse—a mark of
consideration which she certainly would not have
bestowed upon the offspring of their Graces of
Cleveland and Portsmouth.

An excellent idea of a Court ball, which was
given at the Hague on the eve of the Restoration,
is conveyed by a painting of Jannsen's in the
Royal Collection at Windsor. Charles, wearing his
hat, is seen dancing with his sister Mary, widow
of William II. of Orange; the rest of the Royalties,
including the Queen of Bohemia and Princess
Henrietta, are seated, whilst a little boy, the future
William III. of England, is looking wistfully at
the dancers. An opening in the wall shows the
Royal party at supper in an adjoining room.

At Whitehall the Court balls usually opened
with a Branle or a Coranto. The former was in
the nature of a round dance, in which the dancers
joined hands as round a maypole. The Coranto,
or Courante, was a quick dance of French origin;

---

[1] Charles Beauclerk, 1st Duke of St. Albans.

the more stately and sedate minuet being a later introduction which did not attain its zenith until the eighteenth century. Next would come a dance in which the beaux and belles of the Court especially delighted. This was the Pavane, which, as it was more in the nature of a procession than a dance, afforded not only a welcome relief from the more fatiguing movements of the Coranto, but an admirable opportunity for displaying to advantage the splendid dresses worn by the company. Moreover, during momentary pauses, it was not only permissible but customary for partners to exchange kisses. They did the same in the Branle, and " Come Kiss Me Now " was the title of one of the favourite dance tunes. The Pavane was usually followed by a Galliard, a quick step, and towards the end of the evening, when the lights began to burn low, the King would call for a country dance, in which the men and the ladies formed two rows facing one another, somewhat after the fashion of Sir Roger de Coverley, which, I believe, is not even now entirely out of favour at children's parties. It owed much of its popularity a generation or two ago, no doubt, to the stirring tune to which it is performed.

The old English country dance, when properly executed, was a lively affair, and it ensured every dancer taking part in it being the partner in turn of all the others. Thus the Duke of Monmouth was sure of having Nell Gwynne to dance with, and Sir Edward Villiers, the best dancer at Court, was equally certain of little Miss Frazer, and so on. It was danced at Whitehall to the tune of " Maiden Lane " or " Cuckolds All Awry," to name but two out of many ancient airs of which the names are now lost. The homely jig or hornpipe was sometimes danced at Court, but, as it was a *pas seul*, it was probably confined to professional rather than to amateur exponents. It is scarcely necessary to add that Nell was one of the most expert dancers of jigs and hornpipes. So also was Moll Davis, and it is on record that she gave an exhibition of this particular quickstep before the King and Queen. When the saraband was introduced at Whitehall, Grammont said that " It either charmed or amazed every one, for all the guitarists of the Court began to learn it and God only knows the universal twanging that followed."

Before the last strains of the country dance had died away the company were regaled at supper, in the French style, at a long buffet at one end of the hall, and it would be safe to hazard the guess that the dancers, as well as the card-players, much appreciated the newly introduced *vin pétillant* which we now recognise as champagne. It owed its popularity at this period to St. Evremond and the Duchess of Mazarine, and large consignments of it reached the Royal cellars by the aid of friendly French ambassadors, some of whom found it almost as useful to bribe members of the English Parliament with as French gold.

One bad habit the Court had, so far, not contracted. It did not, as a rule, sit up late. And when, usually before midnight, the Queen gave the signal for retiring, it was a case of *rien ne va plus* at the card-tables and, up in the gallery, the musicians began to put away their instruments. Those of the general company who lived at a distance clattered home in their coaches, whilst, in summer time, others took boat to one or other of the riverside mansions in the vicinity of the Palace.

The great officers of state, the ladies-in-waiting, and the maids of honour who lived in Whitehall were borne swiftly to their apartments in sedan-chairs, attended by running footmen, guided, on dark nights, through the labyrinthine courtyards and passages by link-men. Perhaps the King, although he was always an early riser, did not always go to bed quite so early as his guests. Sometimes, accompanied by the indispensable Chiffinch, he would pay mysterious nocturnal visits where we must not follow him. An inquisitive ambassador—of course he was a Frenchman—once reported to his Royal master that the King of England would go through the pretence of undressing, and then, having dismissed his attendants, put on his clothes again and pay

midnight calls in the Palace which were sometimes
prolonged until the small hours of the morning.

Only a few yards away from his own apartments was his neglected wife's bedchamber.
Pathetic in its simplicity, there was nothing of
luxury to be seen in it; only a few religious
pictures (brought, no doubt, from Portugal on
her marriage), several books of devotion, and a
basin of holy water at her head as she slept. An
illuminated clock by her bedside, enabling her
to tell the hour at any time of night, might, we
think, have more appropriately been placed in
the King's room at the other end of the passage.

Choosing as an alternative, at the cost of
some slight repetition, the silent highway of
the Thames and taking boat at Westminster
on an imaginary visit to Whitehall, in 1668, a
good general idea of the Palace, at the time the
Plan was drawn, would be obtained by dropping
leisurely down-stream as far as the garden of
Northumberland House. After passing the Wool-
staple, the first considerable buildings to attract
attention would be Manchester House and Derby
House, the town mansions of the noble families
of Montagu and Stanley. The memory of the
latter is preserved in Derby Street, a narrow
turning out of Parliament Street, guarded to-day
at its entrance by a fierce-looking red lion, one
of the few remaining tavern signs in London,
other than pictorial ones. When the house

was rebuilt this boldly carved beast survived to remind the present generation of an age when few could read though all could see, and signs were of real and practical value.

The next house of any note was the Duke of Richmond's, which stood on the very brink of the river. Shortly before this time the King had been striving might and main to add *la belle Stewart* to his seraglio, but, much to his disgust, the Duke made her an honest woman by marrying her in March 1667.[1]

Mr. Wheatley, in his *London, Past and Present*, assumed that the Dukes of Richmond did not come to this neighbourhood until after the destruction, by fire, of the Duchess of Portsmouth's apartments in 1691, but it will be seen that the last Duke of Richmond of the first creation preceded Louise de Querouaille's son by the King, by some years, although the first of the resuscitated Lennox family to bear that title built himself a new house on the site of Richmond Terrace, years after the husband of *la belle Stewart*, who had three wives before he was thirty, resided hereabouts.

Behind the earlier Richmond House was the bowling-green of the Palace—it had been an orchard in Tudor times—and beyond it again,

---

[1] Charles Stuart, 5th Duke of Richmond, born 1639, died 1672, was in no way related to Louise de Querouaille's son ennobled a few years later under the same proud title.

in King Street, lived old Lady Villiers—Lady
Castlemaine's grandmother. Her house overlooked both the Privy Garden and the bowling-
green, from which it was separated only by a
low fence. A little farther down-stream was a
private landing-place, giving access to Lady
Villiers's garden ground.

We now arrive at the Palace precincts and,
still keeping closely to the river-bank, reach a
suite of rooms which were in Mrs. Mary Kirk's
occupation. She was the younger daughter of
George Kirk and the *chère amie* of the Duke of
York. Her elder sister Diana married the last
Earl of Oxford, and Mary eventually became
the wife of Sir Robert Vernon of Hodnett. Before
her marriage, in addition to a substantial pension
paid to her out of the Secret Service Fund, Mary
had another large suite of rooms fronting St.
James's Park, almost on the site of the present
Admiralty Office.

Her mother having been a Killigrew may,
in part, account for this preferential treatment,
as her father's family had been entrenched in
the Palace since the reign of Charles the First,
and still retained its hold therein.

The Duke of York, though his rooms are
marked upon the Plan, can seldom have occupied
them, as Charles, soon after his restoration, made
over to his brother the greater part of the State
apartments in St. James's Palace. There most of

his children were born, including the Old Pretender, whose entrance into the world excited so much suspicion that the "warming-pan" story of a fictitious child being imposed upon the nation was widely believed at the time.

Continuing our progress down-stream, we find the King's sempstresses enjoying a view of the Thames, and next to them again, before reaching the Privy stairs—alive in summer with beaux and belles embarking in or alighting from gaily decorated shallops manned by stalwart watermen wearing the Royal livery—were the King's private apartments. Adjoining these, as we have already noted, were Will Chiffinch's.

A low wall, with semicircular bastions at regular intervals, extended along nearly the whole of the river front, but as the King's and Queen's lodgings were considerably loftier, this did not interfere with their view of the river. On the farther or northern side of the Privy Stairs were, in addition to the Queen's apartments, those of her chamberlain, Sir William Killigrew. Beyond him lived Lady Arlington, a Dutch lady of good family, and one of Queen Catherine's ladies-in-waiting. Then came the Privy kitchen and the lodgings of a very important personage in the domestic economy of the Palace, the King's master cook.[1] Beyond these rooms again was a lofty stone building (apparently of

---

[1] His name was Sayres.

Tudor date), embattled on the river front, which, at the time of our imaginary visit, was in the occupation of Sir Richard Bellings, the Queen's secretary.

Immediately to the north of Whitehall Stairs, the ordinary landing-place for those not privileged to use the Royal or Privy Stairs, was the Ury office, the "small beer buttery,"[1] the cofferer's office, and a great bakehouse with two huge ovens which are clearly marked on the Plan. Behind these was Sir Stephen Fox's office.

The National Liberal Club is built upon the former site of these domestic offices, but it is important to remember that when the Victoria Embankment was constructed a great deal of ground was reclaimed from the Thames at this point and laid out as a public garden. When the existing houses in Whitehall Gardens were built after the great fire which destroyed the greater part of the Palace in 1698, they stood on the river-bank, and No. 7, the old Board of Trade office, which was Lord Pembroke's house in the eighteenth century, still retains its boat-house.

Halting our own boat at a small inlet from the Thames, called on the Plan "Scotland Dock," we reach a wharf where, for centuries before Wolsey's day, the Archbishops of York were accustomed to land their heavy stores; tuns of wine, barrels of ale, and cargoes of coal and wood

[1] ? Brewery.

being unloaded there from sea-going barges and lighters.

This wharf and the adjoining Deal Yard formed the boundary of the Palace in this direction, and beyond was a large garden belonging to Northumberland House which existed, in a curtailed form, until the formation of Northumberland Avenue.

On festive occasions, when the Court was in residence at Whitehall, Charles would mix freely with the general company, exchanging greetings and cracking jokes in that familiar style which contributed so much to his popularity. Of fine physique, black but comely, and with piercing dark eyes, his features were decidedly pleasing, despite a sensual mouth verging on coarseness. Prudent mothers and chaperons positively dreaded his paying any mark of attention to fair debutantes under their charge, for so deplorable was his private character that even to be seen speaking to the King was enough to compromise a young girl's reputation.

Sir Robert Howard,[1] whose name occurs so often in these pages in connection with Drury Lane theatre, was so well aware of this that he sent his daughter Mary,[2] then only in her nine-

---

[1] Sir Robert Howard was ridiculed by Shadwell in his first play, *The Sullen Lovers*, 1668, as " Sir Positive At All," a foolish knight who pretends to understand everything in the world, and will suffer no man to understand anything in his company.

[2] Mary Howard, born December 28, 1653, entered the English Convent of Poor Clares, became Abbess and died there in 1735, having become known in her later years as Mary of the Holy Cross.

teenth year, to a convent in Paris, merely because she had attracted the King's notice at a play.

When he could tear himself away from the ball-room or the card-tables, Charles would enter into animated conversation with such of his ministers as happened to be present.

Danby, after the break up of the Cabal, was his principal adviser, although he was personally unpopular with the House of Commons.

Corruption was rife in Parliament from top to bottom, every possible device being resorted to by the Court to stifle discussion when the representatives of the people seemed disposed to withhold the granting of supplies.

Danby bribed members of the House of Commons with such assiduity that at the end of a session he once wrote that they came round him "like jackdaws for cheese"! Vacancies were habitually filled by nominees of the Crown, often inferior officials of the backstairs, taking their orders from Will Chiffinch, or by minors who could be counted upon to vote as they were told.[1]

Lord Torrington, General Monk's son and heir, sat and voted in the House, as member for Plymouth, when he was only fifteen, and numerous instances of similar scandals could be cited. Long adjournments and frequent prorogations—

[1] The Parliament which met in March 1679 passed the famous Habeas Corpus Act, the statute which becomes more famous still when it is suspended. It had already been passed by the Commons in the "Pensionary" Parliament, but was then rejected by the Lords.

one of these extended over fifteen whole months
—were Charles's favourite device for silencing the
growing dissatisfaction of the country party.

Whilst the King's private life, owing to his
habits of self-indulgence, was deplorable, his
unfailing good humour, his inborn kindness of
heart (for by nature he was neither cruel nor
ungenerous), combined to make him one of the
most popular sovereigns who ever reigned in
England. On the other hand, his unbusinesslike
methods caused his advisers many anxious
moments. He " could see things if he would "
well enough, whereas his brother James " would
only see them if he could." He possessed abundant capacity for government, but lacked the
necessary inclination. Yet Charles could be
firm enough on occasions. He positively forced
James to consent to the marriage of his daughter
Mary to William of Orange, whom, thus early,
he seems to have regarded as a probable successor
to the throne of England. As an instance of his
remarkable prescience, Charles once told Burnet
that he would not trust James to last four years
when he became King.[1] In arranging his niece's
marriage he was aided by Danby, and to a certain
extent by Bentinck, but it was the King who

---

[1] This was a truly remarkable prediction. Charles the Second died on
February 6, 1685, and on the same day of the same month *four years later*,
at a conference between the Lords and Commons, the throne was declared
vacant. Next day William and Mary were publicly proclaimed King and
Queen of England, France, and Ireland!

carried the project to a triumphant conclusion.
Louise de Querouaille fought hard to prevent the
marriage, and when Louis XIV. heard of it he is
said to have received the news as he would have
the loss of an army. Charles's mind, so far as
it is possible to analyse it, reveals, in addition
to an almost Hibernian insincerity, a preference
for dissimulation, procrastination, and secrecy
in dealing with public affairs which must have
made him the despair of his ministers. They
could never feel sure that he was not about
to enter behind their backs into some fresh
corrupt bargain with Louis XIV., whilst outwardly professing a desire to proceed on con-
stitutional lines. When the Commons declined
to vote any further supplies until they knew
how the money was to be expended, he turned
again and again to France in order, if possible,
to render himself independent of Parliament.
This was the secret of Louise de Querouaille's
power, for, without her, the stream of French gold
which flowed into the Royal coffers might, at
any moment, have been diverted to other channels.[1]

In taking leave of Whitehall as seen from the
river, it may be mentioned that the Thames was
much cleaner in the seventeenth century than it
is now. Salmon for the King's table were caught
in it then, and long after. Nowadays flounders,

---

[1] Yet with all his faults Charles was extremely generous—with his own
money when he had any, and with that of others when this was exhausted.

eels, and, lower down-stream, whitebait, are sometimes taken in nets, but it is to be feared that the Thames will never again become a salmon river, despite the praiseworthy efforts of the Conservancy to make it so.

Charles was fond of bathing in the river and often took a morning plunge off Whitehall Stairs, whilst Sir Dudley North was such an expert swimmer that he would shoot London Bridge at low water without turning a hair. The polite Earl of Chesterfield once addressed a letter to a brother peer: " To The Earl of Pembroke in the Thames over against Whitehall." In more recent years the poet Byron swam from Lambeth to Blackfriars, a distance of about three miles. But with the embanking of the Thames and the introduction of steamboats the importance of the watermen's calling rapidly declined, until, at the present day, no Londoner would dream of taking boat on the Thames for pleasure's sake, much less of bathing in it.

My personal recollections of the Banqueting House date from my childhood, when I used to be taken on Sunday mornings from my father's house in the Broad Sanctuary, under the shadow of the Abbey, to the Chapel Royal. In those days I, naturally, knew little or nothing of the historical associations of Whitehall, nor had I even heard of Nell Gwynne. But I recollect distinctly to this day staring up at Rubens's painted ceiling and wondering when, if ever, the sermon would come to an end.

The Chapel Royal, which was never, I think, consecrated, ceased to be used as such in 1890, and by a happy inspiration Mrs. Edward Stanhope, the wife of the then Secretary of State for War, decided to make use of Inigo Jones's great hall once again for a purely social purpose. On referring to an old diary I find that I was amongst her guests on June 27, 1891, when the invitations were issued to have the honour of meeting H.R.H. the Prince of Wales.[1]

The old hall, which, for the first time in its long history, was illuminated by the electric light and decorated with arms and trophies brought specially from the Tower of London, presented such a brilliant appearance on that summer's night that the scene might well have challenged comparison with the pageantry and profusion of the Restoration era. It is possible that some of the jewels worn on this occasion had been seen at Whitehall before, Nell Gwynne's celebrated necklace amongst the number.

From the same notebook I find that I was present at another historic reception, given by Lady Dalhousie, the young and beautiful wife of the first Secretary for Scotland at Dover House, on the opposite, or Cockpit, side of the road, on May 26, 1886. The fate of Mr. Gladstone's

[1] King Edward VII.

first Home Rule Bill was then trembling in the
balance, and most of the guests were supporters
of the Liberal leader, who was present in person,
looking, as was remarked at the time, worried
and anxious. On the rejection of the Bill by
the House of Commons by a substantial majority
a few days later, not only was Mr. Gladstone
driven from office, but he had the mortification
of seeing his party shattered and split into two
divergent sections for the remainder of his life.
Lady Dalhousie died, at an early age, and in
the prime of her remarkable beauty, in the course
of the following year. As the Banqueting House
is now the Museum of the Royal United Service
Institution and Dover House has become the
Scottish Office, it is improbable that either building will ever be used again for social purposes.

In January 1698 Whitehall [1] was totally
destroyed by fire. All that then remained of
Tudor date (with one exception, mentioned
hereafter), the chapel in which Anne Boleyn was
married to Henry VIII., the death chambers of
Cromwell and Charles the Second, and the Stone
Gallery were swept into oblivion in a few hours.

William the Third made no attempt to rebuild
the Palace, as, owing to his liability to asthma,
his doctors advised him to remove the Court to

---

[1] With the exception of the Banqueting House, the Holbein and King
Street gates, and a few unimportant buildings at the Scotland Yard end of
the Palace.

the more salubrious air of Kensington, and to avoid the mists and fogs of the river-bank.

Whitehall lay in ruins for many years after this disastrous fire, but about the middle of the eighteenth century several substantial houses were built on portions of the old Privy Garden and other vacant spaces.   Of these, No. 7 Whitehall Gardens, late the office of the Board of Trade, which was built for Lord Pembroke,[1] is the most interesting.   I do not know who the architect was, but some of the interior fittings, especially the ceilings and doorways, are of a high order of merit.

Underneath a portion of the site is a fine range of vaulted cellars, once filled with the choicest Burgundy and Rhenish for the Cardinal's high table.   These cellars, which fortunately escaped the German air-raids in the immediate vicinity during the Great War, appear to be of earlier date than Wolsey's time, and were probably built by one of his predecessors in the See of York, whose arms are still visible over one of the doorways. The fact that they have survived, practically intact, testifies to the solidity of their construction, but what is even more remarkable is that whilst an ecclesiastical relic, dating in all probability from the fourteenth century, has survived, every trace of the secular buildings of the Restora-

---

[1] Henry, 9th Earl of Pembroke, who was something of a virtuoso in architecture and zealous in promoting the building of Westminster Bridge, died at his house in Whitehall, January 9, 1750.

tion era has utterly disappeared. It is true that it is only a wine cellar which remains, yet it has outlasted the gorgeous abodes of harlotry and the unsavoury associations of the backstairs which were such conspicuous features of the Palace in the seventeenth century.[1]

The Church, the ancient faith of England, has thus left a more enduring mark upon Whitehall than Charles the Second and his voluptuous court.

A dreary-looking upper room in the old Board of Trade offices has been absurdly called " Nell Gwynne's bedroom," but it is obviously not of earlier date than the eighteenth century.

A mulberry tree, now in the last stage of decrepitude, which stands in what was formerly the garden of Sir Robert Peel's house in Whitehall Gardens, escaped destruction in the Great War when most of the garden ground hereabouts was ruined by the erection of temporary buildings. The mulberry is proverbially a long-lived tree, and as it probably grew in the small garden adjoining the King's private apartments, it is possible to connect Nell with Whitehall as it exists to-day, for, quite conceivably, she may have sat under it when it was in a more flourishing condition than when Sir Robert Peel sought its grateful shade.

---

[1] Cardinal Wolsey's cellars are now in daily use as a luncheon-room for the staff of the Ministry of Transport, and are well worthy of inspection.

CHAPTER V

IT is not always easy to trace in detail how Nelly passed her leisure time after her retirement from the stage, but she continued to attend the theatres with great regularity. There is documentary evidence in 1674 and the following year of her going to the Duke's house to see the *Tempest* on four occasions, and she saw *Macbeth*, *Hamlet*, and *King Lear* once each, and doubtless other of Shakespeare's plays at one or other of the patent houses. It would seem that she made the Treasury pay for her boxes at Davenant's theatre, although at Drury Lane she would, of course, have been on the free list, at any rate so long as Killigrew lived.[1]

A note on her portrait in the National Portrait Gallery credited her until recently with the part of Desdemona in *Othello*, but there being no

---

[1] In the Appendix to the *Third Report of the Historical Manuscripts Commission*, page 266, are bills for Nell's places at the Duke's Theatre and Treasury orders for the payment thereof.

trustworthy evidence to support such a statement, I notice that it has recently been expunged from the label.

She would surely have been present at the reopening of the second Drury Lane, which was built from Wren's designs and bore over the proscenium arch the motto " Vivitur ingenio." But, as all her triumphs had been gained in the older theatre, she can have had no personal interest in the new house.

When, soon after the birth of her elder son, it was decided that Nell should leave her apartments in Lincoln's Inn Fields and be installed in a house of her own in the West End, where did she remove to? The answer is to be found in those invaluable contemporary records, the rate books of St. Martin's in the Fields.[1]

A good deal of misunderstanding has arisen as to the precise situation of the house which was her London home for the remainder of her life. The mistake arose in the first instance from an oversight on the part of Pennant, often an untrustworthy guide as to matters of fact, in supposing that Nell's first West End home was a house formerly included in St. James's Square, but demolished in 1848 to make way for the Army and Navy Club. Pennant, however, confused Nell Gwynne with Moll Davis, who undoubtedly lived for a few

---

[1] St. James's did not become a separate parish until 1685.

years [1] at this house, formerly No. 22 in the Square.[2]

Had Peter Cunningham and his able continuator, Mr. Wheatley, made a more detailed study of the rate books, they would not have fallen into the error of supposing that Nell ever lived on the north side of the street, yet such is the inveteracy of error that in every book which professes to deal in detail with Nell Gwynne's career the mistake has been perpetuated. It was not until a few years ago, when I made an independent study of the entire series of the parochial books so far as they relate to Pall Mall and St. James's, that I discovered the source of the error, which is simple enough of comprehension once the facts have been grasped.

In making his entries for the year 1670, the rate collector accidentally wrote " north " for " south " in his book when enumerating the tenants in Pall Mall, although in 1669 and 1671 the names of the occupiers are entered in their proper places on the south and preferential side of the street. I am afraid that it will come as a shock to the members of the Army and Navy Club to learn that Nell Gwynne's name

---

[1] 1675–1687.

[2] No. 22 St. James's Square has had many distinguished owners, including Spencer Compton, Earl of Wilmington, Speaker of the House of Commons throughout the reign of George the First, and Prime Minister in 1742. At one time it was the Parthenon Club, and at the time of its demolition it belonged to the 1st Lord de Mauley.

and fame can no longer be associated with any portion of its premises. For years they have been worshipping at the wrong shrine. As a compensation, however, they have her portrait by, or after, Lely—a particularly pleasing one— and a silver fruit knife bearing her initials, but the mirror which hangs in the club, if of seventeenth century date, never reflected her fair features, but those of her plainer contemporary, Moll Davis.

The entry in the St. Martin's rate book for 1670 has a distinct bearing on an amusing story, the full details of which Peter Cunningham was unaware of when he wrote his account of her life, to the effect that Nell was dissatisfied with the first house offered to her, and firmly declined to occupy it. After studying attentively the parochial records, I was rewarded by finding that they confirm in every particular the reasons for this refusal.

The first entry of her name refers to a small house towards the eastern end of Pall Mall (assessed in 1670 at the modest figure of sixteen shillings a year), which stood about fifteen or sixteen doors to the eastward of a much larger house [1] then in the occupation of Nicholas Leke, 2nd Earl of Scarsdale. It was to No. 79 that Nell removed when she left Lincoln's Inn Fields. When our heroine—she was now twenty—learned

---

[1] Now No. 79 Pall Mall.

that the house first offered her was only a lease-
hold, she indignantly refused to accept it. She
declared in her usual outspoken way that, having
always conveyed her services free under the
Crown, nothing less than a freehold would please
her. And, of course, in the end she had her
own way. The King not only enjoyed the
joke but applauded the spirit which prompted
her to refuse the first offer. Accordingly,
in the course of the next year, Lord Scarsdale complacently vacated the house he had
only just acquired from Sir William Coventry
(no doubt at the King's instance), and thenceforth, until the day of her death, Nell lived in
it. To this day it is the one and only freehold
on this side of the street, although there are
several on the north side whose proprietary rights
date from the acquisition of the freehold of
St. James's Square by Henry Jermyn, Earl of
St. Albans, in 1665, the year of Nell's debut on
the stage.

With her usual good fortune it was not long
before she succeeded in getting rid of the lease-
hold house she would not accept. For though
in 1671 the entry in respect of it runs, " Mrs.
Gwyn or present tenant," her name disappears in
1672, when it was taken by Colonel Thomas
Howard, who soon came into conflict with the
parochial authorities on their raising the assess-
ment from sixteen shillings to one pound. The

significant word " refuse " is appended to his
name in 1673.[1]

Nell was now permanently installed in the
most desirable position of any that could be
named in the West End of London, and in Pall
Mall she gave birth, on Christmas Day, 1671,
to her second son, who was christened James,
out of compliment to the Duke of York. Her
house was well built, of moderate size, with
ample garden ground at the back. It abutted
on the Royal gardens, which were of much
greater extent before they were curtailed in
Queen Anne's reign on the building of Marlborough House.

At the foot of Nell's garden was a mount
from which she could enjoy the sylvan beauty of
St. James's Park, in which the spangled thorns
and branching oaks were as yet unsmirched by
London smoke.

What a revelation to her must have been this
rus in urbe when contrasted with her early days
in the purlieus of Drury Lane and the vicious
atmosphere of the playhouse! To find herself
secure in the possession of a well-appointed house
in the best part of the best-inhabited street in
the West End might well have turned the head
of a girl of twenty, but, with characteristic kind-

---

[1] Colonel Howard is next met with in St. James's Street, on the east side,
still protesting at the amount he was called upon to pay; and in the same
year the Duchess of Cleveland declined to pay four pounds for her mansion
on the site of Bridgewater House.

ness of heart, no sooner had she the command of ample means than she offered her disreputable old mother a home with her in Pall Mall, fearing that if left to herself, in the sordid surroundings of the Coal Yard, she would drink herself to death. When some years ago a number of Nell's household bills were accidentally discovered amongst the mutilated papers of the Exchequer Office, amongst them was found an apothecary's account for " plasters, glysters, and cordials " supplied for the use of old Mrs. Gwynne.

Whether Nell found it impossible to put up with her mother's failings, I cannot say, but it was not in Pall Mall but at the Neat Houses in Pimlico that she fell into a ditch, when in a state of intoxication, and was drowned in July 1679.

Rochester in one of his scurrilous lampoons, " A Panegyric on Nelly," wrote of her:

> Nor was the mother's funeral less her care,
> No cost, no velvet, did the daughter spare;
> Fine gilded 'scutcheons did the Herse enrich,
> To celebrate this Martyr of the Ditch.

This was heartless enough, but in " The Lady of Pleasure " a lower depth of indecency is reached, neither mother nor daughter being spared:

> The pious mother of this flaming whore,
> Maid, punk and bawd, full sixty years and more,
> Died drunk with brandy in a common-shore.

Other items in the Exchequer Office accounts refer to white satin petticoats, red satin nightgowns, a fine "landskip" fan, scarlet satin shoes embroidered with silver lace, a pair of shoes laced with gold for "Master Charles," and alms to poor men and women.

Another of these interesting documents, recovered by the merest chance from the waste-paper basket, relates to the hire of sedan-chairs from one William Calow, and discloses the fact that Nelly, for doubtless good reasons, did not always make use of her own chair. I have modernised the spelling of the various items which comprise the following details:

1. For carrying you to Mrs. Knight's and to Madam Young's and to Madam Churchill's and waiting four hours . . . £0 5 0
2. For carrying you the next day and waiting seven hours 0 7 6
3. For carrying you to Mrs. Knight's and to Mrs. Cassells' and to Mrs. Churchill's and to Mrs. Knight's 0 4 0
4. For carrying one Lady Sanes [? Sandys] to the play at Whitehall and waiting . . 0 3 6
5. For carrying you yesterday and waiting *eleven* hours 0 11 6

The sum is . . £1 11 6

13 October 1675.
   Received then of Tho. Groundes in full of these Bills and all other demands . £2 0 0
   From Madam Gwynne, by me William Calow.

Chairman Calow's account, which, it must be admitted, was an extremely moderate one for such long hours of service, was settled, apparently, within twenty-four hours of its being rendered. It tells us the names of some of the friends Nell was in the habit of calling upon. I do not know who Madam Young or Lady Sanes[1] or Sandys were, but Mrs. Cassells was her sister Rose, and Mrs. Churchill I take to be Arabella, Winston Churchill's daughter and Jack Churchill's only sister. Winston, the father of the great Duke of Marlborough, was at this time a minor official of the Board of Green Cloth, serving under Stephen Fox, a man of much greater ability, who had acted as an intermediary between Charles and General Monk. He rose to be Paymaster-General of the Forces and a Lord Commissioner of the Treasury. Fox, not Winston, became in due course one of the members for Westminster, and at the time when Nell joined the Royal circle in White-hall both were in receipt of an allowance from the Lord Steward of seven dishes daily at their table, in addition to free quarters in the Palace.

In 1675 Jack Churchill had become a captain in the Guards, having thus early shown promise of military capacity when serving under Turenne in the Low Countries. He was at this time engaged in courting Sarah Jennings, one of the

---

[1] She may have been Lady Sayer, who was a Killigrew; her name occurs in the Whitehall plan of 1668 as Syers; or a friend of Nell's, Lucy Hamilton Sandys.

Duchess of York's maids of honour and the favourite playmate of the little Princess Anne.

Sarah, her elder sister Frances, who became Countess and titular Duchess of Tyrconnell, Jack Churchill and his sister Arabella were all members of one or the other of the Royal households.[1] At the early age of fifteen the future Duchess of Marlborough displayed unmistakable symptoms of that ungovernable temper which, in after years, became so pronounced. She quarrelled violently with her mother, who, according to the current gossip of the day, was ordered to leave St. James's (where her detractors said she had been given rooms as a sanctuary from her creditors) and to leave her daughter at Court.

The course of true love did not run any the smoother when Sarah discovered that Jack Churchill was being talked of as a possible husband for Catherine Sedley. She was a scraggy girl of unprepossessing appearance, but well dowered with worldly goods, which the Churchills certainly were not. The project came to nothing (the idea of the alliance with Catherine, which seems to have originated with Winston Churchill, having been abandoned as hastily as it had been entered upon); and Jack and Sarah were married, after an exceptionally stormy courtship, at St. James's in the autumn of 1678.[2]

---

[1] Another and younger sister, Barbara, married Edward Griffith.

[2] Catherine Sedley sought consolation by becoming the Duke of York's mistress, and eventually blossomed into the Countess of Dorchester. Charles,

Throughout his career Churchill was a careful man in money matters. He invested £5000, which had been given to him by Barbara Villiers " for services rendered," in the purchase of an annuity, and his habitual caution is indicated by a reply which Lord Peterborough, another distinguished soldier and diplomat, once made on being mistaken for him:

" I can convince you by two reasons that I am not the Duke. In the first place, I have only five guineas in my pocket, and in the second, they are heartily at your service."

Nell must have had ample opportunities of observing Sarah Jennings' tempestuous courtship, in which she no doubt endeavoured to be helpful, though I do not think she saw very much of the happy pair after Marlborough's rapid rise and promotion to the peerage which followed on James's accession to the throne.

In her frequent visits to Whitehall she may have been an eye-witness of—perhaps even a party to—an amusing scene in which Tom Killigrew, in his capacity of King's jester, was the leading figure. Habited as a pilgrim, with staff, water-bottle, and cockle-shell drawn from the wardrobe of Drury Lane, he met the King in one of the

---

who could not abide an ugly woman, was fond of saying that he believed his brother's mistresses must have been imposed upon him by his confessors by way of penance, and that there was not one of them whom he could "rest his eye upon." He also declared that Catherine " squinted like a dragon."

many courtyards of the Palace one morning.
"Whither away, Tom?" said Charles, little
suspecting what the answer would be:

"To hell, to fetch Oliver Cromwell back.
He did at least take some care of England,
whereas his successor takes none at all."

No. 79 Pall Mall, as originally built for Sir
William Coventry, must have been a substantial
house, judging from the vaulted wine and beer
cellars remaining intact under the roadway.
Having been privileged to penetrate into their
ample recesses, I can testify to the solidity
of their construction and the excellence of the
brickwork. The house, moreover, contains a
handsome marble mantelpiece, at which Charles
may often have warmed his Royal back.[1] One
of the rooms in Nelly's time was lined with
looking-glass from floor to ceiling, a meretricious
form of decoration presumably borrowed from a
French model. It would be interesting to know
which of the subsequent owners of the house it
was who removed this *salle des miroirs*, and I
should have been inclined to lay the blame upon
the Society for the Propagation of the Gospel
(which had its offices here for thirty years) had
not the house been rebuilt by Dr. Heberden in
the eighteenth century.

Soon after her arrival in Pall Mall began

---

[1] It is now in the Board Room of the Eagle Insurance Company, having
wisely been preserved when the house was rebuilt.

the fierce rivalry between Nell and Louise de Querouaille which continued, in varying degrees of intensity, until the King's death. When, in 1676, the Duchess of Mazarine arrived at Whitehall, Nell promptly went into mourning, as she said, for the eclipsed Duchess of Portsmouth and her ruined hopes.

A few years later,[1] when news reached England of the death of the Cham of Tartary (which occurred simultaneously with that of a French Prince of the blood), Louise appeared at Court all in black, and so, the story runs, did Nell. Being asked in her rival's hearing for whom *she* was in mourning, Nell replied: " Oh! have you not heard of my loss in the death of the Cham of Tartary? "

" And, pray," said her questioner, " what relation was he to you? "

" Well," said Nelly, " he was precisely the same relation to me that the Prince de Rohan was to Mademoiselle de Querouaille."

This was a saying after the King's heart, and he advised the two to compose their differences and to come to an arrangement whereby, in future, they should divide the crowned heads of both continents between them.

Space will not permit of any extended mention in these pages of Nell's neighbours in Pall Mall, but on one side of her, the eastern, lived the

[1] In 1682.

widowed Countess of Portland, and on the other, Edward Griffin, afterwards Lord Griffin, a minor Court official at Whitehall.

A few doors farther west lived Mrs. Knight, a singer, whose name has been linked with that of Charles; and within easy quarrelling distance was Barbara Villiers at Cleveland House, though her numerous infidelities had, by this time, sensibly diminished her influence with the King. There were other doors in Pall Mall and in St. James's Square which conveniently opened to admit " Old Rowley " at all hours, but, in the main, the street of Clubs as it stands to-day was highly respectable when Nell first came to live there.

Nell, who was always fond of pretty things, had a distinct *flair* for silver ornaments and table appointments, most of which were " flourished " with her initials. Some of her plate was stolen out of her house in January 1678, when she offered a reward in the *London Gazette* for its recovery. Massive silver andirons adorned her fireplace, but by far the most elaborate and expensive piece of furniture was a bedstead made entirely of silver, which probably stood in the *salle des miroirs* above mentioned. This she bought from John Coques or Cogues, a noted silversmith in his day, whose shop was on the north side of Pall Mall. He too it was who made the sacramental plate for the Royal Chapels at Whitehall and at Windsor. Nell's bedstead

weighed (with various cunningly wrought ornaments: the King's head, figures of slaves and
cupids, eagles and crowns, and, for some unknown reason, a figure of Jacob Hall, the rope
dancer, on a silver wire) over two thousand ounces.
This truly remarkable bedstead cost over £900, at
2s. 11d. per ounce, the bill for it being accidentally discovered by Peter Cunningham amongst
the mutilated Exchequer papers to which I have
already referred. Other pieces of plate mentioned in Coques's bill, which amounted in all to
£1135 : 3 : 1, were a sugar box, a pepper pot,
a mustard pot, two " Kruyzes," a gold hour-
glass, and two silver bottles, weighing 37 ounces
17 dwt., which were charged for at 8s. per ounce.

Another item of £3 was for repairing and
cleansing two figures made by a Mr. Trahearne,
who was presumably a modeller in precious
metals. Nell had also a warming-pan inscribed:
" Fear God, *serve* the King." All trace of these
household treasures has been lost, and I think
it is likely that the great bedstead may have been
melted down to meet certain pressing liabilities
which confronted Nelly after the King's death.

An eminent goldsmith of the early part of
the eighteenth century was accustomed to relate
a striking instance of Nell's popularity. His
master, when he was an apprentice, made an
expensive service of plate as a present from
the King to the Duchess of Portsmouth, great

numbers of people crowding his shop to inspect it. Some indulged their feelings by cursing the French spy, whilst all were unanimous in wishing that the present had been for Nell's use, rather than for the hated foreign mistress.[1]

Whilst the aversion generally felt for Louise de Querouaille by the English people added greatly to Nell's popularity, the huge sums which the former received from public funds were unfavourably commented upon in the House of Commons by the few independent members who were not subsidised by either Charles or Louis XIV. Though her deportation was advocated in Parliament, Louise contrived to maintain her baleful influence at Court, partly through the good offices of Danby, to whom she is believed to have accorded a share of her favours.

In addition to other sources of income she drove a brisk trade in titles and pardons. The Earl of Bedford is said to have offered her any sum from £50,000 to £100,000 if she could obtain a free pardon for his son,[2] after the exposure of the Rye House Plot. But on this occasion she was unsuccessful, though her avarice doubtless urged her to do her utmost to save his life. This scandalous traffic in pensions, pardons, and honours was revived by George the

---

[1] *The London Chronicle*, August 15-18, 1778.
[2] Lord Russell.

First's ugly German mistresses in the next century.

Once when Nell, accompanied by Lady Harvey, a designing woman who seems to have exploited her for her own ends, visited the Duchess of Mazarine to thank her for her congratulations on the conferring of an earldom on her son, it happened that the French Ambassador was one of the company.[1] Who should enter the room to pay a visit of ceremony to Hortense but Nell's pet aversion, Louise de Querouaille! The utmost cordiality prevailed, at any rate outwardly, between Nelly and her French rival, but on the latter taking her leave, Nelly turned to Courtin and boldly asked him why his master did not make *her* presents instead of showering them upon the " weeping willow " who had just left the room, adding that he must be aware that the King of England infinitely preferred her company to that of Louise! Courtin discreetly omitted to mention in his letter to Pomponne [2] what reply he made, but proceeded to tell his friend that the other ladies present, having heard of the exquisite fineness of Nelly's underclothing, made bold to ask her if they might judge of it for themselves. Without any hesitation she obligingly let them raise

---

[1] The Duchess of Mazarine had a suite of apartments in St. James's, according to an advertisement which she inserted in the *London Gazette*, May 1678, for the recovery of a little dog which she had lost in the Park.

[2] Louis XIV.'s minister.

each petticoat and flounce and examine them there and then as she stood. "Never in my life," added Courtin, "did I see such thorough cleanliness, neatness, and sumptuosity. I should speak of other things that we all were shown if M. de Lionne were still Foreign Secretary. But with you I must be grave and proper; and so, Monsieur, I end my letter."

Though Nell was never at any time of her life a political schemer in the sense that the Duchesses of Cleveland and Portsmouth were, she was always ready to help a friend in distress.

In June 1677 the Duke of Buckingham found himself, not for the first time, a prisoner in the Tower. He had argued with considerable force and skill from his place in the House of Lords that Parliament, not having assembled once in every year, as was the invariable practice in the reign of Edward III., should automatically be dissolved instead of being prorogued from month to month and year to year. His motion was defeated by a large majority, and as he refused to retract his contention or to apologise to the House for his ridicule of its censure, he and three other peers were committed to the Tower. Nell felt sorry for him and, in concert with Lory Hyde and others of the "merry gang," she applied herself to the task of procuring his release. And owing to her influence with the King she succeeded where her early admirer,

Buckhurst—he was Earl of Middlesex now—had failed.

Amongst the manuscripts in the British Museum[1] is preserved a curious letter, without date or signature, which enabled Nell to pass through the prison bars as easily as she penetrated the innermost recesses of Whitehall. This letter ran as follows:

The best woman in the world brings you this paper, and, at this time, the discreetest. Pray, my Lord, resign your understanding and your interest wholly to her conduct. Mankind is to be redeemed by Eve, with as much honour as the thing will admit of. Separate your concern from your fellow-prisoner;[2] then an expedient handsome enough, and secret enough to disengage yourself: obey, and you are certainly happy.[3]

The gist of what Nell said to the Duke may be gathered from a passage in an autograph letter — he wrote an atrocious hand — which Buckingham either sent to the King from the Tower, or got Nell to take to him. This also is in the National collection:

I am so surprised with what Mrs. Nelly has told me that I know not in the world what to say. . . .

---

[1] Add. MSS. 27872, folio 18.   [2] Lord Shaftesbury.

[3] The wax seal still adhering to this letter, on which, on close inspection, is visible a lion rampant, may be that of Nell's namesake, Francis Gwynne, of Llansanor, Co. Glamorgan, and Ford Abbey, in Devonshire, secretary to Lory Hyde in after years, whom I am inclined to think may have been, if not a blood relation, a distant connection of the Welsh family from which she sprang.

What you have been pleased to say to Mrs. Nelly is ten thousand times more than ever I can deserve.

A few days later the Duke was a free man. Nor was this the last service which Nell was to render him, for, when broken in health and fortune, he found asylum in her house in Pall Mall, as I shall show at a later page.

To find Nell described as the discreetest woman in the world is distinctly amusing in view of Burnet's estimate of her character in his *History of my Own Time*.

A letter of slightly later date,[1] from Sir Robert Southwell to the Duke of Ormonde, runs:

'Tis certain that Buckingham passes a great part of his time with Nelly who, because the Lord Treasurer [2] would not strive to make her a countess, is at perfect defiance with him, so that the Treasurer's lady is there acted and the King looks on with great delight. . . . Monmouth takes sanctuary at that place and has all manner of assistance which that place can afford, and all the promises of those that come near it.

A letter from Savile to Rochester, dated June 4, 1678, throws some light upon Lady Harvey's sinister influence over Nell and the current tittle-tattle of Whitehall:

As for Court news you know all prudent persons have ever been wary of writing, especially since Mr. Lane was once turned out about it, but since I am out already, I will venture upon one small piece of

[1] September 22, 1677.   [2] Danby.

intelligence, because one who is always your friend and sometimes, especially now, mine, has a part in that makes her now laughed at and may one day turn to her infinite disadvantage. The case stands thus if I am rightly informed.

My Lady Harvey who always loves one civil plot more, is working body and soul to bring Mrs. Jenny Myddleton into play. How dangerous a new one[1] is to all old ones I need not tell you, but her ladyship, having little opportunity of seeing Charlemagne[2] upon her own account, wheedles poor Mrs. Nelly into supping twice or thrice a week at W. Chiffinch's and carrying her with her. So, that in good earnest this poor creature is betrayed by her ladyship to pimp against herself, for there her ladyship whispers and contrives all matters to her own ends, as the other[3] might easily perceive if she were not too giddy to mistrust a false friend.

This I thought it good for you to know, for though your lordship and I have different friends in the Court, yet the friendship betwixt us ought to make me have an observing eye upon any accident that may wound any friend of yours as this may, in the end, possibly do her, who is so much your friend and who speaks obliging and charitable things of me in my present disgrace.[4]

Savile's meaning, though somewhat obscurely expressed, was that Lady Harvey was trying

---

[1] Presumably a new mistress.

[2] The King. Another nickname often bestowed upon Charles was Chanticleer!   [3] Nell Gwynne.

[4] Historical MSS. Commission. Report on Lord Bath's papers, vol. ii. pp. 162-163.

to get Mrs. Myddleton for the King, and using Nell to this end. The lady in question was a daughter of Sir John Needham and had married Charles Myddleton of Ruabon at the Restoration. She was now thirty-three and well able to take care of herself. Grammont was one of her earliest suitors, but she bade him " keep quiet and look elsewhere." The Duke of York, as well as the King, laid siege to her heart, and so did the Archbishop of Canterbury.[1] To all of them she turned a deaf ear and the breath of scandal never seems to have tainted her reputation any more than it did Miss Blagge's.

Unlike the generality of the ladies-in-waiting at this time, Mrs. Myddleton had considerable literary talent and was a good artist. She was painted in her prime by Sir Peter Lely and also by Largillière, as a shepherdess with a crook and a lamb, the latter picture being now in the National Portrait Gallery.

A curious letter of the same year [2] depicts Nell in the character of friend and adviser to Mary Fanshawe, Lucy Walter's daughter. Mary believed, or affected to believe, that she was the King's daughter and uterine sister to the Duke of Monmouth, who, as will be seen from the text, was not so sure that this supposition was correct.

---

[1] Gilbert Sheldon, whom of all people in the world I should least have expected to find in this *galère*.

[2] Dated November 1, 1677, in Lord Bath's MSS. vol. ii. page 158.

As Lucy's daughter was born in May 1651, and the intimacy between her and Lord Taafe had begun after Charles had left the Hague and gone to Scotland, the King firmly declined to own the child.

Mary married as her first husband Captain William Sarsfield, a brother of the Earl of Lucan, and, after his death, William Fanshawe, a poor diseased creature, whom Charles compassionately made a Master of Requests.

A letter from Henry Savile to the Earl of Rochester at Woodstock, dated Nov. 1, 1677, runs:

If your Lordship was as ill as you told me in your letter, either you are a greater philosopher in bearing of pain or a greater hypocrite in making it more than it is then we can ordinarily meet with in these parts. However the case stands, I was mighty glad to find a man both lame and blind could bee soe merry.   I thought there could bee but one lame thing upon earth in perfect happiness, and that is Fanshawe for his having a daughter, a Princesse, who yet remaines in paganisme for want of baptisme, while the fond father delayes to take some prudent resolution concerning the godfathers.   Hee thinkes the King ought to bee kept for a sonn, and the Duke of Monmouth dos not yet owne the alliance enough to hold his neece att the font, and therefore I beleeve that honour will at last fall upon His Grace of Buckingham. Mrs. Nelly, who is his great friend and faithfull councellour, advised him not to lay out all his stock upon the christning but to reserve a little to buy him new shooes, that hee might not dirty her roomes, and a new periwigg that she might not smell him stinke two storeys high when hee knocks att the outward door. What influence this wholsome advice may have in processe of time I do not know, but noe longer agoe then yesterday hee was out att heeles and stunke most grievously, and putt me very much in mind of a predecessour of his of our English royall blood (as I take it Duke of Exeter) that was soe poor in Flanders (if you will beleeve Phillip de Comines) that hee had noe shooes att all.[1]

Amongst the Duke of Rutland's manuscripts at Belvoir, in a gossiping letter from Lady Chaworth to her brother, Lord Roos, is an account of a silly joke played by Henry Killigrew upon Nell about this time.

" At four o'clock in the morning he disturbed the serenity of her slumbers by knocking at her door in a drunken fit, having come, as he alleged, from the King to acquaint her with the news of the Duchess of Portsmouth's recovery from an illness, rallying her with his abusive tongue extreemly." Lady Chaworth adds that " she [the Duchess] is perfectly well again and they say will lead a new life, at least she has promised it to her ghostly father."

One would like to know what Nell said in reply to this stupid hoax, but, whatever it was, it

---

[1] An allusion to Buckingham's supposed descent from Thomas of Woodstock, Duke of Gloucester, youngest son of Edward the Third.

is sure to have been as emphatic as her extensive vocabulary of expletives permitted. The King was so angry when he heard of the occurrence that he banished Henry Killigrew from the Court.[1]

The next year, 1678, Nell was at Newmarket with the King for the October meeting. At it Charles won a plate, the prize being a silver flagon, the other competitors being the Duke of Monmouth, Mr. Elliot, and Mr. Thynne (Tom of ten thousand).

Charles was not very lucky on the turf, judging from the scanty records of racing at Newmarket which have come down to us, but 1675 was one of his most successful years. At the spring meeting (March 20) he won a plate, " riding three heats and a course," by sheer ability in the saddle, but a month later his horse *Bluecap* was beaten by Lord Suffolk's *Cripple*.

At Easter a match for a thousand guineas, an unprecedented sum in the annals of the turf in the seventeenth century, was to be run between *Bluecap* and Mr. May's *Thumper*, but there appears to be no record of the result.

Only through scraps and fragments culled from old diaries and calendars is it possible to derive any precise information as to the sport of kings on Newmarket Heath at this period. In the

[1] Louise de Querouaille had been advised to try the waters of Bourbon for the sake of her health, and there is a coarse allusion to the cause of her indisposition in " England's Court Strumpets " amongst the *Poems on State Affairs* which I have so often quoted from in these pages.

majority of cases we are left in ignorance of the weights carried, and, almost invariably, information is lacking as to the names of the jockeys and trainers.

Any of my readers who are interested in the subject will find a lively account of a horse race supposed to have been run in Hyde Park in the reign of Charles the First, in Shirley's play entitled *Hyde Park*. In it the bustle and excitement of a closely contested race is admirably depicted, even to the shouting of the odds and the malpractices of the jockeys who rode in it.

At the October meeting at Newmarket in 1682, Sir Robert Carr's *Postboy* beat the King's *Dragon* in a match for seven hundred guineas, after a close finish, *Dragon* having previously been successful in a match for £500, *over a six-mile course*, against Sir Robert's *Why Not*. The earlier race is interesting as being one of the few in which the weights carried by the horses are given, though I am not able to say with certainty if this was a weight for age race or an early attempt to bring horses together on terms by means of a handicap. The King's horse was set to carry seven stone and his opponent only four! *Dragon*, who made a reappearance at Newmarket in October 1684, the date of the King's last visit to the Heath, was unfortunately beaten by *Why Not*, thus reversing the placings of two years earlier.

Other horses known to have been owned by Charles were *Woodcock*, of whom I have already made mention; *Shuffler*, who beat Mr. Griffin's *Ball* over the Beacon Course at the 1680 spring meeting; *Tankot*, who was entered at the same date for a plate confined to six-year-olds over four miles (I should like to see a similar race in the Ascot programme to-day); *Corke*, who beat Sir Robert Carr's *Small Cole*, and *Roan*, who was beaten by Mr. Ryder's *Mouse* at the same (autumn) meeting.

These few entries probably only represent a tithe of the occasions on which the Royal colours were carried.

On her way back to London from Newmarket Nell and Sir Fleetwood Sheppard,[1] who seems to have managed her domestic and financial affairs at this time, were entertained at Cambridge by the Vice-Chancellor, who presented her with an address of welcome in verse, the text of which is, I fear, lost.

An alderman of Oxford, who had gone to Newmarket in order to present a petition to the King in person, was much scandalised, or he pretended to be, when he heard Nell call out to the King as he was walking on the heath: " Charles, I hope I shall have your com-

---

[1] Sir Fleetwood Sheppard was one of Matthew Prior's earliest patrons, and to him the poet dedicated two of his *Epistles*, which won for him the proud title of the English Horace.

pany to-night, shall I not?" Alderman Wright, for that was his name, was presumably a supporter of the country party, and, probably, he did not obtain the concession he wanted, as he continued thenceforth to "speak scurrilously" of his sovereign.[1]

It was ungenerous of the citizens of Oxford not to receive Nell so cordially as the sister University did, for, as I have shown at an earlier page, if Anthony à Wood is to be trusted there is some reason to believe that she was a native of their city.

Instead of being fêted by the Vice-Chancellor, Nell was mobbed in her coach when Charles's last Parliament met at Oxford in March 1681.[2] The crowd, mistaking her for the unpopular Duchess of Portsmouth, was somewhat threatening in its attitude until Nell, quite unperturbed, leant out of the window and said: "Pray, good people, be civil. I am the Protestant mistress." Perhaps she used a monosyllable to the same effect, but anyhow peace was at once restored, and her coach allowed to proceed.

It was on this occasion, after dismissing his Parliament after a session of only eight days,

---

[1] Letter from Humphrey Prideaux to John Ellis, September 29, 1681, printed by the Camden Society.

[2] Charles contrived to attend a race meeting on Burford downs when he went to Oxford to open Parliament this year. The speech with which he opened his last Parliament was one of the best he ever made, but perceiving an undercurrent of hostility to his own views as to the succession to the throne, the King promptly resolved upon dissolution.

that Charles felt himself able to say, "Now am I King of England if I never was before!"

Immediately after the dissolution Charles drove back to Windsor post-haste, taking Nell with him, and there he passed the greater part of the spring and summer, free from care and responsibility to Parliament and sufficiently supplied with French gold to gratify his absorbing love of sport.

As neither Peter Cunningham nor, so far as I am aware, any of Nell's biographers, have devoted much attention to her connection with Windsor, I will now ask my readers to turn their backs for a time upon London and accompany me, in spirit, to a district, unique in the home counties for its sylvan beauty, which it has been my good fortune to know intimately since my childhood. There we shall find Nell in an entirely new environment, in which Charles and she enacted for a while the congenial rôles of forest lovers.

When she quitted the tainted atmosphere of Whitehall, with its perpetual jealousies and intrigues, and removed with her children to the purer air of Berkshire, she was of course no stranger to Windsor. We have already noted her there so early as 1670, when I think that she occupied a house near the foot of the Hundred Steps, for Burford House, her own freehold property, was not built until some years later. But for Nell the real *jour de ma vie* (one of two mottoes adopted by the Beauclerk family on its elevation to the peerage) must have been the day she entered into possession of a country house of her very own adjoining the immemorial home of the Sovereign and his Garter Knights.

Charles must, I think, have invented out of his own fertile brain the surname Beauclerk for Nelly's sons. He had probably read in history that Henry the First, who was called Beauclerk because he could read, whereas his brothers could not, had been the father of more illegitimate children than any English sovereign except himself. The time therefore seemed appropriate for the revival of this patronymic.

Nell, as I have shown, had tasted the joys of country life with Buckhurst at Epsom for a brief period. She had made periodical jaunts with Charles to Burford, Newmarket, Winchester, and other sporting centres, and revelled in the experience:

> A merry heart goes all the day,
> Your sad tires in a mile-a.

But, henceforth, there lay at her doors the manifold delights of a vast tract of virgin forest, wherein every variety of sport and healthful exercise could be enjoyed under ideal conditions.[1]

[1] The forest of Windsor extended in the seventeenth century as far as Guildford on the east, Chertsey on the south, and Henley on the west, the whole area being subject to stringent penal laws, dating from mediæval times, for the preservation of the king's vert and venison.

There were, of course, occasional State ceremonies at the Castle, such as the installation of the
Garter Knights and other Court functions, which
Nell would have had to attend, but, in the main,
her life was now to be occupied with country
pursuits and the enjoyment of wild nature, seen
at its very best. Still in the prime of life, with an
infinite capacity for enjoyment, the freedom from
convention, and that delightful sense of elbow-
room which her latest acquisition conferred, must,
I think, have conduced to her perfect contentment
at Windsor. Yet even there she was not altogether
free from periodical intrusions of the Duchess of
Portsmouth,[1] but as the Frenchwoman cared
nothing for sport and everything for money she
found London her best hunting-ground.

The King had given Nell's boy Charles the re-
version of the hereditary office of Grand Falconer
of England, although Sir Allen Apsley was
actually in possession of the emoluments of the
office until his death in 1683.

The fact that the future Duke of St. Albans
had the care of the King's hawks incidentally
provided Nell with facilities for " going a bird-
ing," to use Shakespeare's phrase, in every Royal
park, chase, or warren in England.

Ladies, as a rule, were content to pursue

---

[1] " Little was done all day but going a-fishing. At night the Duchess
of Portsmouth came. In the morning I was with the King at Mrs.
Nelly's " (Letter of Henry Sidney, July 1, 1679).

larks or partridges with the smaller hawks, like the hobby and the merlin, which they could carry comfortably on their wrists. The higher flights of the larger and stronger falcons (such as the peregrine and the goshawk) at hares, pheasants, and herons were left to their attendant swains.

The neighbourhood of Windsor has never been an ideal partridge country, nor, until the formation of Virginia Water in the eighteenth century, were there any large sheets of water nearer than the lakes at Englemere and Sunninghill Park, where the falconer could always be sure of flushing a heron. The Master of the Hawks had a large establishment under him; in Charles's reign it numbered thirty-three falconers and feeders, but I do not know for certain where the Mews were situated, although they were probably in the immediate vicinity of Burford House.

In consequence of a strenuous Parliamentary agitation for the abolition of hereditary allowances and offices, which in the course of centuries had degenerated into mere sinecures, the Duke of St. Albans' pension of £965 as Master of the Hawks was commuted so recently as 1890–91 for nineteen years' purchase, representing a capital sum of £18,335. This modest amount pales into insignificance when contrasted with the huge emoluments enjoyed by the descendants of Louise de Querouaille and Barbara Villiers.

By letters patent of 1676, the Duke of Richmond, a mere child at the time, was granted by his father a perpetual charge on every ton of coal exported from the Tyne and consumed in England. The subsequent history of this heavy burden on the taxpayer is worth revealing in all its nakedness, far exceeding as it does the sums granted by a grateful nation to the immortal Nelson or the great Duke of Marlborough. In 1799 the Duke of Richmond's pension was commuted into an annuity of £19,000 charged upon the Consolidated Fund. By Act of Parliament this annuity was once more commuted for a sum of £490,833 : 11 : 6, which was invested in the purchase of £633,333 : 6 : 9 of Consols. A portion of this stock was subsequently sold and reinvested in land, and by a further Act, passed in Queen Victoria's reign, power was given to sell the balance and reinvest it in land.

The Duke of Grafton, Barbara Villiers' second son, was also exceptionally favoured by his father. He received a grant of the Prisage and Butlerage dues, which was ultimately converted into an annuity of £6870 charged on the Consolidated Fund. In 1815 this was exchanged for a lump sum of £229,000 in Government Stock, of which, in 1881, there remained in the hands of trustees £30,555 : 16 : 8. It will therefore be seen that, in the long run, Nell's descendants have cost the taxpayer infinitely less than those of the Duchesses of Portsmouth and Cleveland.

The Finance Accounts for 1922–23 reveal the curious fact that £270 per annum is still payable to the representatives of the heir of the Duke of Schombergh, whom William the Third delighted to honour; a fraction of this pension having been purchased by a member of the Gosling family in 1792.

It sometimes happened that the King's hawks, as well as his dogs, were lost or stolen, and I gather from an advertisement in the *London Gazette* that a falcon with the King's varvels on it was lost between Windsor and Burnham Beeches, and that whoever should return it to Will Chiffinch at the Castle was to be " well rewarded." These varvels were metal rings attached to the hawk's jesses, and in the case of falcons from the Royal Mews were usually of solid silver engraved with the insignia of the Crown.

Nell Gwynne's descendants continued to take a mild interest in the sport until quite recent years. One of the last of the old school of falconers, John Peels,[1] a Dutchman by descent, was in the service of the 9th Duke of St. Albans, who died in 1849. Peels trained and flew his hawks at Lakenheath in the county of Suffolk, and in 1845 he made a journey to Iceland expressly to procure gerfalcons, of which he brought home fifteen, eight of them being trained to the lure at Het Loo, the Queen of Holland's charming country seat in Guelderland.

---

[1] Peels died at an advanced age so recently as 1883.

The emoluments granted in perpetuity to Nell's son as Master of the King's Hawks have been abolished by the legislature, and the practice of falconry in England is falling into desuetude, and would ere now have been extinct had it not been for a few enthusiastic amateurs who maintain modest establishments of peregrines and goshawks (mostly imported from Valkensward in Holland) in the New Forest, on the Wiltshire downs, and a few other suitable localities.

In addition to racing, hunting, and hawking, fishing occupied a great deal of the King's time both at Hampton Court and Windsor.

When, soon after Nell's admission to the Royal circle, the hereditary Prince of Neuberg came to England to pay his respects to the King, Charles directed the Lord Chamberlain to invite him to a *souper dansant*, to be held, not in the great Banqueting Hall, but in the Queen's private apartments. Nelly, who was present at this select entertainment, and in exuberant spirits, was the life and soul of the party, her sprightly conversation and merry disposition contributing not a little to its success.

The night being oppressively warm and the Queen's rooms almost unbearably hot, Charles gave the signal for his guests to follow him into St. James's Park, where the company danced *al fresco* by the light of the moon; the flutes, hautboys, and violins being stationed on the greensward.

Such was Charles's phenomenal energy at this period that, when the impromptu dance was over, he insisted on carrying the Prince and the Lords and Ladies of the Household in the Royal barge, luxuriously upholstered in rose-coloured brocade, up the river to Hampton Court, where they arrived not long after daybreak.

Sleep being out of the question, the party began to fish; but the King, not being able to catch anything bigger than a gudgeon or a minnow, Nell laughed heartily at his want of success, adding that she would show them all some rare sport.

When the King said that he would angle no more, since his luck was dead out, she cried: "But see, Sire, you have got a bite at last!" and, pulling in his line, what should he find at the end of it but half-a-dozen fried smelts tied to his hook with a silken thread!

The company laughed loudly at the absurdity of the situation, Nelly declaring that so great a king should have something peculiar above the rest, and that whilst humble fisherfolk caught fish alive, it was fitting that His Majesty's should be ready dressed for table.

When the Prince of Neuberg pulled up his line he found it so heavy that he could scarcely haul his catch into the boat. And no wonder, for at the end of it was discovered a weighty purse of gold, set with precious stones, which enclosed a miniature of a lady with whom the Prince was believed to be head over ears in love.

Nell's practical jokes added to the general hilarity, and the King, guessing who it was that had planned them, told his audacious favourite that whilst Cleopatra caused a sardine to be fastened to Marc Antony's hook, a Naiad of the Thames had surpassed her ingenuity by bestowing, in this quaint fashion, a present of real value upon his honoured guest.[1] On the whole, the German princeling must have found the Court of Whitehall somewhat livelier than his native Bavaria.

" Flatfoot the gudgeon taker," as Rochester impertinently called Charles in one of his lampoons, was throughout his life as keen a fisherman as he was a bold rider. Charles and Nelly often diverted themselves with horse races in the Home Park, or on Runnymede, on the Buckinghamshire bank of the Thames, whilst sometimes an improvised track was staked out on one of those smooth green lawns[2] which are such a pleasing feature of the Windsor landscape.

Races were held on Runnymede until comparatively recent times. At one time old Q's colours were often seen at the Egham meeting, which was held in the week following Ascot.

[1] I have in part abridged this characteristic little story of the frivolous manner in which the Court was wont to amuse itself from the *Court of Venus*, 1716.

[2] Of which Smith's Lawn, near Virginia Water, is the largest.

My uncle, John Delane, once told me that having had his watch stolen on the course at Ascot, and happening to ride over to Egham races the following week, some rascal in the crowd, an accomplice, perhaps, of the actual thief, called out to him, " What's o'clock, Delane? " at which the editor of the *Times* could not help smiling. Delane, who knew and loved every inch of the forest country in which he had been brought up—his father owned a small property at Easthampstead —first followed the Queen's hounds when the celebrated Charles Davis carried the horn. So straight did he ride, that in after years he became known in the hunting field as " the leading article."

Delane lived at Ascot Heath House, immediately opposite the Royal entrance to the stands, from 1858 until his death. The original house had been given by George the Fourth to Lady Harrington, and the arched entrance lodge is of Georgian date, if not earlier. Delane rebuilt the house in 1867–68, principally with the object of entertaining his friends in the race week. This he seldom or never missed, despite his arduous duties in Printing House Square. And when he could spare the time he delighted in running down to Newmarket with Mayer Rothschild to watch the Baron's horses at work upon the Heath. He was fond of talking about the Ascot meetings of his youth, when the races were largely supported by Berkshire gentry living within easy driving or riding distance of the course.[1] His father (and my grandfather) ran a mare, named *Kitty*, in the Wokingham Stakes of 1818. She was not, however, successful in attracting the recognition of the judge, the race being won by the Duke of York's *Vignette*. Run over the last three-quarters of the new mile course, the experiment of a handicap open to horses of all ages had been initiated in 1813, to replace the wearisome heats which had so long been in vogue at Ascot and elsewhere.

The formation of the existing circular course [2] has usually been attributed to the Duke of Cumberland (the breeder of the famous *Eclipse*, who got his name from being foaled during an eclipse of the sun), when in the middle of the eighteenth century the Duke succeeded Sarah, Duchess of Marlborough, as Ranger of the Great Park. But I shall show, at a later page, that Nell's grandson, the 2nd Duke of St. Albans, had some share in the laying out of the new course, which was within the limits of his jurisdiction as Warden of the Forest and Constable of the Castle.

Notwithstanding the vigilance of keepers and

[1] My uncle had in his employ an octogenarian gardener who remembered to have seen the Czar of Russia and the King of Prussia at Ascot in 1814. Firmly implanted in the old man's memory was a number of " tall savage-looking men with furry caps on their heads," evidently the Cossack body-guard of Alexander I.

[2] Its circumference was somewhat diminished some years ago when the late Major Clement was Clerk of the Course, in order to enlarge the paddock and the lawns in front of the stands.

the severity of the forest laws—for stealing the King's deer was a felony — venison was not infrequently found in cottages in the seventeenth century and considerably later, for, in the wilder and less accessible parts of this sparsely inhabited region, the peasantry long retained much of the independence and lawlessness of mediæval times.

Scattered over the length and breadth of the forest, many a village inn still bears the badge of Richard the Second (the White Hart) as its sign; whilst the " Hind's Head," the " Stag and Hounds," and the " Horse and Groom " bear frequent witness to the former importance of the chase in this ancient sporting country.[1]

Hunting the wild red deer—not a tame beast shorn of its antlers and released from a cart, but a forest stag accustomed to find its own food at all seasons—was a favourite sport with King Charles and his friends. Made of stout stuff were these forest-bred bucks which had never known captivity. Not

> Parked and bounded in a pale,
> A little herd of England's timorous deer,

but rather, " moody-mad and desperate stags," which, at the end of a long run, turned on

> The bloody hounds with heads of steel
> And made the cowards stand aloof at bay.[2]

---

[1] The " Green Man," which occurs at Easthampstead, is another sign peculiar, I believe, to forest districts.

[2] First Part of *King Henry VI*. Act IV. Scene 2.

A famous run, in 1684, when a stag started in
the forest was not pulled down by hounds until
it reached Lord Petre's seat in Essex, some
seventy miles from Windsor, must have given
rise to much talk at the Castle. Only five horse-
men were in at the death of this gallant quarry,
the King's brother, the Duke of York, being
one of the number.

When Nell came to live at Windsor the little
red-roofed town, boasting only two main streets,
which nestles at the foot of the Castle, had not
changed much in appearance since Shakespeare
drew his inimitable picture of middle-class provincial life in the *Merry Wives of Windsor*. This
was one of the plays allotted to Tom Killigrew,
and no doubt Nell had seen it acted at Drury
Lane, though I am unaware of the *personnel* of
the cast when it was staged in August 1667, and
in December 1675.

The Castle presented, however, a very different appearance from what it does to-day. The
Round Tower was a squat and stumpy keep,
little altered since it left its builder's hands in
the fourteenth century. Not until the Castle
was remodelled by George the Fourth did it
assume its present lofty proportions. The smaller
flanking towers overlooking the town, which also
date from Plantagenet times, have not been so
much altered, with the exception of the Curfew
Tower, which was provided with what strikes the

eye as an unnecessarily high-pitched roof when the chimes were re-hung about fifty years ago under the direction of Sir George Elvey.

In the seventeenth century, when there is reason to fear that a great deal of mediæval work was wantonly destroyed, the principal entrance to the Castle was, as it is still, through Henry the Eighth's gateway. This gave access to the lower ward and St. George's Chapel, and led up to the great quadrangle round which were grouped the principal State apartments. Though these covered much the same area as they do now, they were almost entirely rebuilt and considerably heightened by George the Fourth and his immediate successor on the throne.

In the town itself, the Garter Inn in Peascod Street, where Falstaff put up, still exists, and is, in part, little altered since Nell Gwynne knew it. Whoever was then " Mine host of the Garter," to whose predecessor, it will be remembered, the ferocious Dr. Caius confided his determination to slay the "scurvy Jack-dog priest," [1] he may have served Nell and her retainers with many a quart of burnt sack, such as Falstaff and his rascally companions habitually consumed in such prodigal measure.

The " White Hart," which must be at least as old as the time of Richard the Second, fronted the Castle as it does to-day, and in the narrow

---

[1] Sir Hugh Evans, the Welsh parson.

cobble-paved streets behind the Town Hall a considerable, if decreasing, number of timbered and gabled houses still stand, presenting much the same appearance as they did two hundred and fifty years ago.

Frogmore, Datchet Mead, to which Falstaff was carried in the washerwoman's dirty clothes-basket, and Eton, are all specifically mentioned by Shakespeare, whilst in the Home Park stood a famous tree—the traditional scene of the fat knight's discomfiture — with which Nell must have been quite familiar, though many worthy townsfolk, men as well as women, feared to walk that way after dark:

> When screech owls cry, and ban-dogs howl,
> And spirits walk and ghosts break up their graves.

In Mistress Page's words:

> There is an old tale goes, that Herne the hunter,
> Sometime a keeper here in Windsor forest,
> Doth all the winter time, at still midnight,
> Walk round about an oak, with great ragg'd horns.

Though this tree of ill-repute was destroyed a century ago, many giants of the forest, gnarled and twisted into weird uncanny shapes, remain to carry on the tradition of Shakespeare's spectral huntsman and the elves and hobgoblins who so grievously affrighted Falstaff on that memorable night.

Descending the Castle hill to reach Eton and

the river, which was spanned by a rickety wooden bridge, were a number of small houses on the right hand clustering under the Castle walls, in one or other of which may have lived Master Brook or Master Ford; but these were swept away in the middle of the last century.

Living so close as she did to Henry's holy shade, Nell must often have visited Eton, which, under Provost Cradock and headmaster Rosewell, was not only in a flourishing condition, but in all probability a bigger school than either Winchester or Westminster at the same date.

Our early school lists are scanty for this period, but it is known that in 1678 there were about two hundred boys at Eton, of whom seventy-eight were collegers and the rest oppidans or town boarders; the mainstay of the school's prestige in after years. Nell's elder son may have received the rudiments[1] of his education at Eton, for it was customary to send boys to public schools at a much earlier age than their *alma mater* cares to receive them nowadays. The great Earl of Cork sent his son, Robert Boyle, to Eton when only eight years old.

We know that in 1682 Charles and Nelly sent the little Lord Burford to Paris to learn French and deportment, and that he was placed under the care of Lord Preston, but he may have been one of Eton's sons all the same, as

---

[1] A word beloved by schoolmasters in past times.

may little Jamie, Nell's younger boy, who, to her great grief and that of his father, died at Paris in the autumn of 1680.

When Cradock was appointed Provost of Eton the poet Waller was an unsuccessful candidate for the post. As a former admirer of Cromwell, the King was a little suspicious of him, and although at the Restoration he composed a congratulatory ode to Charles, it was thought to be somewhat less hearty in tone than his greeting to the Protector. When Charles rallied him upon the discrepancy between the two compositions, Waller scored neatly by replying: "Poets, Sir, succeed better in fiction than in truth," which left nothing more to be said.

Until the forest was enclosed in the reign of George the Third it was divided into sixteen "walks," each under the control of a separate keeper, and within its boundaries were more than a dozen parks in which deer, both red and fallow, were kept and winged game preserved. In all this vast expanse of moor and woodland there were but few towns, of which, probably, the largest and most important was Chertsey, where a market had been held for centuries.

At Wokingham, formerly called Oakingham, a much smaller place between Bracknell and Reading, the forest courts (whereat savage penalties were imposed upon offenders who were caught red-handed disturbing the King's game)

had been held from time immemorial. Wokingham has not much past history of importance
attaching to it, yet it has earned the unenviable
reputation of being one of the last places in
England where bull-baiting lingered; the last
recorded instance of that barbarous pastime being
so recently as 1840, when a bull was tortured to
death in the market-place.

Maidenhead, though little more than a village,
derived some local importance from the fact
that most of the timber grown in the forest was
transported thence by water to London and
other parts of the country.

The wild red deer were found in plenty round
Bagshot, Chobham, Easthampstead, and Sand-
hurst, where, owing to the sterility of the soil
and the paucity of roads, there were as yet but
few inhabitants. These, for the most part, dwelt
in small villages (dating in many instances from
mediæval times), rarely stirring far from their
homes, or holding much intercourse with the
outside world.[1]

---

[1] Of the larger villages in the neighbourhood of the Castle the most
noticeable are Warfield (originally the freehold property of the great
territorial family of Trussell), which possesses a fine fourteenth-century
church, an admirable example of the artistic skill of its Cistercian builders.
Shottesbrooke, which was also owned by the Trussells, is a beautiful early
English church. At Winkfield one of an arcade of oaken pillars in the nave
bears the cipher of Queen Elizabeth, and another that had become decayed
was replaced by Queen Victoria with timber from one of the Windsor oaks.

At Sunninghill and Easthampstead two mediæval churches have given
way to modern Gothic abominations, though in both churchyards are
yew trees which must be many centuries old.

In summer-time the rascal deer (the leaner animals not considered worth preserving for venison or the chase) were weeded out by driving them, with the aid of specially trained hounds, past a "standing" placed in a woodland glade or on a park lawn. Upon this was stationed the marksman, often accompanied by ladies not desiring to take a more active part in the proceedings.

The King had his own pack of otter hounds and another of harriers which he kept at Newmarket, whilst his brother James had what must, I think, have been the first pack of foxhounds in England. But at Windsor the Master of the Buckhounds long reigned supreme. To this day it is the titular Master of the historic pack who performs important social duties at Ascot, requiring infinite tact and discretion when, in every recurring month of June, a social avalanche descends upon the heath.[1]

Within my recollection, and I have known the forest all my life, deer sometimes escaped from the paddocks at Swinley and roamed at large in the dense woods surrounding my father's house at Tower Hill, which, like Cæsar's Camp in Easthampstead parish, commands an enchanting view over the surrounding country. In hard weather they invaded private property—

---

[1] Full details of the *personnel* of the Royal packs will be found in Chamberlayne's *Angliae Notitia, temp.* Charles II.

there were no fences to speak of in the days of which I write—in search of food, whilst, until the character of the forest entirely changed, consequent on the increase of building following on the introduction of railways, not only were black game frequently met with on the purple moors, but the raven, the forky-tailed kite, and the buzzard nested undisturbed amidst the taller trees in Swinley, whilst sometimes a stray eagle would soar overhead in solitary majesty. The enclosure in recent years of thousands of acres of heath-land has not only necessitated the abolition of the Royal buckhounds, but, greatly to the regret of lovers of wild nature, the stricter preservation of game in and around Windsor has denuded the forest of nearly all the larger birds of prey.

These have now been practically exterminated by gamekeepers waging unceasing war on the rarer fauna with gun, trap, and poison, until only the sparrow-hawk, the kestrel, the tawny owl, and the carrion crow maintain a precarious hold, in ever-decreasing numbers, in the more secluded woodlands.[1]

Roads were few and far between in the forest in the seventeenth century until the introduction

---

[1] To give but one instance out of many of this senseless persecution, I well remember that when, some thirty years ago, a wandering eagle made its appearance in Windsor Park, a whole posse of gamekeepers turned out expressly to compass the destruction of the king of birds, lest, forsooth, there should be a single pheasant or a hare the less on their respective beats.

of stage coaches, but when Queen Anne, who inherited the Stuart's traditional love of sport, became too fat to follow the hounds on horse-back, she constructed an elaborate network of gravelled rides (some of which were much extended by George the Third, who also loved to follow his hounds), to enable her to hunt on wheels. The Nine Mile ride, one of the longest of these bridle-tracks, bisected my father's property at Tower Hill, and though now much overgrown with gorse and fir its course can still be traced.

One of the principal roads to Portsmouth, Southampton, and the West of England passed through the forest over Bagshot Heath, which then, and long after, bore a sinister reputation, owing to the depredations of the highwaymen who infested it. One of these light-fingered gentry once stopped Nell Gwynne as she was driving towards Winchester, saying, " Madam, I hope you will give me something for myself after I have took all you have away! " At which Nell, seeing the impudent fellow's simplicity, laughed heartily at his bull, and gave him ten guineas, with which he rode away without further molesting her.

A lonely inn, standing high above the little town of Bagshot, marked in old maps of the district as the " Golden Farmer," is mentioned by Swift to Stella in connection with his walks to London from Sir William Temple's home.[1]

---

[1] Moor Park, near Farnham.

In modern times some wiseacre has seen fit to change its sign to that of the "Jolly Farmer," in ignorance of the fact that the original landlord amassed his hoard of gold by participating in the unlawful gains of the knights of the road who were accustomed to put up at his house.

Nell's name has been associated with a lime avenue at Kingswick in Sunninghill,[1] a few miles south of Windsor. It is a stately avenue of twenty-four tall and evenly grown trees, which may well have been planted two hundred and fifty years ago.

An old hunting-lodge of the Crown which stood hereabouts was pulled down by Richard Fitzpatrick, the intimate friend of Charles James Fox, who, dying in Waterloo year, was buried in Sunninghill churchyard. Though there is no evidence of Nell having lived at Kingswick, it is a singular coincidence that in the reign of Charles the First the property belonged to a staunch Royalist named William Gwynne, but in all probability he was in no way related to his more famous namesake. Still it is conceivable that she planted the avenue to commemorate some *fête champêtre* or merrymaking under the greenwood tree, of which no mention has survived.[2]

---

[1] Sunninghill is famous for its timber, and in the park there is an oak of greater size and as well grown as any at Windsor.

[2] There is a somewhat similar lime avenue in Swinley, opposite to where the official residence of the Master of the Buckhounds formerly stood.

Charles diligently planted trees in and about Windsor, in order to repair, as far as possible, the neglect from which the Royal domain suffered in the Civil Wars. Evelyn, a recognised authority on arboriculture, recommended the planting of oaks rather than elms in the Long Walk, and, had his advice been taken, there would not be so many gaps in the long avenue as there are to-day, when every violent gale causes one or more trees to fall between the Castle and King George the Third's statue (known locally as the Copper Horse) on Snow Hill.

Foresters tell us that the elm becomes " cup shaky " after two hundred years, and the Playing Fields at Eton, as well as the Long Walk, show how short, compared to the oak, is the life of an elm. There are no beech avenues at Windsor comparable to those cathedral-like aisles at Savernake, and Herne's oak is now only a memory; but in the Great Park may still be seen oaks, beeches, and ash trees, which have braved the storms and snows of centuries and yet put forth their crop of fresh green leaves in each recurring spring. One of these giants adjoining Forest Gate on the road through Windsor Park to Ascot bears the proud title of the Conqueror's oak, and may be close upon a thousand years old.

The oak also flourishes in Swinley, a pocket of clay amidst the sterile Bagshot sands, as does the beech, of which there is a particularly fine specimen below the deer paddocks.

The poor neglected Queen Consort, although she took no part in hunting, is said to have been fond of archery, therefore the ladies of the Court professed a devotion for bows and arrows which they probably did not feel.[1] Targets were set up in the Home Park, at which they practised diligently when nothing more exciting was on foot to pass the time away.

In addition to backsword play and wrestling, there was cricket too at Windsor, but only for the servant class, whilst football was left almost entirely to schoolboys and townspeople; the worthy John Stow, in the first edition of his *Survey of London*, published in 1598, summing up the situation in a nutshell when he wrote: " The ball is used by noblemen and gentlemen in tennis courts, and by people of the meaner sort in the open fields and streets." What would he think if he were to come to life again and see the extraordinary hold which cricket and football have acquired over the minds of the English-speaking race!

I had all but forgotten to mention that amongst Charles's household servants was " a goffe club maker," but it was not until the middle of the

---

[1] In Lely's beautiful portrait of the Duchess of Richmond, formerly at Windsor but now at Hampton Court Palace, *la belle Stewart* is depicted with a bow in her hand.

nineteenth century that the game attained its
extraordinary popularity south of the Tweed,
until, at the present day, there is perhaps not a
county in Great Britain or Ireland which has
not its own golf course.

When the weather was too bad to be out of
doors there was plenty of recreation to be had
at the Castle under cover. In 1676 Charles
built himself a new tennis court on a piece of
ground called Old Hawes, conveniently near to
Nell's house. It appears (marked by name on
the roof) in Kip's " View of Burford House,"
as does the parish church[1] and the unpretentious little Town Hall, the design of which has
been attributed, on uncertain authority, to Sir
Christopher Wren.

Nell must have taken especial delight in her
garden—in which was an orangery to remind
her of early days in Drury Lane—for her
pleasure grounds and bowling alleys covered so
many acres (part of which have since been thrown
into the Home Park) that for many years they
prevented the Long Walk from being completed
up to the Castle gates.

This long-deferred improvement of the Royal
domain might have been effected by George
the Fourth, who contemplated spending £100,000
on new stabling at Windsor; but the enormous
sums which he expended on Wyatt's remodelling

---

[1] Rebuilt in atrocious modern Gothic a century ago.

of the Castle, amounting to over a million, and further alterations by William the Fourth, costing approximately as much, postponed the building of the Royal Mews and the completion of the Long Walk—which Charles the Second had dreamed of but could not accomplish without curtailing Nelly's garden, which was of course out of the question — until Queen Victoria's reign.

An Act of Parliament passed in 1839 authorised a maximum outlay of £70,000 towards the erection of an extensive range of stabling on the site of Burford House. It provided ample space for one hundred horses, forty carriages, and a riding house a hundred and sixty-five feet long, which sufficed for the needs of the Crown for many years. I remember, when I was at Eton, going over the Royal stables and seeing the white horses of Hanover, which drew Queen Victoria's State coach on the last occasion on which she opened Parliament.[1] Nowadays I am afraid that the white horses — they were little more than ponies and not at all good-tempered —are gone for ever, since, owing to the changed conditions brought about by the introduction of mechanical traction, the neighing of horses in the Royal Mews has been succeeded by the restless whirring of a fleet of motor cars, which, somehow, never seem to be so well adapted to

---

[1] This was in 1886.

State ceremonial as the well-horsed landaus and barouches of the Victorian regime.

If, as is probable, Nell was familiar with Shakespeare's definition [1] of what an old English flower garden should contain, she would have cultivated " the daffodils that come before the swallow dares," "violets dim, but sweeter than the lids of Juno's eyes," pale primroses that " die unmarried ere they can behold bright Phœbus in his strength," " streaked gillyflowers, which some men call nature's bastards," and last, but not least, carnations, the "fairest flowers of the season." All these and more, not forgetting roses red and roses white, and lilies of all kinds, were to be found in luxurious profusion in Nell's sunny gardens sloping towards the south.[2]

Burford House, which had been assigned to her by Royal Warrant in 1681, reverted at her death to her only surviving son, the 1st

---

[1] In *The Winter's Tale*.

[2] Burford House was not the only country seat which the King settled on Nell. He also gave her Bestwood Park on the borders of Sherwood Forest, a charming woodland estate which had, for centuries, been an appanage of the Crown. No trace has been found of Nelly having ever lived in Nottinghamshire, though local tradition asserts that Nell was promised by the King as large a slice of Sherwood Forest as she could ride round before breakfast! The house was rebuilt by the 10th Duke, and remains to this day the property of her lineal descendant, the present and 11th Duke of St. Albans. In one of the periodical financial crises with which Nelly was confronted in her later years, she mortgaged Bestwood to Sir John Musters, but James the Second, who, to do him justice, always behaved considerately to her, magnanimously redeemed the mortgage after his brother's death. There is an entry in the Secret Service Expenses Accounts of the payment of £3774 : 2 : 6 for this express purpose.

Duke of St. Albans, then aged only seventeen. He seems seldom to have occupied it, and the Princess Anne and her Consort, George of Denmark (*Est il possible*), rented the house furnished, at the moderate rent of £260 a year, together with stabling in Priest Street which had also belonged to Nell.[1]

In Queen Anne's reign, hunt meetings at which the "yeomen prickers" and the local gentry, occasionally reinforced by more important personages, contended for insignificant prizes were held on a track in Cranbourne Chase, the actual site of which it is difficult to identify, though the starting-post is known to have been near Fern Hill, an ancient place name in the forest. It will be remembered that Swift, who was staying with one of the prebendaries of St. George's Chapel at the time, mentions the first of these primitive race meetings in August 1711, riding, he tells us, six miles to the course and six miles back again to Windsor, though, owing to a postponement, he unluckily missed seeing the actual race. The course not being quite ready for use, a Plate of one hundred guineas, given by Queen Anne, was run for "round the New Heat on Ascot

---

[1] There is mention of the infant Prince of Wales, the Old Pretender, being domiciled at Burford House at one time, but I cannot see when this can have been, as on his father's flight from England his mother took him with her to France. It appears that the 1st Duke of St. Albans, when he did not occupy Burford House, occasionally resided at Cranbourne Lodge, where, in after years, the famous *Eclipse* was foaled.

Common" on Saturday, August 11, instead of, as had been intended, on the previous Tuesday. On the following Monday a Plate of the value of £50, given, apparently, by the Corporation of Windsor, was won, I believe, by Nell Gwynne's son, the Duke of St. Albans, with his chestnut horse, *Doctor*. The Queen attended in person, accompanied by a numerous suite. The conditions of both these races had been advertised in the *London Gazette* in July, as was also the notice of postponement. Both are stated to be run for round the " New Heat on Ascot Common ": the entries for the Queen's Plate to be made " at Mr. Hancock's at Fern Hill, near the Starting Post," and those for the Town Plate at the office of the Town Clerk of Windsor. Had it not been for the alteration of date, we might have had a description of the inauguration of Royal Ascot from Swift's facile pen.

Fern Hill, where Charles Greville used to stay for the Ascot meeting with the Claytons, is marked in Norden's map of the forest, *temp.* James I., as being near " Ascot Playne," a very elastic term, as it included the greater part of Winkfield as well, whilst a place called Quelmes (possibly a corruption of Queen's Elms), which is also marked, was, I believe, the site of a gallows.

The present racecourse at Ascot [1] appears to

---

[1] One of the clauses of the Enclosure Act of 1813 provided that Ascot Heath should be kept and continued as a racecourse " for the public use at

be identical with a spot called Burley Bushes in Norden's map, and to this day there are a number of ancient thorns and hollies in the centre of the course.

Before Nelly took possession of Burford House the interior was decorated for her by Verrio, the Court painter, who was also responsible for many of the interior decorations of the Castle at this period.[1] Potevine, her upholsterer in Pall Mall, seems to have supplied the furniture, but whether the celebrated silver bedstead—it was certainly a double one—was brought down to Windsor from London, I know not. To this day the memory of Nell's connection with the house is preserved by St. Albans Street at the town entrance to the Royal Mews, and it has been stated that a small portion of the original Burford House is incorporated therein. She is said, on somewhat doubtful authority, to have lived for a time at Philberts in the parish of Bray, but as the manor house there belonged to Will Chiffinch (who died in it in 1691), she was probably only an occasional visitor.[2]   Bucking-

all times," from which it has been argued that to make any charge for admission to the stands is illegal.   From the cheap stand, an enormous building erected shortly before the Great War, it must be difficult to see much of the racing, owing to its great distance from the winning post, but if it were ever extended farther down the course it would be positively indecent to charge the public for admittance.

[1] These have now, for the most part, been removed, with the exception of some of the ceilings in the State apartments.

[2] Will Chiffinch was Member for Windsor in James the Second's only Parliament.

BURFORD HOUSE, WINDSOR.

From an Engraving by Kip, c. 1690.

ham, as High Steward of Windsor, was in the habit of putting up at the Duke's Head tavern in Peascod Street, which was only demolished a few years ago. A fine bronze bell, dated 1677, brought from Bray school, may now be seen in a dilapidated old house in Church Street at the back of Windsor Town Hall, which has been re-christened by its present tenant " Nell Gwynne's Museum." This house had been in former years the King's Head tavern.

I had thought that the date on the bell might coincide with the year in which Burford House was completed, but not having been able to verify the confident assertion that it once hung there, it seems more likely that it passed from Chiffinch's house at Philberts to Bray school before it was acquired for the " museum " in Church Street. Two larger houses adjoining this unpretentious little building on either side (both of which have some pretensions to architectural merit) have been associated with Nell's name. It may be that one or both were occupied by her servants whilst Burford House was in course of erection, but I cannot imagine that she would have been content with any house which had not a garden attached to it.

Before quitting Windsor it will be advisable to give a brief account of the association of Nell's son and grandson, the 1st and 2nd Dukes of St. Albans, with the Royal borough.

Her elder son Charles,[1] though he inherited his mother's love of sport, did not, I think, spend much of his time at Windsor, and, as I have shown, Burford House was let furnished to the Princess Anne until she became Queen of England in 1702.

The Duke served in the Emperor's army at the siege of Belgrade, the " home of wars for faith," where he displayed both courage and military capacity, when the Austrians wrested it from the Turks in 1688. On taking his seat in the House of Lords[2] he joined the Whigs —his mother, I feel sure, would have been a staunch Jacobite had she attained the allotted span of human life, though it is difficult to picture her at all in a Georgian environment— and having attracted the favourable notice of William III. he was made Captain of the Band of Gentlemen Pensioners[3] and a Lord of the King's Bedchamber.

Like his mother before him, the Duke derived a portion of his income from charges upon the Irish establishment. William the Third gave him £800 a year, to be paid out of the public revenues of Ireland, and he obtained, in addition, a grant amounting to £1642 : 10 : 2½ out of the quit rents of the estate of Lord Antrim, a Catholic, who adhered to James II.

---

[1] 1st Duke of St. Albans. [2] September 26, 1692.
[3] On Lord Lovelace's decease.

At the beginning of Queen Anne's reign a Committee of the Irish House of Commons appointed to inspect and examine the public accounts, ventured to suggest that, in future, the beneficiaries should " attend the duty of their several employments," but I have not found any trace of the Duke having taken up his abode, even temporarily, in Ireland.[1]

When Anne succeeded William he was reappointed Captain of the Pensioners. He lost his post on the Tories coming into power in 1710, when his office was conferred on the Duke of Beaufort.

George I. restored him in the following October and also made him Lord-Lieutenant of Berkshire. On April 30, 1718, he was installed a Knight of the Garter at Windsor.[2] Dying at Bath on May 11, 1726, he was buried in Westminster Abbey, not far from his father's grave, but no inscription marks the site.[3]

His eldest son, the 2nd Duke, who was born in 1696, had a much closer connection with Windsor, having been not only Lord-Lieutenant of Berks but Governor of the Castle and Warden of the Forest, which post he retained until his

---

[1] *Journals of the Irish House of Commons*, vol. iii. pp. 60 and 63.

[2] He was also High Steward of both Windsor and Wokingham.

[3] He had married, April 13, 1694 (being then aged twenty-three), Lady Diana de Vere, daughter and sole heiress of the last Earl of Oxford. By her—she was a noted beauty of her time—he had twelve or thirteen children.

death in 1751. As a young man he sat in the
House of Commons as member for Windsor,[1]
and when the Order of the Bath was revived by
George I. in 1725 he was one of the first knights
to be enrolled.

Like his father before him he married an
heiress, Lucy, daughter of Sir John Werden,
Bt., of an ancient family long seated at Leighton
in Cheshire, by whom he had one daughter and
one son, who eventually succeeded him in the
title.

As Warden of the Forest he encountered
the implacable hostility of Sarah, Duchess of
Marlborough, who, as Ranger of the Great Park,
strove hard to prevent him from even driving
through what she contended was her private
domain, an outrageous assumption, for which
there was never any foundation.[2] Angry letters
passed between the pair, and the Duke must
have felt something of a sense of relief when
she died in 1744, to be succeeded in the
rangership of the Great Park by the Duke of
Cumberland.

During his tenure of Burford House the 2nd
Duke carried out various improvements, and
making a better approach to it from the main
street of the town. Pote, an Eton bookseller,

---

[1] In 1722.

[2] Duchess Sarah lived at the Lodge in the Great Park now known as
Cumberland Lodge.

who wrote a colourless history of the Castle in 1749, describes it as " a stately and handsome seat with beautiful gardens that extend to the Park wall." [1]

The Duke was a favourite at the Court of George the Second, though, apart from his connection with Windsor and Ascot races at a critical period of their history, there is not much mention to be found of him in contemporary memoirs. At the coronation he carried Caroline of Anspach's crown, becoming a Lord of the Bedchamber and, in 1741, a Knight of the Garter. What more immediately concerns us here is that Nelly's grandson played no inconsiderable part in the formation of the racecourse at Ascot, as we now know it. The heath was within the limits of his jurisdiction as Warden of the Forest and Keeper of Cranbourne Chase, although in nearly every book which refers to the origin and development of Ascot races the whole credit of re-founding the Royal meeting is assigned to the " Butcher " of Culloden.

There had been, as I have shown, a primitive racecourse in Cranbourne Chase, as early as 1711, and when the Duke of Cumberland came to live at the Lodge which still bears his name he was only one of a quartette composed of the Warden of the Forest, Thomas Sandby and Ralph

1 Tighe and Davis's *Annals of Windsor*, 1858, vol. ii. pp. 327-441.

Jenison, the Master of the Buckhounds.[1] Jenison was in command at Swinley when the new course on Ascot Heath was formed, and until 1757, when he retired on a pension. His immediate successor was Lord Bateman, who held the post of Master for the exceptionally long period of twenty-five years. This brings our purview down to a time when Nell's descendants ceased to live at Burford House. The 3rd Duke, who married the heiress of Sir James Roberts of Glassenbury in the county of Kent, resigned the Lord-Lieutenancy of Berks, to which he had been appointed on his father's death, and, having dissipated the family fortunes, went to live at Brussels, where he died, without issue, in 1786.[2]

Racing at Ascot, owing to the unsuitability of the track and other causes which I have not space to enter into, languished for some years after 1727 (when John Cheny published the first edition of his Racing Calendar), and there was no meeting on the Heath in 1740 or the three following years. 1747 was another blank year, and in 1750, when the new and improved course was presumably under construction, there

[1] Probably the Master of the Horse had something to say in the matter, for I find that in 1711 the Duke of Somerset paid £558 : 19 : 5 for "perfecting the Round Heat on Ascot Common," though this, I think, refers to the track in Cranbourne Chase and not to the existing racecourse.

[2] His body was brought back to England and interred with much pomp and ceremony in the Ormonde Vault in Westminster Abbey, the 3rd Duke of his line to be so honoured, though I have found no trace of his having taken any prominent part in public affairs.

is again no record of any meeting having been held there.

In 1751 the meeting extended over four days (July 2, 3, 4, and 5), just in time for Nelly's grandson to witness the fruit of his labours, if he was in sufficiently good health to attend, for he died at his London house in St. James's Place (part of which became, in after years, the London home of Samuel Rogers) on the 27th of the same month.

The bold step had been taken of laying out the new circular course—the New Mile was a much later addition, it not being brought into use until 1786—on much higher ground than the old one, but a great and irremediable drawback was, and is still, the natural sterility of the soil of Ascot, which is as barren as the Bagshot sands. Whoever was responsible for planning the new course must have realised the extreme difficulty of making two blades of grass grow where only one had grown before. The soil is poor and sandy by nature, producing little but heather, gorse, and fir. Only by a slow and costly process of reclamation can heath-land be converted into grass. And if the land so reclaimed is not kept in good heart and constantly enriched by artificial means, the heather speedily reasserts itself until not a blade of hard-won grass remains.

This difficulty is one still to be reckoned with

at Ascot. Even after many years of patient effort to improve the track, unless there is a weeping spring, you cannot have good going at Ascot in June. April and May are anxious months for the Clerk of the Course, owing to the porous gravel subsoil absorbing every particle of moisture when the weather is dry for any considerable length of time. The sun burns the grass up faster than it can grow, and, short of relaying the track with a deep layer of imported mould, there is nothing to be done but to wait upon the weather and hope for the best.[1]

If Nelly's grandson, who may justly be entitled one of the founders of modern Ascot, could come to life again and revisit the course, how amazed he would be at the long range of stands and lawns,[2] but what he would, I think, deplore would be the locked gates, unclimbable iron railings, and asphalted roads which have done much to destroy the former amenities of the course and its free and open enjoyment by the public.

With the advent of motors, Saharas of black unyielding asphalt have been formed where formerly were green oases occupied during the

---

[1] About thirty years ago the course at Ascot was as hard as a turnpike road, and several horses never recovered from the shaking they got at the meeting.

[2] These stands, owing to their having been built parallel to the course instead of at an angle, afford but an indifferent view of the racing, especially on the straight mile, with the exception of the Royal stands and Enclosure, which have been entirely reconstructed in recent years.

race meeting by gipsies and roundabouts, where all the fun of the fair was to be found; whilst only within the last two or three years a clump of gorse at the turn into the straight from the old mile, which I remember a blaze of amber in spring and summer, has been grubbed up to form—a motor-car enclosure for only four days —and a blot upon the landscape for the remainder of the year.

Within my recollection Ascot Heath was accessible for legitimate purposes of recreation to neighbouring landowners. Delane, who had many a good gallop over it, used to get his hunters fit on the round course before the opening of each hunting season. Not until a fortnight or so before the races were a few hurdles put up to fence off the straight run in, yet the track did not suffer any material damage, though it is only fair to add that the population of Ascot and Sunninghill in pre-railway days was infinitesimally small compared to what it is now.

It will, I think, come as a surprise to many to learn that before now a classic winner has been trained on Ascot Heath. Yet in 1834 a mare called *Pussy*, owned by Captain Cosby, a young Irish squire from the Queen's County, who was a captain in the Blues, won the Oaks, the winner being trained by one of the Day family and ridden by another. *Bell's Life in London*, in commenting on the race, remarked that Captain

Cosby, who seems to have been a general favourite, was cheered by the company in the Stewards' stand, and that the improvement in the winner's form, whilst doing credit to her trainer, should help to remove the existing prejudice against the Heath as a training ground.

Pussy, who started at the remunerative odds of twenty to one, won by a length, her owner winning £5000 in bets, the stakes being worth £2525. The mare made her next appearance at the ensuing meeting on the Berkshire Heath, when she carried off the Ascot Derby.

Lest it should be thought that I have wandered rather far in this chapter from the central figure of this memoir, I may add that in the race for the Oaks won by *Pussy*, a chestnut mare named *Nell Gwynne*, by Sultan out of Cobweb, belonging to that pillar of the turf the 5th Earl of Jersey, ran unplaced, though she carried off the St. James's Palace Stakes at the Royal Meeting that same year. It is therefore possible to connect modern Ascot and a racehorse with the subject of this memoir, who, in her day, bore away many a trophy at Whitehall and the Court of St. James's.

In recent years the Jockey Club has not encouraged the training of racehorses on Ascot Heath, though about thirty-five years ago the then Marquis of Ailesbury, who had been warned off Newmarket Heath, was permitted to train a few horses at Ascot, not on the track itself but on an inner gallop, which may have been formed before the improvements of 1750.

A summer's day at Windsor in the seventeenth century, such as I have attempted to describe, need not, necessarily, be prolonged until night-fall lest the narrative of Nell's doings, and those of her immediate descendants, should prove weari-some to the most tolerant of my readers. I will therefore quit the fresh air and the fragrance of the forest and return, in company with Charles and Nelly, to the enervating atmosphere of Whitehall and Pall Mall, where, for the most part, the few remaining years of Nell's life were to be passed.

Sharing as she did Charles's fondness for music, she would often entertain the King with a concert at her house in Pall Mall, where, before a select audience, the Duke of York and, possibly, Buckingham amongst the number, Bowman, an actor of the King's Company (who lived to a great age and from whom Cibber received, at first hand, many reminiscences of Nell's career), was usually one of the vocalists who are known to have assisted at these informal gatherings. Once, when the little concert was over, Charles expressed his entire satisfaction with the enter-tainment, whereon Nell piped out in her clear tones: "Then, Sir, in order to show that you do not speak like a courtier, I hope that you will make the performers a handsome present!"

The King, as usual, said that he had forgotten to bring any money with him, and appealed to his brother, asking him if, by chance, he had any in his pocket.

"I believe, sir," said James, "not above a guinea or two," whereon, turning to her other guests, Nell cried out, making use of the King's favourite exclamation: "Oddsfish! What sort of company *am* I got into!"[1]

When Lory Hyde was at the Hague as Envoy-extraordinary and engaged in patching up the peace of Nimeguen, Nell wrote him, some time in July or August 1678, the following letter:

Pray dear Mr. Hyde forgive me for not writing to you before now, for the reason is I have been sick three months, and since I recovered I have had nothing to entertain you withal, nor have nothing now worth writing, but that I can hold no longer to let you know I never have been in any company without drinking your health, for I love you with all my soul.

The Pell Mell is now to me a dismal place since I have utterly lost Sir Carr Scrope never to be recovered again, for he told me he could not live always at this

---

[1] Bowman died on March 23, 1739, aged eighty-eight. One of the most admired songs in his repertoire was Shirley's noble verse:

> The glories of our blood and state
> Are shadows, not substantial things;
> There is no armour against fate,
> Death lays his icy hands on kings,

a prophecy which was only too soon to be verified.

Shirley must have intended the word "armour" to be trisyllabic in order to preserve the rhythm of the line.

rate, and so begun to be a little uncivil which I could not suffer from an ugly *beau garçon*.

Mrs. Knight's lady mother's dead and she has put up a scutcheon no bigger than my Lady Green's scutcheon.

My Lord Rochester is gone in the country. Mr. Saville has got a misfortune, but is upon recovery and is to marry an heiress, who I think won't have an ill time of it if he holds up his thumb. My Lord of Dorset appears worse[1] in three months, for he drinks ale with Shadwell and Mr. Harris at the Duke's House all day long.

My Lord Burford remembers his service to you. My Lord Beauclerk is going into France. We are agoing to sup with the King at Whitehall and my Lady Harvey. The king remembers his service to you. Now let us talk of state affairs, for we never carried things so cunningly as now, for we don't know whether we shall have peace or war, but I am for war, and for no other reason but that you may come home.

I have a thousand merry conceits, but I can't make her[2] write them, and therefore you must take the will for the deed. Good-bye.—Your most loving obedient faithful and humble servant,   E. G.[3]

Mr. Gordon Goodwin, though he skilfully analysed its contents, missed one or two points

---

[1] This word may be "once" and not "worse," as printed in the text.

[2] The amanuensis.

[3] This highly characteristic letter, which was unknown to Peter Cunningham, was purchased by the late Sir William Tite at Samuel Weller Singer's sale in 1858, and has been reprinted in vol. v. of the *Camden Miscellany,* and also in *Notes and Queries,* 4th series, vii. 2.

of interest in this, the earliest of Nell's letters which has yet been discovered.

Her reference to Sir Carr Scrope, whom we have met with before in these pages, is interesting. In calling him an ugly *beau garçon*, Nell makes use of an expression which occurs in one of Rochester's satirical writings. The modern English slang word "rotter" seems to fit it as nearly as possible.

The reference to Miss Knight's "lady mother" (her daughter Moll, the vocalist, was a near neighbour of Nelly's in Pall Mall) was something of a stumbling-block until, on referring to the rate books, I ascertained that the house she occupied was entered in the name of Lady Knight from 1668 to 1670, and in her own from 1671 to 1678, when it appeared for the last time. Therefore, when Nell wrote to Lory Hyde, Moll Knight's "lady mother" had died quite recently, and, in comparing the size of her funeral 'scutcheon or hatchment with that of Lady Green (which the amanuensis spelled "Grin"), Nell refers to another of the King's mistresses, Catherine Pegge. She married, as his fourth wife, Sir Edward Green, but I have not been able to recover much of her history.

Henry Savile did not marry an heiress after all, and the expression "holding up his thumb" is difficult to translate, unless it is an allusion to his intemperate habits.

The reference to the second Dutch war, which was highly unpopular in England, is the most interesting topical allusion in the letter. What Nell evidently meant to convey was that she was hoping that the peace which Hyde was trying to negotiate at Nimeguen would miscarry, so that he might be free to return to England. At this time Hyde was rapidly coming to the front in the Councils of the King, and in the course of the following year he became First Minister of the Crown in succession to Danby.

Lady Harvey's sinister influence has already been alluded to.

The intimacy between Shadwell the dramatist and Lord Dorset was always a close one, and it was to him that the poet is believed to have owed his promotion to the post of poet-laureate.

Though written half-a-dozen years later, another of Nell's few extant letters may appropriately be inserted here:

> These for Madam Jennings over against the Tub Tavern in Jermyn Street, London.
>
> WINDSOR, BURFORD HOUSE,
> *April* 14, 1684.

MADAM—I have received your letter, and I desire you would speak to my Lady Williams to send me the gold stuff, and a note with it, because I must sign it, then she shall have her money ye next day of

Mr. Trant; pray tell her ladyship, that I will send
her a note of what quantity of things I'll have bought,
if her ladyship will put herself to ye trouble to put
them; when they are bought I will sign a note for
her to be paid. Pray, madam, let ye man go on with
my sedan, and send Potevine and Mr. Coker down
to me for I want them both. The bill is very dear to
boil the plate but necessity hath no law.

I am afraid madam you have forgot my mantle,
which you were to line with musk colour satin, and
all my other things, for you send me no patterns nor
answer. Monsieur Lainey is going away. Pray send
me word about your son Griffin,[1] for His Majesty
is mighty well pleased that he will go along with my
Lord Duke. I am afraid you are so much taken up
with your own house that you forget my business.
My service to dear Lord Kildare, and tell him I love
him with all my heart. Pray, madam, see that
Potevine brings now all my things with him; my Lord
Duke's bed, etc., if he hath not made them all up,
he may do that here, for if I do not get my things out
of his hands now, I shall not have them until this
time twelvemonth. The Duke brought me down
with him my crochet of diamonds; and I love it the
better because he brought it. Mr. Lumley and every
body else will tell you that it is the finest thing that
ever was seen. Good madam, speak to Mr. Beaver[2]
to come down too, that I may bespeak a ring for the
Duke of Grafton before he goes into France.

I have continued extreme ill ever since you left
me, and I am so still. I have sent to London for a
doctor. I believe I shall die. My service to the

---

[1] ? Griffith.   [2] Probably a jeweller.

The Countess of Kildare

ELIZABETH, COUNTESS OF KILDARE.
From the Engraving by J. Smith after W. Wissing.

Duchess of Norfolk, and tell her, I am as sick as her Grace, but do not know what I ail, although she does, which I am overjoyed that she goes on with her great belly.

Pray tell my Lady Williams that the king's mistresses are accounted ill paymasters, but she shall have her money the next day after I have the stuff.

Here is a sad slaughter at Windsor, the young men taking their leaves and going to France, and although they are none of my lovers, yet I am loath to part with the men. Mrs. Jennings, I love you with all my heart and so good-bye. E. G.

Let me have an answer to this letter.

This letter is in some respects even more instructive as to Nell's habits and friendships than the earlier one to Hyde. It shows plainly that, in 1684, she was in great and pressing need of money. Probably her Irish pension was once more in abeyance, for she was now obliged to melt some of her plate in order to pay her debts. Yet, in spite of her financial embarrass-ment, she was anxious to make the young Duke of Grafton—he had not yet attained his majority—a present. In May his father sent him to France (after serving two years in the Fleet) to take part in the siege of Luxemburg under Louis XIV., and so greatly did he distinguish himself under the Maréchal de Créqui that, on its fall, Louis presented him with a sword of honour set with diamonds.

Young as Nell still was, the letter shows that she had a presentiment that she would not live much longer.

The Lady Williams referred to in the letter was the widow of Sir John Williams, a Dorsetshire baronet, who lived in St. James's Square, at the house which is now the freehold property of the Windham Club. She had been one of the Duke of York's mistresses before her marriage.

" Dear Lord Kildare " was another resident in the Square, and in the course of this year he married Lady Elizabeth Jones, one of Lord Ranelagh's daughters, who is believed to have been the last of all the King's many mistresses.[1]

The Duchess of Norfolk, whose matrimonial expectations are so pointedly alluded to, does not seem to have given birth to the child so confidently expected.[2]

The Mrs. Jennings to whom the letter is addressed was, I have no doubt, the mother of the celebrated Frances and Sarah Jennings, with both of whom, as we have seen, Nell frequently came into contact at Whitehall.

---

[1] Lady Kildare lived to the great age of ninety-three, and was buried in Westminster Abbey, not far from the King, whom she survived for seventy-three years!

[2] In consequence of her misconduct with Sir John Germain in the summer of 1685, the Duke separated from his wife. A long lawsuit followed, and the case was before the Courts in 1692, when some of the witnesses quoted some extremely lively comments made by Nell Gwynne at the time the guilty intimacy began. Not until 1700 did the Duke obtain an Act of Parliament for divorce, and in the following year he died. *State Trials*, vol. xii. pp. 907, 909, 931.

In 1680 " the wicked Earl," who had so cruelly attacked poor Nelly for a long series of years, died from the effects of his dissolute habits. His ready wit invariably made him a formidable antagonist, but in a verbal encounter he once had with Isaac Barrow, whom Charles made Master of Trinity, the King's chaplain did not come off second best.

Rochester: " Doctor, I am yours to the shoe tie."

Barrow: " My Lord, I am yours to the ground."

Rochester: " I am yours to the centre."

Barrow: " My Lord, I am yours to the antipodes."

Rochester, unwilling to be worsted by a musty old Master of Divinity, retorted: " Doctor, I am yours to the nethermost pit of hell," whereon, turning on his heel, Barrow replied: " There, my Lord, I leave you."

On one occasion Barrow preached an interminably long sermon in Westminster Abbey, so exasperating the vergers, whose prerogative it was to show visitors round the Royal tombs between the services, that they prevailed upon the organist to play until he had " blowed him down "!

The King was wont to describe his chaplain as an unfair preacher because he " exhausted every subject and left no room for others to come after him." Another of Charles's witticisms in connection with the clergy was his saying of Woolley [1] that he was "a very honest man, but a great blockhead—that he had given him a benefice in Suffolk, swarming with Nonconformists—but that Woolley had gone from house to house and brought them all to Church; that he had rewarded him with a bishopric for his diligence, but what he could have said to the Nonconformists he could not imagine, except that he believed that his nonsense suited their nonsense "!

The more famous Stillingfleet once asked the King: "Will Your Majesty give me leave to ask you a question? Why do you read your speeches to Parliament when you could speak them so well? "

" Why, truly, Doctor," replied Charles, " your question is a very pertinent one, and I will tell you; I have asked the House of Commons so often and for so much money that I am ashamed to look them in the face."

This may have been the occasion already referred to on which he naïvely informed his faithful Commons that his debts amounted to four millions. [2]

In another of his speeches from the throne, Charles, who was not often caught tripping,

---

[1] Afterwards Bishop of Clonfert.
[2] This was in 1675, and the House did not meet again until 1677.

made an unfortunate slip when he said that, " by an account which he had lately taken of his expenses, he found that he had not been altogether so good a husband as he might have been "; at which the House could not help laughing, for the unintentional *double entendre* might just as well have been taken to refer to his marital relations as to his financial position.

In the spring of 1682 the King laid the foundation - stone of Chelsea Hospital for aged and disabled soldiers, and no biographer of Nell Gwynne can avoid mentioning, however cursorily, her share in the origin of this charitable institution. To Sir Stephen Fox, who, as Paymaster of the Forces, made a great fortune for himself out of the army, must, however, be accorded the larger share of the credit attaching to the initiation of the scheme. Evelyn, who refers at some length to the history of the foundation, makes no mention of Nell in connection with it, but then he never did have a good word to say of her at any time.

The story runs that when Nell saw Wren's original plan she induced the King to extend its size, asking him, in the first place, to make it at least as big as her pocket-handkerchief. Hastily tearing this into strips she made a hollow square with them, into which she fitted Wren's draught, and thus ingeniously persuaded Charles to double the size of the projected building.

Whether this pretty story is apocryphal or not, the traditional belief in Nelly's benevolent device lingers in Chelsea to this day. And, when Lysons wrote his *Environs of London*, the signboard of an adjoining public-house bore not only her likeness (with the lamb which figures in so many of her portraits), but an inscription definitely awarding her a share in the origin of this labour of love.

The public-house remains, but the inscription has disappeared; yet there are so many well-authenticated instances of her sympathy with the necessitous and the afflicted that the persistent tradition linking her name with Chelsea and its poor pensioners must not be hastily dismissed as altogether unworthy of credence.

There may have been something a little theatrical in Nelly's presenting Oliver Cromwell's tall porter with a Bible, as he was in Bedlam at the time and suffering from acute religious mania. But it was pure kindness of heart and sympathy with suffering which prompted her to give a hundred pounds towards the relief of a number of poor people who had been rendered homeless by a disastrous fire which occurred at Wapping in the bitter winter of 1682. The King contributed the handsome sum of £2000 to the same charitable purpose, and "a person of quality," who desired to remain anonymous, gave £500, but I take leave to doubt if the identity of either of their Graces of Portsmouth or Cleveland is concealed under that heading.

Yet another instance of Nell's kindly nature was her discharging in full a debt incurred by an unfortunate parson whom she saw being dragged to prison by his creditors as she was driving up Ludgate Hill. He, at any rate, must have appreciated the truth of the saying that kind hearts are more than coronets. This impetuous desire to prevent a total stranger from being sent to prison lends some colour to the belief that her father had died in an Oxford gaol. Moreover, Nell left £100 in her will towards the relief of poor prisoners in St. James's and St. Martin's, and to provide them with warm clothing in winter time.

In and after 1680, in the autumn of which Nell lost her younger son, many a link snapped in the long chain of her friendships. Sir Peter Lely, who, more than any artist of his time, has immortalised her features on canvas, died suddenly of apoplexy at his house in the Piazza on November 30, 1680. John Lacy, an original member of the King's Company of players, who first taught her to dance, died at his house near Cradle Alley in Drury Lane in September 1681.[1] In 1682 Prince Rupert died.

---

[1] About this time an unfounded rumour that Nell had been secretly married to Slingsby Bethell, an unsuccessful candidate for Parliament at the Southwark election, gave rise to much discussion in Court circles. There never was a word of truth in the story, for no wreath of orange blossom

Charles Hart,[1] who shared in so many of her triumphs on the boards, and Tom Killigrew, who gave her her first chance at Drury Lane, both joined the majority in 1683, whilst in 1684 died Michael Mohun, another of the original members of the cast of *The Indian Emperor*.

But an infinitely greater catastrophe, so far as Nelly was concerned, was now near at hand. After the exposure of the Rye House Plot, which caused a great revulsion of feeling in Charles's favour in the country, he seems to have taken a dislike to Newmarket and to Audley End, which he had been in the habit of making a half-way house on his journeys to the Heath. He had a so-called " Palace " at the headquarters of the Turf on or adjoining the site of the Jockey Club Rooms, and a house not far off is still pointed out as having been occupied by Nell Gwynne, though she can only have used it for a few days at a time.

Charles now applied himself assiduously to the task of building an entirely new Palace at

was destined ever to adorn her fair brow, her sole connection with the " Hesperian fruit " having been when she stood in the pit of Old Drury with a basket of Chaney oranges on her arm.

[1] Mr. G. Thorn Drury, K.C., discovered a contemporary broadside entitled " An elegy on that worthy and famous actor, Mr. Charles Hart," of which only one other copy appears to be known. It is the sole authority as to the date of Hart's death (Thursday, August 18, 1683), and, after making mention of his success in comedy in the character of Celadon, it concludes by saying: " Hart ne'er made exit yet without applause." This curious fragment of theatrical necrology will be found with many others in Mr. Thorn Drury's *A Little Ark*, 1921.

Winchester, in the centre of a fine sporting country,
where races had been held on Worthy downs from
time immemorial. Nell accompanied him to the
Cathedral city in August 1684 to see how the
work was progressing, only to encounter a stub-
born opposition on the part of one of the King's
chaplains,[1] who objected to her being lodged
in his prebendal house in the Close. On Nelly
declaring that rather than leave he might take
the roof off, the Dean [2] proved more complaisant
than his subordinate, and temporary accommodation for the King's favourite was found
for her in the Deanery.

From the Cathedral Close Nell removed to
more spacious quarters at Avington, the country
seat of Lady Shrewsbury,[3] notorious for the
shameful part she played, a few years earlier,
in a duel in which her husband was killed by
Buckingham.

When, a little later, Ken's name was mentioned as a suitable candidate for a bishopric,
Charles bore no malice for his uncompromising
attitude at Winchester, and exclaimed: " Oddsfish! Who *should* have Bath and Wells but the
little black fellow who would not give poor
Nelly a lodging? " [4]

---

[1] Thomas Ken.   [2] Dr. Meggot.

[3] Lady Shrewsbury is said to have held Buckingham's horse and to
have looked on whilst her husband was fighting for his life with her
paramour.

[4] Plumptre's *Life of Thomas Ken*, vol. i. pp. 158 and 178.

The new Palace was destined never to be finished, although, after the King's death, a secret hoard of £90,000 — I expect it was mostly French gold—was found in a strong box at Whitehall, which Charles had intended to devote to its completion. His once robust constitution was now somewhat impaired by the reckless dissipations of nearly forty years, and this Royal progress to Winchester was the last of his provincial excursions in Nell's company of which any record has been found. He spent the winter of 1684–85 at Whitehall in much the same state of voluptuous indolence as I have depicted a decade earlier, but it was evident that the end was approaching and that the days of Nell's empire would soon be numbered with the past. Instead of taking active exercise in all weathers, as had been his invariable practice up to this date, he lolled upon sofas and dozed in the boudoirs of his mistresses, causing his entourage to realise that a premature decay of his physical powers had succeeded his former phenomenal activity. Embarking as he did on the troublous sea of dissipation at the age of sixteen, he did not regain *terra firma* until stretched upon his death-bed.

Despite his undoubted fondness for Nell, he now spent much of his time in the company of Mazarine and Portsmouth, and to this period belongs one of the last letters which he ever wrote to the latter. A mere scrap of paper, recovered from the archives of Goodwood House, affords convincing proof of his persistent neglect of the Queen Consort. Hastily scribbled in pencil, the note ran as follows:

My dear Life—I will come to-morrow either to dine, or immediately after, and then will settle all, but certainly I shall not mind the Queen when you are in the case.—Adieu, I am yours.

In Charles's declining years Louise was evidently his mistress and his master too.

More interesting for our purpose would have been, had any such survived, one of his *billets-doux* to Nell. No doubt he wrote her scores of them, but, unfortunately for posterity, the Dukes of St. Albans—there have been eleven holders of the title since 1684—do not seem to have been so scrupulous in preserving these sidelights on the history of their time as were their Graces of Richmond.

On Nell's thirty-fifth birthday [1] Charles was struck down with an apoplectic seizure, and on the following Friday (February 6)

The first English born, that has the crown of these three
   kingdoms worn,[2]

died at half-past eleven in the forenoon, in the thirty-sixth year of his reign, aged only

[1] February 2, 1685.
[2] In Waller's felicitous phrase.

fifty-four.[1] On his death-bed, surrounded by his
children, with the exception of Monmouth, who
was in Holland at the time, Charles asked his
wife's pardon for his shortcomings, forgave every-
body, including his creditors, expressed a wish
that the window curtains should be drawn aside
so that he might look once more upon the dawn,
and expired—with a fond remembrance of Nelly
upon his lips.

From the day he entered Whitehall, amidst
the acclamations of his subjects, his mistresses had
exercised a greater influence over him than any
of his Ministers, with the possible exception of
Clarendon in the earlier years of his reign. Yet,
in spite of his deplorable moral instability, he
had so endeared himself to his people that the
news of his death was everywhere received with
genuine sorrow and regret.

No doubt Nelly was aware that he died a
Catholic, for kings, like humbler individuals,
often tell their mistresses more than they tell
their lawful wives. The fact that Father Huddles-
ton, who once saved his life, came at the last
moment to save his soul—he was brought to the
King's bedside disguised as a lawyer in wig and
gown—may, in part, account for the shabby

---

[1] Evelyn chanced to be present at what was the very last of the gay
assemblies in the Banqueting House, on the night before the King was
seized with his fatal illness. He noted with sorrow and amazement the high
play at cards in which the Court indulged, and wrote in his diary a few
days after: " Six days later all was in the dust."

funeral accorded him by the English Church.
The Deans of Westminster have always been
masters in their own house, though they have
not always been so broad-minded as, for instance,
Dean Stanley, who not only tolerated but encouraged pilgrimages to the shrine of Edward the
Confessor. Yet, owing to an unreasoning jealousy
of the Catholic faith on the part of the Anglican
clergy, Charles was literally huddled into his
grave at dead of night, unhonoured and unsung,
and without any of the stately ceremonial
customary on the death of a sovereign of Great
Britain.

Troubles and disappointments now came thick
and fast upon Nelly, and, though invariably cheerfully borne, life had, I think, no very absorbing
interest for her after Charles's death, except where
her son's interests were concerned. It is said
that though she received more than one tempting
offer of marriage she refused to listen to any suitor
for her hand. Without attempting to justify
Nell's attitude during those happy years which
she spent in the comparative seclusion of
Windsor, free from the jealousies and sus-
picions of Whitehall, I am bound to admit
that her mode of life, viewed strictly from
a moral standpoint, was not only irregular but
indefensible. Yet when it is remembered that
Charles had married, at the early age of twenty-
nine, solely for reasons of State, a Consort whom

he could respect but whom he found it impossible to love (owing, in part, to her proved incapacity to ensure the succession to the throne), is poor, irresponsible Nelly to be blamed for accepting the situation as it presented itself to her? The answer must surely be " in the negative," as Ministers of the Crown are, I am told, in the habit of saying in the House of Commons when they do not wish to give a more explicit reply to inquisitive questioners.

It was no conventional mourning which Nelly put on in the spring of 1685. Yet, scarcely had the new reign begun before she received a sharp reminder that her position would henceforth be widely different from that to which, for so many years, she had been accustomed. Sir Cyril Wyche, writing to Ormonde less than a fortnight after the King's death, tells us: " Nell Gwynne has been forbid to put her house in mourning, or to use that sort of nails about her coach and chair which it seems is kept as a distinction for the Royal family on such occasions, and had else been put on by her command." And so the chair, studded with gilded nails, in which I have pictured her ten years earlier, was not allowed to display the outward and visible signs of her regard for her late lord and master, though mourning was in her heart sure enough, despite any vexatious regulations which the new Household officers might impose.

Whitehall, the scene of so many brilliant assemblies in the late reign, was henceforth a dull and dreary place, not only for Nell, but many others, compared to what it had been for the last quarter of a century. James and his second wife seldom entertained on a large scale either there or elsewhere during the brief space of time which elapsed between Charles's death and the bloodless revolution which placed William of Orange on the throne.

The savage reprisals, instituted by Jeffreys after Monmouth's execution, shocked and horrified public opinion, whilst the intimidation of the Judicial bench and the senseless persecution of the Anglican bishops led the English people to deplore the advent to power of a gloomy religious fanatic, who passed rapidly from blunder to blunder, and was every whit as immoral as his brother, but without a spark of his magnetic geniality.

Whilst it is easy to guess the regret with which Nelly received the news of Monmouth's execution, for she had always a friendly feeling for "Prince Perkin," the death of Otway,[1] which occurred only a short time before, must have been a real and poignant grief to her; the more so as he died, practically of starvation, at

---

[1] Otway, who had been the little Earl of Burford's tutor, died on April 14, 1685, and Monmouth was beheaded on Tower Hill exactly three months later.

a moment when Nell's own finances were in such disorder that she was unable to relieve his most pressing necessities.

Poor Nelly, though not actually arrested for debt in 1685, was outlawed for the non-payment of sundry small bills for which her creditors were clamouring. Shortly after James the Second's accession Nell addressed two pathetic letters to him, in which she said: "God knows I never loved your brother interestedly. Had he lived he told me before he died that the world should see by what he did for me that he had both love and value for me" (an evident allusion to the title, Countess of Greenwich, which Charles intended to confer upon her). "He was my friend, and allowed me to tell him all my griefs, and did, like a friend, advise me and told me who was my friend and who was not."[1] James, to his credit be it remembered, came to her rescue and made himself responsible for her debts, and the comparatively small sum of £729 : 2 : 3 duly appears in the Secret Service Accounts for their discharge in full. Whatever his sins of omission or commission may have been, he certainly did not fail to translate into action his brother's dying request: "Do not let poor Nelly starve."

What must, I think, have been a bitter blow to Nell was that she was now compelled to part with many of the jewels which Charles had

[1] Additional MSS., British Museum, 21483, pp. 27 and 28.

given her, or which she had been able to acquire
from time to time out of her own resources.
The great pearl necklace with a ruby clasp, which
in happier days she had given " Peg " Hughes
upwards of £4000 for, was now to pass to the
neck of another wearer ; and I have been fortunate
enough to discover, whilst the proof sheets of
this volume were passing through the press,
where this celebrated row of pearls now went to.
John Manners, 1st Duke of Rutland, bought it
privately and presented it to his third wife.[1]   A
portrait attributed to Lely, preserved at Belvoir
Castle, shows Lady Grace Manners, who married
Lord Chaworth, wearing the identical pearls and
ruby clasp, and they remain a valued heirloom in
the Duke of Rutland's family to this day.[2]   Not
even Marie Antoinette's diamond necklace can
lay claim to a more interesting pedigree.

About this time it was rumoured that Nell,
as well as Dryden, had become a Catholic.
Her reported conversion to the ancient faith
is alluded to by Evelyn, who was of opinion
that " such proselytes were of no great loss to
the English Church." As regards Nelly the
rumour was unfounded, although she may have
gone so far as to attend Mass occasionally in her
later years, in company with Dryden, who was
always a welcome guest at her house in Pall Mall.

[1] Catherine, daughter of Baptist Noel, Viscount Camden.

[2] From information kindly communicated to the author by her Grace
the Duchess of Rutland.

Many Protestants are in the habit of attending Catholic churches at the present day. The late Father Bernard Vaughan, one of the most gifted orators who ever entered a pulpit, told me that when he preached at Farm Street a large proportion of his congregation was Protestant. In like manner the beauty of the music at the Brompton Oratory, where the organ is second only to that at St. Paul's Cathedral, never fails to attract a large number of non-Catholics.

That Nell was essentially broad - minded in matters of religion, when in the days of her bereavement she began to think seriously of a world beyond the gay one she knew so well, is apparent from a bequest which she made by a codicil to her will. Therein she left it on record that " for showing my charity *to those who differ from me in religion* I desire that fifty pounds may be put into the hands of Dr. Tenison and Mr. Thomas Warner [1] who, taking to them any two persons of the Roman religion, may dispose of it for the use of the poor of that religion inhabiting in the parish of St. James's." How many Protestants, I wonder, either in the seventeenth or the twentieth century, better educated and brought up than Nell had been, would give a moment's heed to those who differed from them in their religious convictions? I should as

[1] Her private chaplain.

soon expect to find a Catholic endowing a Protestant church!

Nell had probably become acquainted with Tenison through Richard Lower, the most sought after physician in London, who, in consultation with other eminent members of the profession, attended her in Pall Mall when her health began to fail. " Send Dr. Burnet to me or I die " is a line in one of the contemporary satires in which her name occurs, but it was not the Bishop of Salisbury but the Vicar of St. Martin's who attended to her spiritual needs. Lower was an uncompromising Protestant, of whom King James pithily remarked that " he did him more mischief than a troop of horse." He became a frequent visitor at No. 79, and, as Kennet gathered from Tenison's own lips, " he picked out of her all the intrigues of the Court of Charles the Second."

Tenison had attended the luckless Monmouth before his execution, and as he was present with him on the scaffold Nell and he may have shed a tear together over his tragic end, for it is unlikely that the whole of their conversations were confined to religious topics. From an entry in the accounts of her executors [1] it appears that Nell had taken into her service the late King's cook at Whitehall, Lamb by name, so that her guests were always sure of finding good entertainment in Pall Mall.

[1] Printed in Appendix II.

It would be uncharitable to assume, in view of the kindly feeling which Tenison avowed for Nelly, that she was insincere in regretting the frailty of her early life.

To part with her beloved pearls was mortifying enough in all conscience, but, in her dire necessity, Nell had to pawn her plate in order to raise money at her bankers. Could she only have foreseen how enormously the value of her possessions would be enhanced in years to come, she would, I think, have clung with desperation to her artistic treasures, if only for the sake of her heirs and descendants. But necessity knows no law, and to Fleet Street they had to go. At her death Messrs. Child and Rogers valued the silver which Nelly deposited with them at only *five shillings and threepence an ounce*. If sold at Christie's to-day it might well fetch twenty pounds an ounce, and probably more. Merely to read the details of such a priceless inheritance would be enough to make a connoisseur's mouth water at the thought of such treasures coming into the open market. Over fourteen thousand ounces of the finest silversmith's work of the period, comprising as it did complete table services of plates and dishes, tureens, wine-coolers, sauce-boats, ewers, castors, sugar-basins, salvers, high-standing cups and salts, cups, bowls, and candelabra, with dozens and dozens of three-pronged forks and rat-tailed spoons, all of them

" flourished " with Nell's cipher and coat-of-arms, would attract buyers from all parts of Europe, for a service of household plate with such a pedigree might well realise £25,000 if sold as one lot. But there is reason to fear that most of Nelly's treasures went eventually into the melting-pot, for in the seventeenth century no one ever dreamed that in days to come old silver would fetch pounds where it then only brought shillings.[1]

In the spring of 1687 it was evident to all around her that Nell was, as Etherege coarsely puts it, " past all galley pot relief." " Her time was come and then there's no delay."

In April the Duke of Buckingham, broken in health and fortune, joined the majority. Nelly and he had been closely associated for twenty years. In order to spite his kinswoman, Barbara Villiers, Buckingham had been instrumental in bringing Charles and Nelly together, and a chance acquaintanceship, founded originally upon frivolity, deepened into an enduring intimacy.

So many of her friends and acquaintances died between 1680 and the crowning catastrophe of Charles's sudden death, at an age when many men

---

[1] The remarkable record of this transaction, preserved in the archives of Child's Bank, printed in 1902 in *The Sign of the Marygold*, by F. G. Hilton Price, is reprinted in Appendix II. To their eternal credit, be it recorded, Messrs. Child do not appear to have charged their clients interest on overdrafts !

are still in the prime of their physical and intellectual powers, that life can have held but little attraction for Nelly after 1685.

Buckingham's fine lines:

> Methinks, I see the wanton hours flee,
> And, as they pass, turn back and laugh at me,

may often have been present in her thoughts towards the close of her life. The fact that her son, the Duke of St. Albans, had been betrothed, in Charles's lifetime, to Lady Diana de Vere, a prospective heiress as good as she was beautiful, was, no doubt, a consolation, although the marriage was deferred until many years after Nelly's death.[1]

On July 9 Nell made her will, to which three months later she added the codicil already referred to. Mr. Gordon Goodwin discovered a second, which was proved in the Prerogative Court of Cànterbury a month after her death. From this document we learn that it was Christian Harrell, " Doctor of Physicke," and not Lower, who attended her at the last. He had been one of the many doctors present at Charles's deathbed. Nell left him twenty pounds, and his

---

[1] Charles was always keenly alive to the expediency of marrying his children to the best advantage. He betrothed most of his natural sons to prospective heiresses when they were mere children. Only one of them, the Duke of Northumberland, broke away from this well-established custom and struck out a line for himself after his father's death. Charles was equally careful in the selection of rich husbands for his daughters, and, as a rule, their marriages were uniformly happy.

nephew, "Mr. Derrick," ten pounds. To her near neighbour in Pall Mall, Dr. Joshua Lefevre, who had also attended the King in his last illness, she gave twenty pounds to buy himself a mourning ring. Harrell's bill for medical attendance amounted to £109, and from the receipt for it, which has recently been discovered amongst Messrs. Child's papers in Fleet Street, it appears to have been paid by her executors on the day of her funeral!

As Nell's will has been often reprinted, I have not thought it necessary to give its terms *in extenso*. It contains, as might be expected, abundant evidence of her charitable and kindly nature, shining brightly through a maze of legal jargon. She forgot nobody; every servant in her employ, and there were a great many of them, was remembered, from the highest to the lowest. Even her nurses were handsomely rewarded and given suits of mourning.[1]

Her executors were Lory Hyde, now Earl of Rochester; Sir Robert Sawyer, an ex-Speaker of the House of Commons, and His Majesty's Attorney-General; Thomas, Earl of Pembroke,

---

[1] Sir Charles Lyttleton, writing on March 29, 1687, gives a highly exaggerated estimate of her probable fortune, placing it at £100,000, made up of £2000 in revenue, and the remainder in jewels and plate. As a matter of fact she was in straitened circumstances at the time of her death, otherwise I have no doubt that her charitable bequests would have been much larger than they actually were. She had mortgaged her pension in 1680 to a Mr. Frazer of Westminster; according to Rochester he was a notorious usurer; and I am not certain whether this liability was still undischarged.

a President of the Royal Society; and Henry
Sidney (afterwards Earl of Romney, and the
" handsome Sidney " of Grammont's *Memoirs*)
—as distinguished a quartette as could be met
with in the great world of London at this date.
To each of them Nell bequeathed £100.

For more than six months before her death
she suffered acutely. In March she had an
apoplectic seizure which practically paralysed
one side. Although her ultimate recovery was
doubted, Harrell's skill prolonged her life until
the autumn. But on November 14, as recorded
by Narcissus Luttrell, she breathed her last in
Pall Mall.[1]

Little more remains to be said of " pretty,
witty Nell." At her earnest request, Dr. Tenison
preached her funeral sermon at St. Martin's,
whither her frail little body was carried, to the
mournful accompaniment of a muffled peal, to
be laid to rest in the Vicar's Vault on the night
of November 17.

In complying with her request Tenison found
much to say in her praise, although, as Peter
Cunningham aptly remarked, it was courageous
of him to preach such a sermon. But know-

---

[1] By a singular coincidence the Duchess of Portsmouth died on the
same day of the same month, but at an interval of no less than forty-seven
years! Moll Davis, another thorn in Nelly's side, who had faded into
obscurity some years before, also appears to have died in 1687, as I cannot
find her name in the parochial books, in respect of her house in St. James's
Square, after that year.

ing, as he did, Nelly's worth, he was not afraid
to speak out. No doubt the view he took was
the eminently charitable one that the errors of her
many-sided life were due to her having been
tempted beyond her strength, and not to any pre-
dilection on her part to embark on an irregular
mode of life. Yet his *apologia* provoked much
difference of opinion at the time it was delivered,
as well it might. No transcript of this sermon
has yet been discovered; yet it must, I think,
have been printed, for a piratical version of it,
which the Vicar promptly branded as a forgery,
was hawked about the streets.

Though Tenison's eloquent tribute to Nell's
merits is, I fear, irretrievably lost—since it is
the common fate of sermons to find a resting-
place in the waste-paper basket — an eminent
authority [1] on the Restoration drama has, by
way of compensation, unearthed a copy of an
" Elegy " [2] on the death of Nell Gwynne. This
roughly printed broadside, headed by a conventional *memento mori*, consisting of a most
repulsive-looking skull and crossbones, a winged
hour-glass—to remind the living of the uncertainty of life—a sexton's spade and pick-axe,
all of which had no doubt done duty a score
of times before, was presumably sold in the
streets by itinerant hawkers on the day of the

---

[1] G. S. Thorn Drury, K.C.

[2] It has been republished in facsimile in *A Little Ark* of seventeenth
century verse, 1921, to which I have already expressed my indebtedness.

funeral. Having served its purpose, few copies can have survived, and it may be that Mr. Thorn Drury's is unique.

The Elegy states correctly the date of her death, and bears witness to her wit, beauty, charity, and good temper, but does not make even a casual reference to her stage career; another proof, if any were needed, of the ephemeral nature of theatrical reputations.

When some years after Nell's death the See of Lincoln was vacant, Lord Villiers,[1] in his zeal to advocate the claims of Scott, the rector of St. Giles's, in addressing Queen Mary, put forward as a reason for Tenison's exclusion that he had preached a notable funeral oration in praise of Nelly. But the daughter of King James and the wife of William of Orange, whose ear he had gained, administered a salutary reproof to Tenison's detractor. The Queen had her own sources of information, and she replied to Villiers: " I have heard as much and this is a sign that she died penitent. If I can read a man's heart through his looks, had she not made a truly pious end, the Doctor could never have been induced to speak well of her." [2]

Villiers should have been the last to take exception to the Vicar of St. Martin's preferment. Instead of casting aspersions on his

[1] Afterwards 1st Earl of Jersey.
[2] *Biographia Britannica*, vol. vi. part i. p. 3926.

character, he should have remembered that his own father-in-law and mother-in-law were the pimp and the *entremetteuse* who had charge of the notorious " Backstairs " at Whitehall.

Scott never attained to a mitre, but Tenison became Archbishop of Canterbury after filling the See of Lincoln for three years.

Queen Charlotte in the next century was not so charitably minded as Queen Mary. When asked if she remembered a famous picture of Nell Gwynne, which formerly hung at Windsor, she snapped out: " Most assuredly since *I* have resided at the Castle there has been no likeness of any such person there." Strange to say, there is no portrait of her there now, or at Hampton Court, and, so far as I know, the only relics of her at the Castle are a pair of tiny slippers and, in the Royal plate room, a pair of silver bellows which probably came from Burford House.

No doubt old St. Martin's Church was crowded from end to end on the night of November 17, for Nell's name and fame were as household words, to rich and poor alike, and Tenison was such an eloquent preacher that there can have been few dry eyes amongst the congregation. Many who were present must have been struck by the remarkable resemblance between Nell's seventeen-year-old son—he was the youngest Duke in the British peerage at the time—and his Royal father, as he walked with measured steps behind his mother's coffin. Black but comely, if not so tall as Charles, he bore himself with much of the dignity which distinguished the late King.

The funeral was not an ostentatious one as the times went, yet the expenses of the paraphernalia of woe—the sable scarves and hatbands, the nodding plumes and velvet palls, so beloved of ghoulish undertakers in all ages— amounted to £375, the bill being promptly defrayed by Sir Stephen Fox out of the £1500 a year which King James had settled on his brother's favourite.

Nell's career has now been traced from her birth, through the dark hours of sin and temptation which clouded her girlhood, until she emerged, after a brief apprenticeship as an orange-girl into the fierce light which beats upon the stage.

Only relinquishing her profession in the prime of youth and the hey-day of her popularity, at Charles's urgent solicitation, she became a sleeping partner in the ship of State whilst still in her teens, to maintain a firm hold upon such affection as Charles was capable of feeling, until the day of his death.

The sharp contrasts which her life presents, passing rapidly, as she did, from poverty and neglect to affluence and power, from tears to laughter, and from obscurity to notoriety, such a life as hers could not fail to excite wonder and envy in any age. Madame de Sévigné, who I believe never visited England, was nevertheless singularly well informed of all that was passing at the Court. Writing in 1675 [1] to Madame de Grignan, she speaks of the King being *ensorcelé* where Nelly was concerned. To be able to bewitch a man of Charles's peculiar temperament, Nell must have possessed some extraordinary power of attraction denied to her rivals near the throne. For, in spite of strenuous efforts to weaken and destroy her influence, in that same state of mind the King continued so long as life remained to him.

Her earliest admirer, when she was quite a little girl, is believed to have been a linkboy—who shared her poverty and with his own hands knitted a pair of warm stockings to clothe her naked feet—her latest the King of England and the most fascinating monarch who ever occupied the throne! [2]

Cibber's tribute to the warmth and sunshine of Nell's disposition [3] is especially valuable, based as it is on material derived from contemporaries who had known Florimel and Jacintha in her habit as she lived:

[1] The year of Nell's official introduction to Whitehall.

[2] The pathetic but possibly apocryphal story of the link-boy and his whole-hearted devotion to the waif and stray of the London streets will be found in an annotated copy of Waldron's edition of Downes' *Roscius Anglicanus* in the British Museum.

[3] In Cibber's *Apology* for his own life.

If the common fame of her may be believed, which in my memory was not doubted, she had less to be laid to her charge than any other of those ladies who were in the same state of preferment. She never meddled in affairs of any serious moment, or was the tool of working politicians, never broke into those amorous infidelities which others are accused of, but was as visibly distinguished by her particular personal inclination for the King as her rivals were by their titles and grandeur.

None of her biographers have succeeded in bettering old Colley's appreciation, neither have they been able to detect a flaw in its reasoning.

The time has come to bid farewell to this fascinating girl, whose life and times I have endeavoured truthfully and impartially to portray in these pages. I have quoted the first words which Nell ever spoke upon the public stage, and given my reasons for thinking that she made her last appearance at Old Drury early in 1671, when she was still not more than twenty years of age.

Not in the tragic rôle of Almahide " by kings adored," but as Jacintha, the sprightly Spanish beauty, she shall pronounce her own befitting epitaph, for:

> Like a mistress she must stand or fall,
> And please you to a height or not at all.[1]

---

[1] Epilogue to *An Evening's Love, or The Mock Astrologer*, revived at Drury Lane, 1671, in which Nell spoke the last words she ever uttered on the public stage.

APPENDIX I

CHRONOLOGICAL LIST OF PLAYS ACTED AT DRURY LANE IN WHICH NELL GWYNNE APPEARED, NOT INCLUDING REVIVALS OF NEW PLAYS

DRAMATIST.	TITLE OF PLAY.	CHARACTER.	APPROXIMATE DATE OF PRESENTATION.
Dryden	The Indian Emperor	Cydaria	c. March 1665
James Howard	The English Monsieur	Lady Wealthy	December 8, 1666
Beaumont and Fletcher	The Humorous Lieutenant	Celia	December 20, 1666
Beaumont and Fletcher (as altered by the Duke of Buckingham)	The Chances	Constantia	February 5, 1667
Rhodes	Flora's Vagaries	Flora	February 14, 1667
Dryden	Secret Love, or the Maiden Queen	Florimel	March 2, 1667
James Howard	All Mistaken, or The Mad Couple	Mirida	? April 1667
Sir Robert Howard	The Surprisal	Samira	April 26, 1667
Sir Robert Howard *	The Committee, or The Faithful Irishman	?	May 13, 1667
Beaumont and Fletcher	A King and no King	Panthea	? September 1667
Lord Orrery *	The Black Prince	Alicia	October 19, 1667
Sir Robert Howard	The Great Favourite, or The Duke of Lerma	Donna Maria. To this play Nell spoke the prologue (with Mrs. Knepp) and the epilogue alone	February 20, 1668
Sir William Davenant	The Man's the Master	Lucilla	May 7, 1668
Sir Charles Sedley	The Mulberry Garden	? Victoria	May 18, 1668
Beaumont and Fletcher	Philaster, or Love lies a-Bleeding	Bellario	May 30, 1668
Dryden	An Evening's Love, or The Mock Astrologer	Donna Jacintha	June 12, 1668
Lacy *	The Old Troop, or Monsieur Raggou	Doll Troop	July 31, 1668
Flecknoe	Damoiselles à la Mode	Lysette	September 14, 1668
Ben Jonson	Catiline's Conspiracy	To which Nell and Mrs. Knepp spoke the prologue	December 19, 1668
Shirley	The Sisters	Pulcheria	c. 1668–1669
Dryden	Tyrannic Love, or The Royal Martyr	Valeria	Spring of 1669
Dryden	The Conquest of Granada by the Spaniards	Almahide	Part I. December 1670 Part II. January 1671

* The part of Alicia has also been assigned to Ann Quin, and Nell's appearances in both *The Committee* and *The Old Troop* are somewhat doubtful.

APPENDIX II

The Accounts of the Executors of Madam Eleanor Gwynne
1687–1692

Cr. 1687	£	s.	d.	Dr.	£	s.	d.
Dec[r]. 19. Rece[d] p[r] Sir Steph Fox ...	2300	0	0	Paid Lent on Plate...	4600	0	0
Jan[ry]. 7. Rec[d] p[r] 14443[oz] of plate,				Paid Lent at several times p[r] acc[t]			
[1688] 5s. 3d. p[r] oz	3791	5	9	given in to y[e] Exe[trs] and for Interest due	2300	0	0
					6900	0	0
					6091	5	9
	6091	5	9	Rest due from Mad[m] Gwin ... £808	14	3	

The Accompt being stated between Mr Child & Mr Rogers on y[e] one part and y[e] Execut[rs] of Madam Gwin on y[e] other part there appeared to be due for principall and Interest y[e] Sum of Six Thousand nine hundred pounds whereof was paid to them by Sir Steph Fox on y[e] acc[t] of y[e] Duke of St Albans Two Thousand Three hundred pounds and by y[e] sale of 14443 ounces of plate which y[e] Execut[rs] doe absolutely Sell to them amounting to Three Thousand Seaven hundred ninety one pounds five shilling and nine pence So that there remains due unto y[e] s[d] Mr Child & Mr Rogers onely Eight hundred and Eight pounds for y[e] Interest whereof untill y[e] same be repaid y[m] Mr Child & Mr Rogers do agree to accept of Five Pounds p[r] cent in Witness whereof y[e] Execut[rs] have hereunto put their hands this Seaventh day of January 1687[-88].

Rochester
F S Sydney
R Sawyer
Pembroke

The Accounts of the Executors of Madm Gwynne

Cr.			
1687	£	s.	d.
Dec. 10. Recd less	5	o	6
19. Recd of Sr Stevn Fox ...	2300	o	o
Feb. 8. Recd of Mr Wm Scarborough	150	o	o
1688			
Ap. 7. Recd of Benj Bartlett & Mr Wm Waterson ...	500	o	o
30. Recd of Mr Scarborough	100	o	o
May 1. Recd of his Royall Highnss Prince George for halfe a yeares Rent Due at Lady Day last	130	o	o
Octr. 15. Recd of the Farmers of Logwood	500	o	o
	3685	o	6

Dr.			
	£	s.	d.
Jan. 7, 87. Brught over Due from Madm Gwynn ...	808	14	3
Dec. 24. Paid for Proveing the Will	7	14	10
Jan. 11. Paid Mr Tho Casey ...	100	o	o
Mar. 18. Paid Mrs Edlin	13	o	o
17. Paid Mrs Hannah Grace	26	o	o
Paid Mr Grigson Feb 20	22	o	o
23. Paid Mr Christian Murry	10	o	o
Paid back in the Former acct the money recd of Sir Steven Fox ...	2300	o	o
May 1. Paid Sr Benj Bathurst six pence in the pound ...	3	5	o
9. Paid the Lady Holyman ...	10	o	o
11. Paid Mr Tho Caray ...	120	o	o
28. Paid Sam Helton Cook ...	12	1	4
June 2. Paid Mr Stokes for Mr Danvers ...	13	o	o
„ Paid Mr Rob Johnson ...	34	5	o
8. Paid Mrs Rebecca Mee ...	36	o	o
„ Paid Mr Wm Wheatley ...	71	o	o
15. Paid Mr Re Beauvoir ...	207	o	o
„ Paid Mrs Elizth Robinson	15	16	o
16. Paid Mr Sam Aubery ...	258	o	o
22. Paid Mrs Frances Sherrock	100	o	o
July 4. Paid Exeors of Pr Geedren	59	10	o
6. Paid Lady Holyman ...	6	o	o
7. Paid Elizth Hawks Wed ...	5	7	o
Octr. 23. Paid Mr Waltr Baynes ...	50	o	o
24. Paid Lady Holyman ...	6	10	o
„ Paid Wm Barnesley Esqr...	120	o	o
Nov. 10. Paid Mr Fer Watkins ...	10	o	o
15. Paid Mr Dan Skinner for L Dover	33	10	o
17. Paid Dr Christian Harel ...	109	o	o
24. Paid Jam Joyce	17	o	o
	4584	13	11
Dec. 24. Paid to Robt Sawyers ord to Mrs Grigson ...	10	o	o
Dec. 29. Paid Mrs Russell in full	162	o	o
Paid Lady Holyman ...	6	10	o
31. Paid Guy Foster Esqr and his Wife	200	o	o
„ Paid Mr Jos. Fells for Elizth Leverett ...	6	o	o
„ Paid Lady Fairbourne ...	50	o	o
„ Paid Hen Robins in full ...	68	o	o
„ Paid Dr Tennison ...	100	o	o
„ Paid Bridgett Long ...	10	o	o
	5227	3	11

THE ACCOUNTS OF THE EXECUTORS OF MADAM GWYNNE

		£	s.	d.
CR.				
Brought over Received		3685	0	6

		£	s.	d.
DR.				
1688. Brought over Paid ...		5227	3	11
Jan. 4. Paid Mr Grigson charges for probate of second codicile		11	1	10
„ Paid Mr Guy Foster and Rose his Wife		240	0	0
„ Paid Bridget Willson, Widow		25	0	0
„ Paid Mr. Hen. Ridgeley...		18	0	0
5. Paid Mr Derrick ...		10	0	0
„ Paid Mr John Renny and D. Campbell		190	0	0
„ Paid Mr Math Cupper ...		20	0	0
„ Paid Mr Quan DOllivier ...		57	0	0
„ Paid Mr Kneller ...		90	0	0
„ Paid Dr Le Fevre ...		60	0	0
„ Paid Dr Harrold		60	0	0
„ Paid Mr Moreton ...		15	0	0
„ Paid Elizth Hawkes ...		10	0	0
„ Paid severall small Debts p^r Mr Grigson		97	1	4
8. Paid Mr Chase, Apothecarry		26	9	0
9. Paid Edm^d Bowlesworth		30	0	0
11. Paid Dr Lower		50	0	0
12. Paid Mr Fuller, Seedsman		11	0	0
„ Paid Mr Cross, Picture Drawer		31	0	0
„ Paid Mr Ja^s Whitfield and Mrs May Jan 7 ...		36	0	0
16. Paid Dr Lister		60	0	0
17. Paid Mr Lambe, Cook ...		29	0	0
„ Paid Mr Gaultier for Wine		39	0	0
21. Paid Mr Richd Grigson to pay Debts		138	17	6
23. Paid Hen: Kent, Footman		6	0	0
„ Paid John Berry, Porter...		8	0	0
25. Paid Mr Warner... ...		50	0	0
„ Paid Mr Warner for Mr Will: Cholmley ...		100	0	0
„ Paid Dr Tennison and Mr Warner		50	0	0
26. Paid Mr Math: Phillbois		17	0	0
„ Paid Mr Fran: Isaack ...		12	0	0
Feb. 6. Paid Mr Chalmer ...		10	0	0
12. Paid Mr Pryor		10	0	0
18. Paid Mr Rich: Grigson ...		122	0	0
20. Paid Mr Eaton		13	0	0
„ Paid Sedgwick		20	0	0
Mar. 1. Paid Mrs Edlyn		10	0	0
„ Paid Mrs Lyons p^r Mr Grigson		15	0	0
„ Paid Mrs Bridgett p^r Mr Grigson		17	0	0
		7041	13	7

The Accounts of the Executors of Madame Gwynne

Cr.	£	s.	d.		Dr.	£	s.	d.
1689. Brought from fol 167 Rec^d	3685	0	6		1688. Brought from fol 161 P^d ...	7041	13	7
April 8. Rec^d of Mr Benj Bartlett p^r Wm Waterman ...	500	0	0		Mar. 19. Paid Wm Read p^r Mr Grigson	31	4	0
Octr 17. Rec^d Left Logwood money	500	0	0		,, Paid Wm Pickering p^r Mr Grigson	8	5	6
1690.					,, Paid Hen: Coates p^r Mr Grigson	14	10	0
April 8. Rec^d of Mr Benj Bartlett p^r Mr William Waterman	399	9	2		30. Paid Lady Holyman ...	6	10	0
Octob.21. Rec^d of Wm Waterman	425	0	0		1689. Paid Mr Grigson May 6th	10	0	0
					27. Paid Earle of Pembroke ...	100	0	0
	5509	9	8		29. Paid Lord Sidney Visc^t of Sheppy	100	0	0
					May 1. Paid Rob Sawyer	100	0	0
					2. Paid Earle of Rochester ...	100	0	0
					June 20. Paid Lady Hollyman ...	6	10	0
					July 23. Paid Mr Long	20	0	0
					Octr 18. Paid Lady Hollyman ...	6	10	0
					Nov. 15. Paid Mrs Bridget Longe ...	20	0	0
					27. Paid Ann Smith ...	12	0	0
					Dec. 2. Paid Robert Wing ...	3	12	0
					20. Paid Edm^d Cox ...	12	5	0
					24. Paid Lady Holyman ...	6	10	0
					,, Paid Jno Molins	13	8	0
					,, Paid Mr Grigson ...	20	0	0
					1690.			
					Jan. 20. Paid Dr Teneson ...	24	1	10
					Mar. 29. Paid Lady Holyman ...	6	10	0
					June 26. Paid Lady Holyman ...	6	10	0
					Octr 20. Paid Lady Holyman ...	6	10	0
					Nov. 14. Paid Mrs Bridgett Long ...	20	0	0
					Dec. 24. Paid Lady Holyman ...	6	10	0
1691.					Jan. 2. Paid Mr Grigson ...	20	0	0
20 Rec of Mr W. Waterson	489	12	0		Paid Lady Holyman ...	6	10	0
					Paid Back of this acc^t as p^r Bill of particulars is given to ye 25 June 1691	384	17	6
					Sume Paid ...	8114	7	5
					Sume Rec^d ...	5509	9	8
					By acc^t given on to ye Execut^{rs} of Mrs Gwynn there rested due from them	2604	17	9
					June 26. Paid Lady Holyman ...	6	10	0
					Octr 19. Paid Lady Holyman ...	6	10	0
					Nov. 16. Paid Mrs Bridget Long ...	20	0	0
					Dec. 24. Paid the Lady Hollyman ...	6	10	0
					Jan. 11. Paid the Duke of St Albans ord S. Robt Sawyer ...	300	0	0
					Feb. 3. Paid the Duke of St Albans	200	0	0
					27. Paid the Duke of St Albans	200	0	0
					Mar. 3. Paid Mrs Bridget Long ...	150	0	0
					4. Paid Lady Holyman ...	225	10	0
					Paid Into ye 26 Ap 92 ...	83	12	3
						3802	19	0
						489	12	0
					Ap 26 1692 ...	3313	17	0
July 20. Rec^d of Duke of St Albans pursuant to a decree in Chancery in full of all Acc^t	3355	7	0		For Interest since ye taking ye acc^t	41	10	0
						3355	7	0

From these Accounts, which extend and amplify the provisions of her will, it is evident that Nell's Executors paid away a great deal of money to doctors. In addition to Christian Harrel's bill for £109, Dr. Lefevre's was £60, Dr. Harrold's £60, Dr. Lower's £50, Dr. Lister's £60; and Mr. Chase, an apothecary, received £26 : 9 : 0.

Dr. Tenison, in addition to the £50 paid to him and her chaplain, Mr. Warner, received two separate sums of £100 and £24 : 1 : 10. Her last illness, therefore, cost £365 : 9 : 0.

Mr. William Cholmondeley, whom she styled "her kinsman" in the will, received £100, and a pensioner, Lady Holyman, whom I am not able further to identify, was paid various small sums, amounting in all to £326.

The Accounts reveal the interesting fact that Nell had her portrait painted by Sir Godfrey Kneller at a cost of £90, shortly before her death, and a Mr. Cross, "picture drawer," also received £31, but neither of these likenesses can now be traced.

Her wine merchant, Mr. Gaultier, received £39; her cook, who had, I think, been in King Charles's service, received £29.

The very last entry in these instructive accounts, April 26, 1692, shows that Messrs. Child only charged the Executors £41 : 10 : 0 in all by way of interest!

The estate took a long time to wind up, possibly owing to the difficulty of tracing the smaller creditors. From there being no mention in these interesting accounts of the sale of any furniture, pictures, or household goods, either from Pall Mall, Burford House, or Bestwood, it would seem certain that these were retained by Nell's son and heir, the 1st Duke of St. Albans, though, unfortunately, much of Nell's property was dissipated by her great-grandson, the 3rd Duke.

INDEX

Abbot, George, Archbishop of Canterbury, 113

Albemarle, George Monk, Duke of, 125, 129

Aldwych, 99

Alexander, Harry, of Mains Menstrie, nephew of 5th Earl of Stirling, 107

Alicia, part created by Nell Gwynne (or possibly Anne Quin) in Lord Orrery's *The Black Prince*, 94, 96

All Mistaken, or The Mad Couple, comedy by James Howard, in which Nell Gwynne created the part of Mirida, 74

Almahide, character in Dryden's *Conquest of Granada*, created by Nell Gwynne, 89, 90, 91, 92, 300

Almanzor and Almahide, or the Conquest of Granada by the Spaniards, Dryden's tragedy, 90, 91, 92

Amies or Amis, maiden name of Aphra Behn, 97

Anglesey, Arthur Annesley, Earl of, lived in Drury Lane, 109

Anne, Queen, 245, 252

Antrim, Alexander M'Donnell, Earl of, 256

Apsley, Sir Allen, Master of the Hawks, 227

Archer, Lord, his house in King Street, Covent Garden, 35

Argyll, Archibald Campbell, 7th Earl of, lived in Drury Lane, 106

Argyll, Archibald Campbell, 1st Marquis of, lived in Drury Lane, 106

Argyll, Archibald Campbell, 8th Earl of, lived in Drury Lane, 108

Arlington, Isabella, Countess of, 142, 186

Arlington House (now Buckingham Palace), 145

Army and Navy Club, Pall Mall, 198, 199, 200

Ascot Heath, early race meetings at, held in Cranbourne Chase, 252, 253, 259, 261

formation of the existing circular course, 235, 259, 260, 261

the new mile formed, 261

formerly a training centre, 263, 264

Ascot Heath House, given by George the Fourth to Lady Harrington, 234

John Delane lives and dies at, 234

Ascot Plain, in Cranbourne Chase, *temp.* James I., 253

Assignation, The, or Love in a Nunnery, comedy by Dryden, 92, 93

Astrological indications at Nell Gwynne's birth, 29

"At All, Sir Positive," Sir Robert Howard ridiculed as, by Shadwell in *The Sullen Lovers*, 188

Atlay, James, Bishop of Hereford, 24

Avington, near Winchester, 279

Bagshot Heath, 245, 246

Barnes, Mrs., "Bonny Black Bess," 76

Barrow, Isaac, 273, 274

Bateman, John, 2nd Viscount, Master of the Buckhounds, 260

Beauclerk, origin of the name, 226

307

THE END

1. Lodgings belonging to His Majesty.
2. To His Royal Highness.
3. His Highness Prince Rupert.
4. The Duke of Richmond.
5. D. of Monmouth
6. D. of Ormond.
7. D. of Albemarl.
8. Earl of Bath.
9. E. of Lauderdale
10. Lord Peterborough
11. Lord Gerrard.
12. Lord Crofts.
13. Lord Bellasis
14. The Ld Chamber^ln.
15. The Ld Keeper.
16. Councill Office.
17. Sr Edwd Walker.
18. Treasury Cham^br
19. The King's Labadory & Bath.
20. Ld Arlingtons
21. Sr Robert Murray
22. The Ward Robe
23. The Comptrollers
24. Groom Porters.

25. Her Majesties Apartments
26. Maids of Honour
27. Count^ss of Suffolk.
28. Queens Wardrobe
29. Mad^m Charlot Killigrew.
30. Lady Arlington

PART OF THE CANAL

PARK WALL

PART OF THE [PARK]

THE COCK PIT

THE TENNIS COURT

ENTRANCE TO COCK PIT

THE STREET

PART OF THE TILT YARD

PART OF KING STREET — TO THE LADY VILLIERS

THE BOWLING GREEN

THE PRIVY GARDEN — THE SUNDIAL

THE STONE GALLERY

PART OF THE [THAMES]

57. The Pages of the Back Stairs.
58. Queens Waiters
59. Privy Kitchen.
60. To the Mr Cook.
61. Sr T Clifford's Kit
62. The Scullery.
63. King's Herb Ho.
64. Mr Bryan.
65. Ushers Larder.
66. Flesh Larder.
67. Fish Larder.
68. Sr Henry Wood.
69. Sr Geo Carteret.
70. Gen^tn of Privy Cham
71. Groomes of P.Cham
72. Office of Sewel Off
73. Quarter Waiters
74. Signet Pr.Seal Off
75. Confectionary.
76. Esqr of the Body.
77. Sr John Trevors.
78. Treasurer's Off
79. Chandlery.
80. To Mr Chase.
81. D^r of H
82. M^r Li
83. Mr V
84. Ld Cha
85. Mr Li

Joan Kingsford del.

Plan of the Palace of
WHITEHALL
from a survey taken in
1668

DROIT

THE · NORTH ·

THE
SPRING
GARDENS

PARK

THE PASSAGE INTO THE PARK

GATE
STABLES
STABLES

HORSE
YARD HOUSE

HALL

SIR JOHN DENHAMS

NEW
BUILDINGS

THE
CLOCK
HOUSE

STABLES
CORN COOPERS SHED

DR WREN'S
COACH HO:

SCOTLAND
YARD

SCOTLAND
YARD

SHED

SAND
PIT

THE
DEALE
YARD

THE COURT

THE PASSAGE

PART OF

THE SPICERY

THE SPICERY

CHARCOAL
HOUSE

DUKE OF YORK'S
WOOD
YARD

THE
WOOD
YARD

THE
GREAT
HALL

THE CHAPELL
VESTRY

THE KITCHEN

THE PANTRY

THE
OUT WARD
LARDER

PART OF

THE BUMBARD

THE KING'S COAL YARD

THE DRY OFFICE

THE SMALL BEER BUTTERY

GREAT BAKE HO:

SCOTLAND DOCKS

THE
WHARFE

R   THAMES

31	Lady Silvis.
32	Countess of Falmouth.
33	Queen's Waiters
34	Queen's Secret?
35	Mrs Kirks.
36	Count^{ss} of Castlemains Kitchen.
37	Colonel Darcy's
38	Sr Phil Killigrew
39	Captain Cooke.
40	Lady Sears.
41	Mrs Kirke.
42	Mr Hyde.
43	Mr Povey
44	The K. 2 Sempstress
45	Mr Chiffinch.
46	Sr William Killigrew.
47	Sir Francis Clinton.
48	Dr Frazier.
49	To the Gardiner.
50	Passages into the Park.
51	To the Sutlers.

52	Porters Lodge.
53	Groom of the Privy Chamber.
54	Fath^r Patricks.
55	Ld Chamb^ns Cell^an
56	Sr T. Cliffords Cel?

Neale.	91 Scalding House	96 Yeo^r of Scullery.	101 Sr Step Fox Coach Ho	106 Mr Dupper.	111 Comptrol^r of Works
usic Ho.	92 Yeo^n of Wood Yar^d	97 Cofferers Office	102 King's Lock Smith	107 Surveyors Off^ce	112 Master Glazier.
offers Of.	93 Mr Early.	98 Sr Stephen Fox.	103 Almnery Office	108 The Surveyer.	113 Master Mason.
House.	94 S^r T Cliffords Lau^n	99 Queen's Laun^y	104 Mr London of Beer Cellar	109 The Mr Carpent^r	114 Clark of Works.
ock.	95 L^y Churchills Lau^y	100 Mrs Churchill	105 Porter.	110 Poulterers Off^ce	115 Sheds & Store Ho.

Emery Walker Ltd Sculp.